# PLANNED COLLAPSE OF AMERICANISM

## PRES. TRUMP'S BIG CHALLENGE

### - AND SURVIVING THE COMING AMERIGEDDON -

## EDWARD A. GLINKA

Planned Collapse of Americanism

[Type here]

## In appreciation and acknowledgements

Special thanks go to my amazing wife Dale, whom patiently and fully supported me as well as helped in the writing corrections of this book during my three + years of full time study and writing of this work. The success and professionalism of this new second edition would have been impossible without her patience, especially to editing.

Irreplaceable historical insights came from 89-year young Paul Cook, PhD., world historian whom spent countless hours offering me unusually profound insights into little covered histories leading to today's conditions. Much appreciation to Ralph and Betty Affatati lasting friendship and support of my works.

Special thanks to the world community of concerned fellow truth seekers and concerned patriots out there trying to make a difference in the world, just as I am. Eternal Vigilance!

Special appreciation and respect goes to the ultimate truth-seeker and trailblazer Alex Jones as well as respected and independent writers consisting of a wide spectrum of thought, current and past. Such as Michael Snyder, Chris Hedges, Professor Antony Sutton, Rep. James Traficant, Jon Rappaport, G. Edward Griffin, Katherine Austin Fitts, Professor Carroll Quigley, Mark Steyn, Jim Marrs, Naomi Wolf, John L. Casey, Lew Rockwell, James Rickards, Joseph E. Stiglitz, Michael C. Ruppert, Michael Savage, Noam Chomsky, Dinesh D'Souza, Mark Levin, George Orwell, David Horowitz, Paul Craig Roberts, Karl Marx, Joseph Stalin, Ludwig Von Mises, George Soros and such others included in reference section and as quoted. Not to forget Mike Maloney's incredible YouTube series on money and the Seven Stages of Empire, not to be missed by any who really want to know how the money machine really operates.

# TABLE OF CONTENTS

Planned Collapse of Americanism

[Type here]

Camp FEMA, Here to Help You?


CHAPTER TWENTY-SIX:  THE FIGHT TO REGAIN OUR COUNTRY

FINAL WORDS

# PREFACE

*"During times of universal deceat, telling the truth becomes a revolutionary act. "*
**George Orwell**

One must wonder who 'they' are? Who in America today is at work destroying our traditions, our family bonds, our religious beginnings, our reinforcing institutions and indeed, our entire culture? What is it that is changing our American civilization?

Indeed, a thoughtful person should ask himself or herself whether or not all this 'change' away from America's traditional culture is simply a random set of events played out by a random set of players, all independent of each other, all disconnected from any central premise or guidance. It is entirely possible that chance is at work here and all of these 'threads' of American culture are the random workings of the human intellect (the pursuit of what is possible, vice-versa, what is appropriate) in a free, democratic society.

But suppose you were to learn that nearly all of the observations made in this series of essays are completely consistent with a design that is a concept, a way of thinking, and a process for bringing it about. And suppose one could identify a small core group of people who designed just such a concept and thought through the process of infusing it into the Americana culture. Wouldn't you be interested in at least learning about such a core group? Wouldn't you want to know who they were, what they thought, and how they conjured up a process for bringing their thoughts into action? For Americans with even a smidgeon of curiosity, the answer should be a resounding yes!

If such a core group could be found, then it would still depend on your personal 'world view' as to its significance. If you believe in the 'blind watchmaker,' that is, all cosmic and social events are random and guided only by the laws of nature, 'evolutionary' in the sense of competing with other random events for survival in a 'stochastic' world, you may choose to believe that such a core group was meaningless. It may have existed but so what? It may have been only one of an uncountably large number of such 'groups' in the world's history. And you may believe that any particular groups 'window of opportunity' to influence future generations was passed by and did little to influence the course of America's history.

If you believe instead that nature has a 'design,' and that all events can be connected, and we humans can make sense out of many of them if we will only 'connect all the dots,' then you may believe that this small core group has great influence, even today, in American Culture. If this is your world view, you may (but not necessarily) even believe in a 'conspiracy. and 'conspirators who aim to alter our culture on a vast scale.

It is clear, however, that irrespective of one's 'world view,' it is informative to at least know if such a core group, or groups exist. One should explore their roots, their driving ideology and belief systems. One should strive to find out exactly what it is that they have set out to accomplish, and what methods they might use to carry out their plans for you and me.

## Planned Collapse of Americanism

[Type here]

Well, I'm here to tell you that such core group(s) did, and indeed still do exist. And that their aims have, to large extent, been fulfilled at the time of the writing of this book. I expose who they are, their agenda, their deceptions and how they secretly operate in their attempts for ultimate control over our lives. This book is written for my love of Americana, and as a huge sounding alarm to all whom cherish this country.

.

*The most dangerous man to any government is the man who is able to think things out... without regard to the prevailing superstitions and taboos. Almost inevitably he comes to the conclusion that the government he lives under is dishonest, insane, intolerable.*

*H. L. Mencken*

# INTRODUCTION

Are you ready for the purposeful coming takedown of President Trump and his great saving grace the economy? What about the evil forces that are going to intentionally create the conditions that will likely force his removal before or during his re-election campaign of 2020? The times we are living through are liking to be perhaps the most dangerous our nation has experienced in all its history.

It is time that the public turns off the Mainstreet media for awhile. It is also known as the MSN. I must warn readers that this book is the one that the Mainstreet media and deep state do not want you to read. Those that actually love the status quo agenda who still believe all the msn delivers, well, these types often have their ears shut off to the reality of their own governments sabotagings and the constant lies coming from the agenda driven media's they have trusted all their life perhaps. Many still have a hard time believing that there is in fact a real "deep state", filled with many anti-American traitors who have a completely different vision for America than the one our founding fathers laid out, or our parents loved! Even with all the continual Washington D.C. scandals that fill up the airwaves and the internet every single day, many people are too busy to pay attention to the news, or have just become apathetic to politics. They have given up on truth for it is so rare in the media. Many, out of share habit, have just chosen to automatically check the D box or the R box come election time. They have decided it easier to just choose the party they have always felt personally persuaded by. That, my friend, spells disaster for a nation that, according to its founders, demanded plenty of public involvement in order to survive against the con men who get into office.

Occasionally a liberal will slam this book with a short, hate filled bogus review while leaving the receiver absolutely no specifics as to the broad claim. Embarrasingly, a few admit they did not even read the first 20 free pages of this book! Even with this being the case, this book has sold more books than 98% of all new books by new authors! Why have politics become so very polarizing? What, and who, has been behind the systematic breakdown of that feeling of Americana that was at one time shared by all who came here? What happened to the once widely shared common ideals and belief in the U.S. Constitituion and what it stood for amongst all who called themselves Americans? Could it be that this hateful, anti-Constitutional American ideology that America is witnessing today was actually well-planned over 100 years ago employing certain strains of gradualism? Indeed, there are many lessons to be learned simply by noticing a pattern that is nearly always used by past despots, and their followers, in order to reach their dream of socialism or communism. Would you believe that such a pattern is simply a long repeated "cookie cutter" plan that follows the same guided instructions to achieve success? Yes, there is an abundance of forever truths to be learned from in order to save the America we have been losing! Our learning institutions have failed to divulge to its students the modus operandi of most communist or socialist revolutionaries! You will learn this modus operandi and finally begin to recognize and see this pattern when watching or hearing news, history and commentaries focused on world events. Especially American events.

Just to clear things up at the beginning here, my research has come to blame both the Republican and Democrat parties on many of the most important counts. This is primarily because according to respectable surveys, most of our representatives in Washington D.C. rate lower than used car salesmen and attorneys! Most all such surveys rate the honesty of our leaders in Washington only at a 6-8 percent approval! We must realize that Washington and state governments together have become one big dysfunctional, systemically broken system run by "kleptocrats and corporatcrats" (my words). Change seems impossible to accomplish. This includes both parties for they are both sponsors and water carriers of deep state and elitism in their quest for personal advancement.

The American political landscape is pretty well divided, yet today far too many on the left and the right have made it clear that they don't wish to engage in true dialogue anymore. It is as if neither ever learned in school how to debate, or even carry on an intelligent dialogue! Perhaps the truth is that our education system and media outlets have failed to offer citizens objective analysis or honest coverage of the news. For those that don't like to tolerate the free expression of ideas, these might want to consider that the true premise of liberalism during the early and mid-1900's meant full toleration of free thought, openness and diverse ideas. Around World War II the word "liberalism" and the entire liberal movement began to change what it stood for forever. By the 1970's, most real liberals had largely "left the buildings" of free thought. What replaced true "liberalism" is what we see today with little to no room for other ideas. Group think has taken over both parties in fact. The illusion of a true two-party system in America is a similar subject I cover for the reader to be dismayed by. Those responsible for this shift are clearly exposed herein as never before.

The amazing, somewhat unpredictable election of outsider President Donald Trump brought to light the fact that there is a huge mandate now taking place across America. This mandate was specifically aimed at attacking so much of what has been going wrong in Washington, D.C. politics for years. Yes, a new Sheriff in town! Quite a shift from a Washington that only made promises, never keeping them! For some, a vote for Donald Trump was more of a vote against Hillary or any of the status quo candidates. It seemed anything was better than what we had to endure for the last several presidential elections. Middle America had enough, and Trump's message resonated with those left out of the top 10% who had not seen a real pay raise in years.

Whether you personally like him or not, will the Donald really be able to pull off a systemic turnaround in the Washington politico, perhaps even draining the swamp? Why is it that nearly half the country still fails to give him a chance without a fair shot? Initially, he was mocked by the liberal press and much of the establishment politico's, even being called a clown by scores of top libs and renegade Republicans. Well, the man took the hits without slowing down and now Republicans have both Houses of Congress. Writer John Rappaport had this to say before the election: *"Trump succeeding as president would be equivalent to forcing Progressive vampires to walk through Death*

*Valley at high noon.*" The statement came to be oh so true, for we have all witnessed the absolute hysteria in the media, colleges and other houses of liberalism and neoconservatism. All these were shocked beyond belief and it appears that they will never acknowledge him as President of the United States.

After reading this book, shock is likely to take hold in many readers minds. Realized will be just how tough a job, nearly an impossible job it will be for anyone, let alone outsider Pres. Donald Trump to make the real and systemic changes needed to reverse America's present course towards disaster. Yet not impossible! For the elites and the status quo, this big brother government machine grew to unbound proportions, filling the largess of the current gravy train. For the far, far left their progressive, even Marxist utopian vision was almost at the finish line called victory by the time Pres. Obama was at the end of his term.

Ever since Pres. elect Trump's election win, deep state water carriers on both sides have been hell-bent at crippling his ability to carry out the Trump agenda he was voted in to accomplish. Washington elites, GOP Rino's, liberal Democrats, the Deep State itself, and Main Street news sources have proven to be hell-bent at crippling his ability to carry out his populist agenda. Yet from most accounts, he seems able to carry out the agenda. We all see his enemies taking drastic and truthfully desperate measures to pull him down at all costs even if at great personal inflictions upon their legitimacy. This Washington war of words and lawsuits is going dwarf any other such example in history. Both sides of the political realm seem to be hanging to their party platform even though most in the camp are simply sheeplings who have been following a plethora of political untruths from the state endorsed medias for the most part. Actually, there is no other such extreme example of this in American presidential history! Made up lawsuits, corruption accusations, divisions and splits, backstabbing's, scandals, lies, historic rallies and protests, anything in the world they can come up with that just might get some traction with the media and somehow, some way make a connection to our President.

The America that we remember not too long ago assuredly is fading into the horizon if nothing is done. People know something is terribly wrong. President Trump was elected exactly because of his agenda, not to kowtow to the old guard, the statists. He owes no one anything. That is, besides the promises he has made to those who elected him President of the United States. Even the Republican 'rinos' are standing their ground at around a 50% rate in order to keep the good old boys club from closing shop. Trump realizes that wage inequality is the worst it has ever been, worse than even the Great Depression. For instance, in 2009 there were fewer than one thousand billionaires. Since that time the number has moved up to nearly three thousand! I sincerely believe that at his age he has realized that the rapid growth of the billionaire class has come at the expense of middle Americans, still struggling with inflation that has destroyed the purchasing power of a near stagnant paycheck since the 1980's.

I explain how all of this has happened and what needs to do be accomplished very soon, for most of this billionaire bonanza is fueled not by brick and mortar businesses that make things. The truth is that most of these are making their fortunes in financial transactions. But here is the shame of it all: America's largest corporations are sitting on top of more cash than they have ever experienced in their long histories. Unfortunately though, this fact, as well as the great run up in the stock market during Trump's first two years shows again that workers are again, just as is always the case, the top 10% are receiving nearly all of the gains in real wages, by a long shot! As much credit must go to the Trump economy, will he be able to keep it on an upward trajectory, and for just how long? The biggest question remains "How long will the Trump economy continue? And, will the average worker ever get back to the real and fare wages received in the 1970's ever again?." Is the American and world financial system, loaded with debt as never before, just too far along to actually stay ahead of the curve? The real numbers spell NO.

Are we really so sure that our country could never morph into something that is the opposite of what our Founding Fathers envisioned? Could it ever be possible that America might not return to its splendor of earlier years? Some in Washington D.C. and around the world say America's best days are over. Many socialist academic prophets claim that the experiment of capitalism and democracy has run its course, that the greedy capitalist cabals have gone as far as they can with their expansionisms and plunders around the world, and we soon will have nowhere to escape to besides a communistic one world globalist state perhaps.

Unbeknownst to most, this epic transition into full blown worldism is now in its final stages of implementation without but a few realizing it, nor the extent that the deep state has accomplished. According to my reliable sources, ever since Trump's election win, the "deep state" has made plans to engineer serious institutional changes even if at great cost. At some point before his reelection, they are ready to go so far as to carry out a financial "coup-de-ta" upon Trump's one saving grace…The stock market and economy.

*"Each generation imagines itself to be more intelligent than the one that went before it, and wiser than the one that comes after it"*. **George Orwell.**

The above quote was told nearly 100 years ago by George Orwell, famous and renowned American writer of the time, whose name you might recognize. Being a bit of a dreamer philosophical politicist and novelist, he wrote in 1949 the hugely famous, forward looking book entitled '1984', warning of a big brother government to come. Millions have read it and it is now a classic. Unknown to many is that Orwell was already an ardent supporter of **Fabian socialism**, a popular political movement of that time that is in fact still very much alive, especially in the halls of the White House. The book was built as a fictional look into the futuristic dystopian world that we see emerging today, otherwise known as communist styled globalism and the one world order, yet Orwell and most of his readers knew it was actually a warning to the world. The entire deep state moves we have seen since that books release follows the Fabian agenda and its "slow as a turtle" tactic to effectuate hardly noticed changes toward a socialist one world oligarchy. This silent Fabian agenda deserved a chapter of its own.

It should be clear to anyone today that America and the world is being completely re-engineered on every front to reflect top down state control over everything. Global this, global that, is there anything that is not becoming part of global something? Few realized at the time that this new, fictional world Orwell talk of was "as serious as a heart attack" actually. Fabianism is the long slow roadmap to bring the world into a communistic, top down, neo-feudal society to be run by a top .001%. Yes, the old order is moving over into a new one of sorts. This information I present will shock most readers.

America is at a dangerous and highly unprecedented juncture as never before. And reality dictates that it matters little as to whom is elected 'President of The United States'. For the Deep State and the 'Empire" has historically allowed very, very limited amounts of real change insofar as what the elites primary goals are. If it appears that any real change comes about, the elites usually have their own counter measures, such as in chess. Past Presidents have entered office with high hopes of systemic changes and soon learned that it was not them that really made many of his decisions. The top .001%, the long reigning hierarchy of the world agenda will only allow changes that help to grow the state and the globalist agenda.

President John F. Kennedy was one that the deep state got rid of. Like Trump, he was an extremely liked populist president by his base, even taking on the establishment. But Kennedy went too far. He stepped on one too many establishment toes. Is history ready to repeat? By mid-2018 it seems extremely possible we will see large and violent protests, even a civil war between the far left and the rest of us. Many experts are sounding the alarm. For the pissed off far left and the deep state, preparations are in order. Global billionaire George Soro's has verifiably been putting up billions of dollars in funding this evil agenda to take America into the one world arms!.

President Trump promises to accomplish far more change across the board than Kennedy ever thought of. Normally, the political system insures that a one world globalist leaning candidate (or one that can be made pliable to their needs) wins every major election or else. American history is replete that there are dire consequences for the spoilers who come along and try to bust up the empire. And Trump may not avoid that fate.

Let the reader remember, as long as there have been kings and rulers, they have promised "freedoms" and "rights" unto their people's. But history shows us that basic freedoms are rarely experienced for longer than a blip on the radar screen. Almost without exception, the elites promise of "freedoms & rights" actually result in those only being available with the explicit sanctions of the state. Are we not beginning to see a bit of this in America?

The American Revolution, the experiment called America, finally offered the new idea of God given individual rights as never before dreamt of or offered. A great experiment in history for sure! People were promised a basic right to life, liberty, and the pursuit of happiness. As we know, the states (republics) were to be left alone. Federal Government powers were granted primarily to provide for defense of the nation against enemies foreign and domestic, and granted such enumerated powers as provided in Article One of the Constitution as well as article 10 of the Bill of Rights. Our Founding Fathers would turn in their graves to see how the Constitution of the United States has been bastardized and stepped upon, even by our Supreme Court. The "politically correct" and "historical revisionists" have contaminated America with Fabian gradualism that has fooled the masses much like the frog in hot water!

# Planned Collapse of Americanism

Yes, the globalist and greedy elites have been purposely infiltrating politics since the country's beginnings, creating a slow growing socialist cancer upon our system. The right to practice truly free speech, earn a living of one's choice, not to be overtaxed and over-regulated, own a gun, to use one's own private property as one see's fit, even the right to choose an unregulated medicine to save one's own life—these are all now treated as 'privileges' the government may grant or withhold at will. But thanks to President Trump, this last item is slated to finally be turned over. Now, thousands of terminally ill patients are able to make their own final choices as to the type of healthcare they choose! It is sad indeed that tens of thousands of people have been denied the freedom to explore other options to treat their disease or ailments for so many years. Prior administrations were obviously so tied to healthcare profits that they could not see their way to pass this legislation. Trump has done it.

Sadly, the 001% elites of the world have had different ideas for some time. For America it is time for its peoples to wake up and stop the bleeding. The Trump victory for now has pumped up half the country with more hope than they've felt in a long time. Perhaps this is a step in the right direction, but neither he nor his agenda will be successful unless Americans put tremendous pressure on their representatives in Washington D.C. to face the raw facts of corruption and greed. Even then, there is so very much systemic damage to the entire system that many agree its nearly an impossible job to accomplish. Especially so when much of the news we receive is twisted and out of truth about the causes, effects and roots of the many problems being spun by spin masters.

Adults, teenagers and college kids should consider reading this book as part of their required readings in order to truly understand exactly how the world really works today. This is not the fairytale version that the state run, liberal leaning school system has imparted to them when their minds are still mushy! The young will learn that the cultural and identity politics of emotion is the trick used by extreme leftist liberals to suck them into their web of lies.

For most readers, this book could be the most important read for a long, long time. It exposes the reasons for the real and actual state of our world perhaps as no other book has dared to go. It explains the real who's, how's and the why's behind most of the dangerous shifting's taking place all around us. Going behind the curtains of public deception, this book will help the young in particular to really understand the forces behind what we see going on in the news daily. That is if you can convince them to get away from mindless entertainment just for a while! If you can, they may likely be able to actually disseminate and deal better with the multitudes inequalities, brainwashing's, and problems they will see thrown their way far too often. I will even go so far as to claim that this information, if taken seriously, will help them to thrive. Instead of falling for the politics of emotional driven dribble and identity politics they will be able to spot the lies of many of our politicians, medias, schools and so forth.

Now you will know who the groups, the leaders and their true and unspoken ideologies that have long been behind the collapsing of America and the world's footings. These are often names you know nothing of, yet often you will. You will discover who these are that have purposely designed our failing school systems and why. I expose their names, their roots, their one world founders, their monetary funders and their evil histories. Often, the same names and ideologies work in coordination with each other. The same names keep coming up again and again when it comes to the funding of most of these groups. There are no surprises if you know what you are looking for. I offer up to the reader who these main players are, the psychopathic "leaders" of the globalist movement that are hell bent on taking America into their socialist one world arms! These groups, in conjunction with a comprehensive worldwide network of socialist globalists include the leaders of many of our world's nations, and these are who we need to worry about. You see, it's all by unified design, and being in the dark is not pleasurable.

With a little patience, you will see how the puzzle has been orchestrated under sheets, with slick psychological disinformation campaigns upon the mass public in order to keep them in line and docile. For instance, why don't more realize that the movement to end border walls and welcome everyone into our country is based upon a silent plan created by the far left one world Marxist planners? You, the reader will see every step of their devious and dishonest plans that they have been building upon for over 100 years. Unbeknownst to most, today these are at least 90% complete in the scheme. We have perhaps 5 years before they have completed their job no matter who is elected president unless Americans create a mass movement upon Washington to change the tide and go back to Constitutional government! We know that the far-left action groups, their political disruptors and their huge war chests have grown exponentially in the last few years. Regular patriot citizens must unite and use every lever of power available to push back the radicals, the anarchists and socialist groups who are making such headway within the medias, the courts, the halls of Congress and on the streets of America The Beautiful. History is replete with the failures of these types of ideologues. Communism has never worked, socialism has never worked as a complete system, and just forget anarchy.

Few realize the extent of the many socialist and Marxist inspired groups that are operating effectively under one name or another here in America and around the world. These anti-American groups often have nice, kind sounding titles to fool us. These are sometimes recognizable names, yet these are so very dangerous when one realizes their anti-American histories and hidden agendas. While most of us are minding our own business as Americans, these are constantly at work arranging the next sinister attacks against basic American expectations, our very own Constitution and past protocol.

You'll learn the primary perpetrators of treasonous acts against everything America stands for. Yes, name by name. Many have for years been involved in the many decades of scientific and long-term brainwashing techniques created to produce a population of dumbed down citizens who largely believe all the lies coming out of the mouths of our leaders. Sometimes these programs have been released to the public. Those of course are covered as well as others. Often, even some of our leaders don't even realize that they are being fooled, manipulated, played and controlled by the elites whom often follow the status quo. I explain who, how and why the private and governmental think tanks have for years been shaping our world, using slick psychological techniques to lead the masses, the public, and individuals into predetermined attitudes, directions and thought processes!  Much space is lent towards exposing the crooked and biased medias, the end of real journalism and the many styles of disinformation apparatuses used on both sides of the political and corporate agenda.  This information alone should be worth the price of the book.  Let's just remember this quote when we see nicely dressed politicians trying to tickle the ears of voters:

*"The revolutionaries do not flaunt their radicalism.  They cut their hair, put their suits on and infiltrate the system from within."*  Saul Alinsky, radical American Marxist, famous author of "Rules for Radicals", a playbook for radical anti-American types.

Time is past due that Americans turn off the television set a bit more often, ignore the Mainstreet "press-titutes" (my word) for a while, and begin reading what is REALLY going on.  It is time for readers like you to learn what that a huge urgency exists, even though the deep state is busy lulling us into a false state of complacency or even pacifism.  And forgive me if you mind all the quotes from leaders of past.  Such are often like little gems of enlightenment!

I love America.  I am willing to make the fight to keep it, aren't you?  Please take your time to absorb the oft-hidden findings within. There is so much valuable hidden information that neither our government nor the media's dare share. It will amaze and help you to fight these enemies of the American dream who wish to take us into a new and despotic direction.  Discover their long-drawn plans and agendas for America. Now get ready for a giant and rare lesson in the most hidden histories and secrets that exist inside the real American political machine.  Time is not on our side!


*"Power tends to corrupt, and absolute power corrupts completely"* Lord Acton

# .1
# SWAN SONG OF GLOBALISM

*"The conscious and intelligent manipulation of the organized habits and opinions of the masses is an important element in democratic society. Those who manipulate this unseen mechanism of society constitute an invisible government which is the true ruling power of our country."* – Edward Bernays, book Propaganda, 1928

Globalism sounds like such a nice thing for many, it even has a nice ring to it! At least to the naïve, whom actually believe that if the world could just get together and work out its problems under one big umbrella, all would be great. The globalism that this world has become nearly immersed in is a mechanism that, in reality, is intent on creating a one world integrated planet under a top-down, locked-down, political and economic management system backed up by coercion. It will be run by a partnership of the top .001% elites and administered by the United Nations. International rules and laws for every single decision will nearly all come under the auspices the United Nations.

President Trump has vowed to buck these one world globalists. So far, he seems to have accomplished about as much as any one president ever could accomplish when walking into a room of entrenched den of thieves! Washington is not going to be a part of solving the problem of globalism, for they and the globalists are in bed together. Part of the problem remains that the establishment agenda is overrun by statists who walk in lock-step with their leaders and party platforms even if corrupted. It is just too profitable for them to ignore. Yet, the truth is that statism has no sense of proportion. These sometimes-well-meaning politicians, once they are put into power, knowingly, or unknowingly become slaves to their corporate owners. This is corporatocracy, and it is unsustainable. The one world corporate pirates, comprising a collection of the largest 100 or so family dynasties, do in fact control approximately 90 percent of the wealth of the world, hidden inside a complex web of very complex structured organizations and corporate nameplates. Such makes it very difficult, but not impossible to truly figure out who the real owners are behind the maze. This is perhaps the reason why I contend that outsider President Trump, an outsider, may be our last chance. Most of these types hate Trump because he is hitting them where it hurts on most fronts!

Corporate socialism aka globalism such as the world has been increasingly been immersed in for the last many years, is a growing and controlled oligarchy as such it affords both the supranational capitalists and the world's governments to profit together as a baseball team would. To work together with one unified grand vision for the profit and powers of both. Globalism is the name. We already see how nearly everything around us is becoming part of the so-called global order. These, creating quid-pro-quo systems of control over the entire world economies, whom create wars for profit, create inflation to inadvertently benefit themselves and enact so-called "free-trade partnerships" that portend to help creates jobs here at home, only succeed occasionally of creating low wage service jobs in large part in the parts of the world that the globalists venture with their self-serving con-game. Limiting competition, being on the inside, having power over others, this is what the global government and one world monopolistic corporations are all about.

What the true elite globalists want is unbridled control over nearly everything in order to unite us into a global world of subservient slaves unto them. So, what's the answer? It is easy to witness that the far leftists often do not divulge they are socialists at all. Many are in government and we can easily spot them if we compare their voting records and compare them to the promises made when running for election! So, before you get too comfortable with politicians who come off as infectiously kind and compassionate while using the words 'fairness', "world community", "social equality", "open borders", "free trade", "globalism", "justice" and other such pleasantly attractive catch-phrases, be careful. Although Democrats will usually fall into this category of globalists, many Republican so-called 'servants' also play the same game to deceptively suck the unsuspecting into their globalist one world order agenda.

Government / corporate partnerships, whether formal or consensual, create insanely profitable fortunes for their owners while too often screwing over not only Americans but the worlds taxpaying citizens and their industrialized countries as well. Who do you think the prime contractors are who build and supply trillions of dollars of military weapons to the huge, high testosterone American military machine? These war factories are largely owned by billion-dollar super elites whose huge goliath corporations very often operate under a duplicity of names that largely hides the true identities of the owners behind them. These true owners often use layers of sub-corporations operating under various, differing names and locations providing legal and illegal tax havens around the world. Apple pays zero US taxes for example using such a scheme. This is just one case amongst thousands. Often the tax havens are claimed are justified by the existence of a foreign post office box. Seldom are these caught or fined by our U.S. authorities. When they do occasionally get caught, the fines are typically just a miniscule part of the total savings they have accumulated over the past years.

With a little research we can find many of the same board members appearing again and again on the rosters of the quietly interconnected mega corporations. This creates the long-time problem of immoral collusions that often allow shifting of profits to other tax havens, allowing American profits to go untaxed and shifting the responsibility fully onto the American worker. Does it not make sense that a corporation that makes ridiculous record profits such as Apple and others do, that they should pay their share? This globalist mindset of the elites creates record profits at the expense of American workers and their spending powers.

Within our public "screwling system" as I call it, students are increasingly taught that "globalism" is a new religion of sorts, a "cure-all" for world discourse perhaps! Those with enough power to create massive changes in culture are behind the politically correct culture, the green movement and most other leftist power grabs. These are often the very same supra-national corporations and political kingpins who wish to undermine the America we remember, its legal system while creating a monopolistic economic and totalitarian one world state. It is wise to remember the confirmed beliefs and admissions of the godfathers of the one world order. I am speaking of the Rockefellers, J.P. Morgan and dozens more of the wealthiest families of the world whom have for centuries verifiably acted and talked of such plans. Their heirs, as well as the new titans such as Bill Gates and his types are nearly all on board vocally with a one world order system of governance. I will cover this much more further on.

For over 100 years much of American education has been stealthily entrenched in anti-Western "cultural Marxism" propaganda and other damaging indoctrinations (as I document later). Public schools have long promoted the globalism lie, teaching such as the yellow brick road towards acceptance of a one world order that delivers utopia. It is hard indeed to find a young person today in America who still believes strongly in traditional values and ideas of self-responsibility, detest government interference in their lives, loves the Constitution, what it stands for and protects. They have been indoctrinated by our schools to the point that common sense no longer matters, for honest discourse in discussions are heavily discouraged in the classroom. I prove further along that most of the liberal ideology being increasingly touted by the left is borne out of a long dreamt of socialist utopia carried out by a partnership between the corporate globalists, the U.N. and those elites who desire power over the world. And I can guarantee to you that these are getting impatient. These, their cohorts/devotees are those whom desire to make the choices as to everything you buy, eat, drive, live, your job destiny, how much or how little you make, etc. etc. Most of this agenda is not so hidden, contained already within the prime vehicle to bring about the one world order with the United Nations Agenda 21 policies taking place around the world.

Considering that at least 50% of the world's wealth is verifiably controlled by the top 1% consisting of only 67 of the world's wealthiest individuals (and shrinking), this is pretty good evidence that we are essentially being controlled by a very small corporate global elite club designed and run for the few. These stats are verified later. The pace of their destruction is staggering.

Today, the top 200 corporations are bigger than the combined economies of 182 countries and have twice the economic influence than 80 per cent of all humanity as I prove!

Globalism has come very far in rendering world with greatly reduced amounts of anything amounting to a capitalistic system that comes with practical safeguards against abuses that place too much harm to the hard working stiffs. Increasingly, we witness wage inequalities worse than in the Great Depression. Truly, the top 10 percent earners have left everyone else in the dust increasingly over the last 50 years. The top 1 percenters incomes during this time has gone to the moon at the expense of the masses.

Globalism is the vehicle to achieve the elite globalist goals of a one world order, separate, nationalistic and independent nations with their own borders must be eliminated, which shouldn't be too much of a problem to accomplish in much of the world, especially in the current socialist run countries in and around the European continent and America who largely embrace socialism. What is ironic is that socialist Briton's have turn their backs on Brexit, meant to centralize nearly all power to the elite globalists. Little did they realize that you can't have both, at least in the long run.

The League of Nations was the precursor of the United Nations. From their beginnings, the primary long-term reason for both of them had always been to be the primary central agency of the world, an assemblage of the top global power brokers created to steer and carry out the new world order which has been dreamt of for millennium. Its creation has not been, as it touts, "to create a harmonious and peaceful world". No, the U.N.'s overarching goal has been to create a one world government using the ploy of globalism. There are ample records dating back before its very creation, direct from the U.N.'s own publications and top officers and founders to support this statement which I document and prove. They have with much ambition endorsed and sanctioned one world inspired leaders, corporations, groups, agencies, NGO's and billionaires from countries all around the globe in a long term unified vision of this new world order. It is this cabal that are the enemies of true freedoms, Americanism or any other type of governance besides their one world order. These are the world's Deep State who are in fact the worlds corporate powered global power structure.

The global multinational corporatist leaders have pushed their un-free trade treaties, long creating a horrid record of killing millions of good paying jobs across America and nearly everywhere they venture. These stealing of good jobs have swelled the bank accounts and powers of these globalist multinational corporations while boosting their wealth into the top 1% largely at the expense of the masses who now work for far less. lowered wages.

Using the false promises that socialists promise, the globalists new world order plan requires a complete breakdown of the required systems that allow a nation to prosper as well as selling the purposeful, slow overloading the wholesale belief that big government can fix everything. Such promotes self-interest above all, using deceptive techniques as I cover. It requires a break away from traditions that bind us with our neighbors and family. It requires a growth in narcissism, self above God, so much so that we can now see pedophilia becoming mainstream! Since President Trump's reign, thousands of pedophilia people and groups have been arrested as never before! This is just one of many actions by this President that leads to my belief that our new President is legit! History is replete with all the immense damages that the globalist movement has brought upon the world. These have sold the lie that globalism is the answer to the inequalities between the haves and the have nots. While the opposite is the real truth! The truth is now evident when one looks at the condition of the world they have pushed upon all of us over the last many years.

The elite new world order operatives have infiltrated all the major nations governmental agencies, top positions of power. Led by the lure of power, connectedness, money, these are often not aware that they are actually perpetuating a deadly ending if the globalist elites they serve should get their way. The fact remains that political expediency and promotions come with compliance. The heads of nearly every major country are working together with this huge one world apparatus machine that is enclosed within the UN, World Bank, IMF, European Union, Trilateral Commission, Council on Foreign

Relations, the Royal Family, the corporation called America, and hundreds of other governmental and non-governmental centers of power. Many of these hide behind nice sounding, humanitarian nameplates. Nearly all the crises we see play out are ones they actually create, (of which American hegemony around the world is a large player). For these, the ends always justify the means.

Continual non-stop conflicts around the world, of which America is often at the forefront of are exponentially increasing. I will explain why and how America's endless war policies has been implemented over the last many years, but I cannot divulge my take on who and what is behind much of the openly visible powers working behind much of the news we hear.

Explained will be real, actual reasons why America has spent over 15 years in Iraq, Afghanistan and Libya with nothing to show besides disasters and deaths, while earning a bad reputation around the world as a bully. Be assured that the elites and banking system have made trillions of dollars from these three examples. And lives mean little. Psychopaths don't care about anything beyond their own desires and powers, and many of these are psychopaths indeed. They use false justifications as a passport to sell many of their warring's and destructions. This is globalism.

I predict that the CIA, (a globalist arm of the U.S. Government and deep state), armed with an unlimited budget and trillions of dollars derived from their years of secret, under the radar dirty operations, are likely to be the agency to be reviewed, revamped or remodeled within the not so distant future. The truths behind this clandestine, above the law and corrupted agency may finally be surfacing, and when a real investigation is ever conducted, it will bring a firestorm of controversy and change more momentous than anything in American history, hopefully. President Donald Trump has his work cut out, but his years in office have shown he is no typical deep state establishment fixture of either political party! What we are witnessing is perhaps the last and only chance in American history that will determine whether America and the world rejects conservativism, or on the other hand embraces it again. So, we must ask ourselves, how did this all come to such a historic moment as we are living in?

## THE SELLING OUT OF AMERICA

*"The civilization may still seem brilliant because it still holds an outward front, the work of a long past, but is in reality an edifice crumbling to ruin...destined to falling at the first storm.*   Gustave Le Bon, The Storm

Before we jump into this important section, I want to drive home the fact that most Americans do not yet realize that there is a liberal one world ideology behind a large percentage of the world's leaders and lawmakers. It should be obvious to anyone paying attention to the actions of the Democrat Party in particular that their agenda has in recent years swung to the far, far left position that touches on the edges of Marxism if they could get all they want, and if one can be completely truthful. One thing can be said of these new democrats. Come vote time they are usually 100 percent lined up the same.

# Planned Collapse of Americanism

There is no room anymore for compromise from the Democrat leadership or its sheeplings. Democrat leaders such as Nancy Pelosi, Chuck Schumer and their close allies have declared that socialism come Marxism is here to stay and they are not going to let go! The old order must be overturned using whatever method they see fit!

Between having ninety percent of the leftist media pumping out their fake news lies on a daily basis, as well as a majority of colleges teaching the same lies while restricting free thought or expression, the younger set of Americans are being largely led by social revolutionaries who think in terms of the destruction of the existing social order in order to create a new social order in the world. These revolutionaries are the New Age Elite Boomers, the New Totalitarians, and it certainly didn't start with President Barack Obama, whom has often described as a Marxist/Leninist in many ways. They now hold an amazing amount of control over nearly every public institution in the United States of America. And like Obama, they are experts at lying at every turn in order to push their agenda on the unsuspecting youth in particular. Their 'quiet' revolution, beginning with the counter-culture revolution of their youth during the 1960's forward, is nearly complete. It was based on the intellectual foundation of the 'cultural Marxists' of the Frankfurt School. Its completion depends on keeping the American male in his psychic 'iron cage.' The confluence of radical feminism and 'cultural Marxism' (upcoming chapter), within the span of a single generation, that of the elite Boomers (possibly the most dangerous generation in America's history), has imposed itself upon Americana. If we allow this subversion of American values and interests to continue, we will (in future generations) lose all that our ancestors suffered and died for.

We are forewarned. A reading of the histories of nations tells us that we are about to lose the most precious thing we have, our individual freedoms. Washington D.C. politicians and the elites have created a state seized by a tiny cabal of oligarchs and tyrants of the U.S. corporation. Most of these types have no concept of what our lives are like. These types don't use regular commercial airlines, definitely not in passenger class! Many take a helicopter to work. Many have never been to a grocery market, instead always being catered to. Pres. Bush admitted this about himself.

Obviously, the members of Congress lack the capacity to fix our mess. For some members, it is purposeful. To make it worse, they only know how to piecemeal problems without having any concept or willingness of how to replace a failed system to a new one or truly fix the present one. Arguably, many of these same sold out souls believe that the the Fabian gradualism way to a new world order is an inevitability, so why try to fix the unchangeable? With this thought process, perhaps they escape any guilt to their predatory and self-serving largess. These petty, timid and uncreative bureaucrats are trained to carry out systems management, seeing only piecemeal solutions that simply move the chairs around on the titanic! They are too busy favors to satisfy the corporate and banking structures that finance their re-elections. Their entire focus is on numbers, profits and personal advancements. I contend that a large majority lack a moral & intellectual core. They are able to deny gravely ill people to medical coverage to increase company profits as they are to peddle costly weapon systems to blood soaked dictatorships who pledge to kill us. The human consequences never figure into their balance sheets. The democratic system, they believe, is a secondary product of the free market, which they slavishly serve, and it applies to both parties.

Each political party claims to have the cures, but Americans have finally learned to not believe them anymore. We see that it's largely just theatre and they are the actors. It's like having buyer's remorse after the elections are done, with the realization that things won't change except to move even farther over to the one world globalist agenda for another 4 years, no matter who is in power. Whatever mix of President, House or Senate you like, nothing seems to move towards good commonsense changes that everyday people can appreciate. For proof that both political sides belong to the corporatists, consider that even though the House Republicans fought against Obamacare with theatrical fortitude, even when they won the House and in fact finally have powers defund Obamacare, they didn't. This act is repeated time and time again, with Republicans acting and talking like they just couldn't overcome the opposition!  But wait! Republicans have owned the House for years, so they have had full control of the nation's purse strings as well!  Yet, they never seem to use their powers to get anything accomplished as far as really turning government around, creating a true economy, cut waste or nearly anything else that Joe Six-Pack could appreciate. How about real reforms to align our country with the U.S. Constitution, use restraint before going into warring's, effectuate fairer campaign reforms, instilling true and honest Wall Street reforms, or balancing of the budgets.  Isn't that odd?  Once we realize that there are powers above them all, it isn't so odd at all.

It definitely appears that the "New World Order" is really just the "Old World Order" but on steroids.  It's been a long game of the wealthy minority working against the working majority whom are confounded by unpayable national debt, a controlled mass media and political confabulation on both sides of the political isle whom have fooled the masses into believing their purposeful deceptive policies are working. Regardless of Pres. Donald Trump's presidency or anyone else of good intent filling that high office, there will of course be temporary spurts of improvements in some people's lives, particularly for the wealthy again. The real systemic problems.  Financial policies in American politics are much like an addict who, with every fix, the next fix must be increasingly stronger, in order to keep the body from imploding.  Unless the addict kicks the habit, bites the bullet so to speak, then the addict will die. This too is America today.

Within this corporate inverted fascism we are witness around us here in America today, any substantial changes for the good of the country is difficult to achieve, to say the least. As with so many problems America faces, many times we witness many controversial laws being codified into law by liberal judges without a public vote or congressional vote. Sadly, in such cases we see that it is not necessary for socialist and communist activists and leaders to re-write the Constitution.  It is easier for these cockroaches to exploit legitimate power by means of judicial and legislative interpretations.  The courts, populated by justices put behind the bench by those such as the leftist corporate culture and plain old liberals alike, greatly helps that their needs are met without contest from the other side of the political aisle.  This is part and parcel to the Fabians plan to destroy the democratic system from within while the electorate is asleep.

# Planned Collapse of Americanism

A recent example of the above statements follows: The Citizens United Supreme Court decision provided the Democrat Party in particular a godsend. Without much fanfare or public knowledge, this decision insures that huge corporate campaign contributions are protected speech under the First Amendment. Now, corporations are treated by the state as persons. Yes, even though corporate misdeeds are allowed to escape personal prosecutions, somehow the court decided this was a good and logical decision! These nice corporations have over 35,000 lobbyists in Washington who shape and write legislations in exchange for campaign contributions. Now it is possible for campaign donors to make unlimited campaign contributions to Super Pac's, for their corporate status allows them to do such.

Tens of millions of Americans are catching on to the extent of this takeover of our court system and our country during the last couple of decades and are rising up, even though they often don't really understand the crux of the problems and those behind the smoke screens of political deception. Answers and fixes will not come unless people learn who the real enemies of freedom are. They must engage in peaceful but loud revolt en-masse, if that is what it takes, or else we shall face the music. In these situations, revolution is called for by our Founding Fathers.

We are at fault for falling asleep and allowing the real powers around the world to fall more and more into the hands of the elites. We are now witnessing how effective their slowly acquired manipulations and their acquisitions of power over state have led us to this abyss. If allowed to continue, it is hard to believe but we will be faced with even more laws, edicts, governmental oversight and new trade agreements that will water down and surely eliminate most freedoms that we can still claim to have. Such will also elevate the costs to small and medium American businesses to the point that they can no longer operate. Citizens will face even larger losses of liberties, freedoms and economic inequalities than what we see today.

Corrupted partnerships between Congress and corporatisms have increased so immensely in the last 25 years that in one way or another, nearly all bills passing thru Congress today are summarily stuffed with pork filled, anti-Constitutional, even foreign favoritisms aimed against America's best interests in large part. And they are usually typed up by the corporate lawyers! These silent partnerships between Washington and corporations are not slowing, quite the opposite.

It has been no mistake that since the 2008 stock market and economic crash, Americas economic system had still not recovered by 2017 but for the top 10%, and it won't. Trillions of dollars in un federal reserve bailouts to the banks robbed the American economy of nearly all its strength, and all we are left with is a propped up, false economy built upon the Federal Reserve's zero interest lending environment, jacked up by a fiat money printing machine of which the big traders on Wall Street borrow much of their gambling money from at next to nothing!

Just as in 2008, the un-federal reserve, the bankers and Wall Street are again playing even larger risks with other people's money obtained through near zero interest rate policies. For without the near zero un-federal reserve rates, this anemic economy would have crashed years ago while the national debt exploded. Many claim as I do that only because of the near free interest rates has the American economy not crashed and burned. has been on life support, never truly recovering for the largess of Americans. Only the top 10 percent have seen real, inflation adjusted gains in income since before the 2008 crash. The official economic indicators we hear on the television and news sources are largely fabrications. Official economic numbers such as the unemployment rate, new jobs creation, inflation, money supply, GDP, GNP, are all massaged by whoever is in power. The formulas and the metrics that have been used for so many began changing around the time of President Bill Clinton (that can be verified).

**Have you ever wondered** why the CPI, GDP and employment numbers run counter to your personal and business experiences? The problem lies in the biased and often-manipulated government reporting. The quality of government reporting has deteriorated sharply in the last couple of decades, largely for political gain in a particular year and who is in office. Reporting problems have included methodological changes to economic reporting that have pushed headline economic and inflation results out of the realm of real-world or common experience. Many statistics have been massaged with new metrics that often do not take into consideration many of the factors of the old methods, often leaving out inconvenient facts, and thus making it possible for the governmental accountings to look so rosy. I am one of the many who feel confident that the coming crash will have the job of not only wiping clean the current world debts, but also the leftovers of the corporate, state and federal debts of the 2008 world economic crash that were never fully flushed out of the system! Taken from Shadowstats/John Williams/shadow government statistics and other sources.

The big banks have been back at their old games of leveraging for about 10 years since the last crash. They have been quietly expanding and ravaging the financial markets, increasing their risk takings far beyond that of 2008. They never learned any lesson it would seem. Or perhaps we should consider that they actually are very smart indeed. With government guarantees and other incentives, could it possibly be that those stellar bankers whom own those thirty story swanky buildings in Manhattan might be complicit in purposely gaming the system AGAIN? Before the next financial Armageddon takes place? Could this consortium of big banks, most of whom are largely fronts for just a few mega wealthy families of the world, be partnering with the un-federal reserve insiders as well? Could the run up of reckless behavior by the banks really consist of an intentional act by the banking elites to rob the very same system that propped them back up last time they took a big fall? The answer is obvious. It isn't real money after all. They ran off with trillions of dollars of taxpayer's bailout money first time around, and from all indications they will recover all of their paper losses during the next crash of 2017-2018.

This time the new world order elites have engineered a coming economic crash that will many financial analysts believe will be a boon for those on the inside. This will be on a scale as the world has never seen. It will make the 1929 Great Recession look like a picnic! The bigger they are, the harder they fall as the saying goes. We have seen every recession since the 1960's takes longer to take place, but always larger and with more downside. Without fixing the systemic problems of a unfederal reserve and an out of control government, each one builds upon the last one. If that's an indication, we are going to face financial Armageddon!

Before I go into the next section, I must preface it by explaining to the readers that I am not anti-capitalism at all! Capitalism and democracy must work together, and government must restrain capitalism from becoming a mechanism to be enjoyed only by a few. What we are witnessing today is just the opposite of that widely desired ideal. I believe we can all agree that too much of one or the other is dangerous. Karl Marx had even predicted the path that the corporate elites have taken. He prophetically claimed as well that it would all end up as a monopolized capitalism cabal if not stopped.

America and major nations have been duped into, or knowingly accepting, the globalists callings for so-called free trade agreements, allowing these mega national corporations to consolidate their trade rules under one big unregulated umbrella that only they benefit from. The free trade argument has never really been about fair trade, it was about "managed trade" devoted towards a monopolized market system. The following two quotes below come from two Rockefeller globalist pigs and surely hit a cord with what has been talked of above. These past tyrants and many like them run on the same old abusive tactics of their past lineages whom share their last names They are the proven grand masters and architects of the global elite's one world cabal. Forgive me if I have already included these two. These are just too good to not be repeated often! PLEASE don't make the common mistake of thinking that these old geezers are pass`e and those days are gone, not relevant anymore for they have been extremely good at hiding their secrets for all these years, at least for those too busy to pay attention and really follow their trailing's for many years as some have. The plan has worked so well, we are on its doorsteps! After what you now know, do not the bankers really run the world? The quote below may help with that decision…

*"The supranational sovereignty of an intellectual elite and world bankers is surely preferable to the national auto-determination practiced in past centuries."* -David Rockefeller, Memoirs

Regarding free trade treaties and international corporatism, chew on this one:

## *"Competition is a sin!"* John D. Rockefeller

# MARX KNEW!

Karl Marx warned that unfettered capitalism is a revolutionary force that consumes greater and greater numbers of human lives and whatever else it needs until it consumes itself. Uncomfortable and unpopular as it might be for die hard in-the-wool capitalist lovers to admit it, the huge mega capitalists of the world today do not care about individual nations or sovereignty. They care not if they exploit the very poor, leave their more expensive workers unnecessarily behind to suffer. Unrestrained capitalists are notorious for destroying forests, habitats, lives, causing massive and avoidable oil spills, and basically whatever got in way in their quest for profits. History is replete with examples. This is the uncomfortable bad side of capitalism if not regulated properly.

Perhaps it was Jim Cramer on CNBC's Mad Money who admitted that what happened in the 2008 crash was in part a late stage symptom of capitalism written about by Karl Marx. His exact words were *"The only guy who really called this right was Karl Marx!!"* It has become more and more obvious since the 2008 crash that most of the "experts" don't have a clue in understanding the underlying actions of the markets and the forces that manipulate it or how bad they damage it, but Kramer obviously knows.

So, should we do away with capitalism? <u>Of course not</u>! It by far offers the best economic system of any other to benefit the good of mankind! It is a miraculous system that, if practiced with common sense restraints and fair rules of trade, does benefit both the corporations, the smaller businesses, workers and the general welfare of most all. Only capitalism can offer so many benefits to so many, but it needs to be tamed with laws that restrain those excesses. Today's globalism represents a style of capitalism that helps but for a few. Unfortunately, for the last 100 years the global capitalist elites have ever increasingly abused everything in their path, laws or not. The largest and most egregious violator of plundering the nation's wealth has of course been our friendly un-Federal Reserve, an entity not commonly thought of as a "corporation", but it is in fact a branch of the British /Rothschild's privately owned central banking system around the world, a.k.a. the Bank of International Settlements. This entity is the godfather of the entire central banking system. It controls the flow of money around the world in most respects, as is explained elsewhere.

As their final push for total control is almost complete, the globalists already have numerous, far reaching "free trade treaties" like the TPP, GATT, NAFTA, SPP, CATFA, PNTR, TAFTA and a myriad of past trade treaties already in place all around the world. Such complicated agreements are drawn up by the banker hired trade attorney's whom draft up legalese that few besides them can decipher, purposely. Often being thousands of pages long, members of Congress are rarely given enough time or energy to read these behemoth agreements.

The end game is to meld these varying trade agreement into just 4 major regional master agreements that will cover the entire planet. The most ominous example of late is the TTIP (a companion agreement to the TPP), standing for the "Transatlantic Trade and Investment Partnership" which is being implemented. It is a trade deal that melds together the American TPP and the European Union. The TPP is the big daddy that drives even more American jobs offshore. It dwarfs what NAFTA was in scope. Officials claim it is drafted to "provide multilateral economic growth." Growth for who I ask?

During President John F. Kennedy's speech about *"All boats rising"*, he was not talking about pure, unfettered capitalism to achieve that goal, but a more restrained, less concentrated type of democratic capitalism perhaps, combined with proper laws that kept it from abusing human rights while protecting good jobs. He knew too that if we could get rid of the private Federal Reserve system, America could retake the powers over its money creation, thereafter ridding ourselves paying interest on our debts while slowly become debt free!

# Planned Collapse of Americanism

President Trump has taken a tough, nationalistic fair play stance on the extremely unfair tariff disparities that current exist between countries that import their products into the U.S. and the high tariffs America pays to those same countries when shipping to them.  For instance, for years America has only charged a 2.5% tariff to import cars.  He persuaded China to lower their 25% tariff down to 15% effective July 2018. Canadian President Trudeau has been told to expect his tariff to be raised to 25%. Of course, that will likely entail negotiations, but the result is the same.  Good news for America!  Other deals are in the making to create a fair playing field finally!  Since when have we had a president that was not part of the good old globalist boy's club?

Trump promises a lot of things and I am sure he is doing his best.  Whatever political persuasion you are, remember he is still our President and give him the respect he deserves as leader of the greatest country on earth.  Not perfect for sure, but he and the country don't stand a chance of maintaining the freedoms we have enjoyed for two centuries if sanity does not return to sound policies on borders, government spending, setting priorities that are more nationalistic in nature and much more.  We must stop the far leftist, sometimes communist extremist groups right here in the United States who have been playing Americans as fools with their stealthy tactics that mislead their followers using created crises and panics (the 2018 fake news event on illegal children kept in cages (hiding the fact that the photo was from back in 2014 during Obama's term) all the while blaming Trump!  Once Americans understand who backs these slickly nefarious and anti-American stand-ins, the easier it will be to ban the evil George Soros and his Open Society Foundation out of America!  As a tribute to this man's evil deeds, in 2018 Soros was banned from operating in his own native country Bulgaria!  They know how evil he is. Americans should wake up and learn about this $50 billion dollar anti-American one world order philanthropist/butcher.

# POLITICALLY CORRECT MALEDUCATES

The years 2017-2020 will be a time that the leftists and the deep state government push harder than ever before in history to squelch free speech, push the pc agenda, and spy on us. Even with Pres. Trump cleaning house, we see instances of free speech being squashed more and more so not only in America, but within countries all around the globe. This is the silencing of the opposition to the new world order with politically correct speech derived from the cultural Marxism revolution that came out of the Frankfurt School and flowed into our universities as I elaborate elsewhere.

Reporters Without Borders is a group that monitors freedom of press around the world. It took notice of Obamas administrations stifling of the press. What did they find? Since Obama's administration, freedom of press had dropped from 32nd to 46th among the 180 countries measured. This is from the same Obama that had promised his would be the "most transparent" administration in American history.

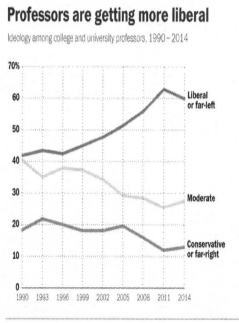

## Professors are getting more liberal

Ideology among college and university professors, 1990 – 2014

Presidential candidate Donald Trump learned the hard way that saying the wrong thing could come at a high cost. Example: South American Univision's airings of his upcoming Miss America pageant was threatened by that leftist media outlet. His sin was saying that he wanted to build a wall along the length of the Mexican border. Eventually he worked it all out, but it just shows how the big networks try to control anyone who bucks their agenda of open borders and one world agenda. What happened to free press? The globalist owned media's really do have immense sway as to what can be said, or they'll make sure you pay a price! Many accuse these liberal universities as a leading force toward the "standardization of culture." This term is their plan to squelch real free speech and regional cultures in exchange for their one size fits all global world and singular rules on conduct for all. It is in its essence Cultural Marxism at its core.

The chart above is a very conservative graph showing the predominance of liberal professorships at colleges and universities from the time period of 1990 until 2014. The reason I say it is a conservative look at the problem is that many studies have been done that show the problem of heavy handed liberalism in schools as being much, much worse. If you believe that todays college education is going to turn your Susie or Johnnie into a balanced young person with a healthy skepticism of radical ideas, forget the whole premise of college I suppose. If you really want to mess with their head, perhaps send them to one of the Ivy League schools such as Harvard, Princeton, Columbia for example. Yes, they will likely learn how to succeed in the world of finance, academia or any number of other specialty occupations that are generally lucrative. But I can nearly guarantee you that their outlook on life, morality and such will be much different than before. I think you know where I am going with that statement.

On August 4, 2015 it was reported on mainstream news that a student attending the Texas Christian University was suspended for criticizing the terrorist group ISIS, the Baltimore Rioters and illegal immigrants. Even though it was only posted on social media, not school property. But the 'politically correct' staff at the university held firm. The student stated that he might take it up a lawsuit against his first amendment rights. Some call this type of word discrimination as the beginning of the 'Word Police state, and/or the Thought Police state." Every day in the news we see this play out at increasing frequency.

The PC crowd is always at work. In 2013 national news networks discovered that University of New Hampshire (UNH) students and staff got together and came up with what they called the 'Bias Free Language Guide', placing it on their website in 2015. It was developed to dictate, or rather 'recommend' speech parameters on gender, race, immigrant status in order to be politically correct and not 'offend anybody! Recommended is the following: We should use the term "American citizen", not "American". Instead of calling a person "poor" we should call them a person living at or below the poverty line. Instead of using the term "rich" we must call them a person of material wealth. Don't use the term "illegal alien", but rather a "person seeking asylum". As to the word "gay", instead use the term "same gender loving". Do their cash strapped parents know they are paying for this type of politically correct garbage as part of their education? Just as alarming is the increase of universities and upper learning centers where professors discourage, even disparage students who want to dig a little deeper, question the popular anti-Western world dogmas preached by the far left. This is Cultural Marxism's core indoctrination technique.

In America today, our own police, Sheriff's and virtually all law enforcements are often required to force outdoor public protestors to only speak their minds in "set aside free speech zones", preferably far enough away from the public that hardly anyone notices the cries for justice! One infamous event that brought forth this change in police enforcement was the infamous 2013 Bundy Ranch incident in Nevada. Since when do we as citizens have to move into special zones to practice our Constitutional Rights provided in our first amendment? This is an unsettling trend.

After much objections by freedom loving Americans, the newer American Security Act (formerly the Patriot Act) was passed. The newly revised act was in large part supposed to end the ridiculous privacy abuses that had been found within the NSA by Edward Snowden. In reality, it just shifted the stolen information duties over to public phone companies, Facebook, Google and others to collect and turn over to the N.S.A. As with so many other things coming out of the Oval Office these days, real and actual change wanted by the majority is just a mirage, a juggling act. If the powers want to enact a devilish new law, they have dozens of ways to slip it through with only a few even realizing its dishonesty, i.e. placing it inside a new bill with a saintly title that has nothing to do with it! When it seems impossible to get anywhere while arguing with a liberal minded socialist, remember that their main argument comes down to Saul Alinsky's infamous playbook entitled 'Rules for Radicals'. Item #13 says "Pick the target, freeze it & personalize it". There it is in a bottle. Instead of discussing the issue and being truthful, a liberal will often stop any further discussion (freeze it), make scathing attacks on your ideas, frame you as a bigot, racist, an uncaring capitalist or something of the sort, (personalize it). These types don't believe in free speech because their ideas can't stand up to a frank, non-biased, actual discussion and they know it.

The Republican Presidential debate on the night of 10/28/2015 was a watershed moment exposing the neo-liberal bias. Sadly, for the libs, the CNBC moderators of the debate made themselves fools in the eyes of the American people. Americans have become sick and tired of the liberal political gamesmanship as was so visibly apparent and directed towards the questionings of the 2015-16 Republican runners. The common-sense approach of Donald Trump was disparaged. Being so, it was interviewer John Harwood whom asked of Trump "*Is this a comic book version of a presidential debate?*" At another time the talk was of fantasy football for goodness sakes! This was the implementation of Alinsky's tactics which mirrors the instructions given in the communist manifesto. Likewise, if a lib doesn't like a discussion, the idea is to disparage or berate the opponent, rather than engaging in non-p.c./intelligent debate. If the tables were turned upon the democratic debaters, such questions would not be tolerated! Bottom line, politics has purposely been boiled down to the lowest common denominator directed to an ever-growing dumbed down public whom can only understand general mantra's using simple and generalized words such as 'equality, race, glass ceiling, women's rights and other platitudes without any exact specifics. Sound like Hillary Clinton's campaign speeches? Their endgame has been to create a "standardization of culture", albeit their culture of failed ideas!

Kors, A. C.; Silverglate, H (November 1998). *"Codes of silence – who's silencing free speech on campus – and why"*. Reason Magazine. Archived from the original on 3 August 2004. Retrieved 20 August 2015 Friedman, Marilyn; Narveson, Jan (1995). *Political correctness: for and against*. Lanham: Rowman & Littlefield. *ISBN 0847679861*. Retrieved 31 October 2015

# A CONSPIRACY?

*"The high office of the President has been used to foment a plot to destroy the Americans freedom, and before I leave office I must inform the Citizen of his plight."* PRES. JOHN F. KENNEDY (10 days before his assassination)

As you can read at the top of this page, President Kennedy knew who ran the world. At the very time he made the above quote, he had begun the process of eliminating the unfederal reserves hold over our money. Kennedy made a huge statement to the Rothchild's fiat money operation. He began backing the one, five and ten-dollar bills with real silver backing. He knew the truth of the Rothschilds Federal Reserve conspiracy. Within a few days he was shot. The very next day after his death, the new President Johnson immediately rescinded the silver certificate plan. The Rothschild banking cabal were dead serious in maintaining their hold over America's money. They will never end the fiat money extraction machine. After all, they can create money out of debt! Kennedy was also intent on taking out Castro as well as clamping down heavily upon the Mafia, and other noble efforts to end the corruptions in Washington government. The man was a real game changer much like the new President Trump. The Deep State had enough. He lasted as President for just two years before being taken out under a surgically perfect murder, likely by the CIA.

To really be convinced that this long talked of world government is not just another conspiracy theory, you must absolutely need to read the history behind the makings of today's crazy upside-down world. Even if you don't like reading history, you might learn to like it after reading this. It will serve you well to read the plots, the deceptions, the big calls behind the scenes for the last 100+ years that have been purposely carried out in order to get us to where we are already at today, and what the carnage we are about to witness. When it comes to the whys and how's of America's decline, most only know a few things they heard at the coffee shop and of course on the paid media outlets. Much heard is old news and doesn't seem even relevant as far as most of the young are concerned. Todays are amazingly dumbed down by their failed state-run school systems, and by large they verifiably don't know jack about basic civics nor America's history. This is no mistake. After considering the following problems below, you might see how all of these systemic problems in America have a common connection. And although much of the brief intel in this important chapter skims on details, there is much more to learn about these claims in further chapters.

Newsweek reported a couple years ago that of 1,000 U.S citizens that took America's official citizenship test, 29 percent couldn't name the vice president. Seventy-three percent couldn't correctly say why we fought the Cold War. Forty-four percent were unable to define the Bill of Rights. Six percent couldn't even circle Independence Day on a calendar! Students spend 50% less time studying than two decades ago. Most other such surveys figures are worse. Disparagingly, seventy-five percent of young adults cannot find Israel on a map of the Middle East, but they sure know how to find a smut site on the internet or check out the latest on the Rapper-Illuminist Jay-Z and Rihanna (Obama's good friends)! Is there any question as to how and why the young have been brainwashed into believing the globalists lies on so many issues? Today, over half the country are believers in the false doctrines turned religion global warming, bigger government, socialism, wars being fought for democracy, etc. Its starts with young, for the globalists and the far left (acting as their useful idiots) appeal quite successfully to the young's feelings, not facts.

The elites of the world know that 99% are just too busy to pay attention to mundane matters such as politics unless is spoon fed to them in a ten-minute synopsis by their local mainstreet media which is controlled by official and leftist sources on how to report their stories. Nielsen ratings service reports that the average person now spends a total of 10 hours a day plugged into some form of electronic media! That includes four and one-half hours watching television alone. Needless to say, all those hours aren't spent looking beyond the headlines. If you let anyone to pump programming into your mind for 8 to 10 hours a day, it is going to have a dramatic impact, aka social conditioning.

It was Adolph Hitler whom said, *"Great for rulers that men do not think"*.

The following is just so important to take special note of…Communist Karl Marx knew, and had written truthfully, about how communism takes hold…

*"To accomplish Communism, it requires democracy first, followed by socialism, naturally falling into communism"*. **Karl Marx**

Is it any mistake that essentially all countries who call themselves a 'Democratic Republic' or 'Peoples Democratic Republic' are communist or hyper socialist? Isn't America always referred to as a democratic republic or vice-versa? Think about it. China, Cuba, North Korea, Soviet Union, Korea, Japan, Yemen, Libya, Ethiopia, Yemen, Congo are examples that use these important words to describe themselves! All are complete failures as to human rights and economic prowess, China being an exception as to the wealth equation of itself. Of course, America was not set up to mimic the examples above. The Founding Fathers realized that a democracy is always susceptible to falling into a socialist state or communism, especially if we were to stray from the Constitution and its principles. Principles that came from wise men that had once lived under the British monarchy that left them with little liberty or freedoms.

Marx, Lenin and other Marxists & dictators like them around the world have always known that a democracy system is soon followed by socialism, and next comes communism. This is nearly always the case. This is just the natural progression as a result of alpha man's quest for evermore and growing power over others. Such leader types understand the everyday average man's vulnerabilities and his misled trust of power. The choices between freedom, self-responsibility, and security/tyranny are never put together for the oppressed to understand or appreciate how much they give up for big government.

Few people realize just how powerful the big banks and corporate interests really are! The bankers have rigged the game going back the Knights Templars during the eleven hundreds. They now own us in effect. They destroy the currency, create debt and we become their slaves. The big money in the stock markets today is largely money put in there by the same heavyweights that are taking money from the unfederal reserve and multiplying it.

How many know that the banks and the corporate bottom feeders make far more money with the current worldwide socialism that exists today. It is indeed sad that the great American economy they left behind for years turned into the perfect breeding ground for them to thrive on the sufferings they themselves helped to create. Job offshoring turned down the faucet of tax dollars coming into the Treasury, thereby creating a debt-based economy for the bankers to thrive upon. Who benefits from a debt based anything? The Rothschilds, their banking crony's, the government, and nearly every part of the economy in the short term. The more debt, the better, as I demonstrate in the Federal Reserve chapter. Simply demonstrated, the Federal Reserve simply types in their money order to the Treasury and presto! "Money" is created from nothing but debt! U.S. bonds in particular. When the federal reserve has to pay interest on the bonds, how do they pay it? With simple electronic entries again. That's it! Never does anything real get passed on.

What do the bankers do with the "money" they borrow from the unfederal reserve? They loan it or invest it of course. When they make loans, they are allowed to lend out their deposit monies ten times over! So, from a one-hundred-dollar deposit they can lend one thousand dollars, sometimes even more. Again, money from nothing! It's called fractional lending and it goes on every day. Once this loaned money goes out into the economy, it is spent repeatedly to infinitum. Can we see how much money came from nothing? I wish I could take my paycheck and cash it in for ten times its face value! As we can see, the unfederal reserve banking system is nothing but a Ponzi scam. This is who Americans supposedly owe $20 trillion dollars to! The unfederal reserve creates inflation, boosting their profits many fold as well. Their money schemes go on and on. Going back to the 2008 crash it wasn't long after that the unfederal reserve posted their biggest profits ever! Coincidence? I think not.

The unfederal reserves ability to create inflation and manipulate interest rates is just one more way they manipulate money for themselves and their closest banking allies to benefit from under sheets. Inflation can be a friend of big business and big money investors, but it hits hard at working folks who find that their paychecks seem to be getting smaller. Inflation allows them to manipulate the *value of money during the time between monies creation and its use. Inflation by its very* definition is the destruction of your buying power over a period of time.

The reader will see how the Federal Reserve is not federal and it does not have a "reserve" either! But for the laziness of many Americans, they don't have a clue how the un-Federal Reserve, our banking system, globalism and so many other entities have been destroying the ability of America to be what it should be. Instead we are played for fools by the global money elites! It may be boring stuff for some and some may wish to call much of this little discussed 'boring' information. And those like myself who are trying to expose the conspiracy unto their fellow Americans, we are often called 'conspiracy nuts'. Just because you don't know yet about this information doesn't mean it doesn't exist for darn sakes! These architects of corporate and global takeover don't want you to know the long-running plan that is now taking shape.

Obamacare is another con game set up from the get-go to primarily serve the money interests of everyone involved, of which there are many. Is it any wonder that health insurance companies in large part have had record profits under Obamacare? The socialist democrats and republicans have always wanted a nationalized healthcare system in order to increase dependency upon the mother's milk of the state while the global corporates who run the biggest companies have in America have turned over the responsibility of healthcare to the state (boosting their profit margins). Meanwhile the corporate insurance industry can charge exorbitant insurance rates inside of a market nearly void of much competition, especially in states like California! The leftist hopes of eventual single payer could lock in permanent profits to all those involved with such a monopoly. Perhaps if Obamacare, or single payer actually was successful at cutting health and drug costs, we might believe at least a little bit of the lefts arguments for its very creation. Instead the opposite has occurred as anyone with a brain could have envisioned. Can we see a pattern of big money interests steering nearly the entire economy here? Great deceased talk show host George Putnam always opined, "Follow the money!"

As America predictably continues to flitter along with very little, if any, <u>real</u> income growth for average workers, the top 10 percent, as well as most government workers have done very, very well. This demographic of earners are beholden to the big state architects that have padded their pocketbooks through big government programs, jobs. Their incomes have outstripped inflation many times over as shown further on. The corruption and has been a trend going in for several years now whereby many cashed starved cities, counties, public utility companies and similar public entities are opting to sell their properties to huge and often foreign corporates and globalist entities in exchange for cash, leasing back the property. These transactions are often taken in order to feed the overly generous, expensive retirement plans, overcompensations and waste. This is just one simple example of how big bureaucracies are often shortsighted, gorging on the banquet plate called corruption.

As we witness more and more sales of American companies and public infrastructures unto the laps of wealthy private investors, especially big foreign and national corporates, we will soon wake up to a country that is no longer America. America will just another dot on the map of the world along with all other countries. It will be sold out and bereft of its soul. It will meld into what will have become a one world globalist economy with a one world central body, police force, laws, and nearly zero semblance of the America that our founding fathers risked their lives for. Our independent spirit will have left the property as well as many of our freedoms and liberties. The way we get there? The new world architects usually create a crisis in order to rebuild what they tore down into their visions. How crafty indeed for the world change agents. They create the conditions we are witnessing, then they slam the hammer down. Nobody knows the date that is for sure. Communists call this process "planned deconstruction before reconstruction." The Mainstreet talk speaks won't utter a sound, that we can be assured! No, instead all you will hear about are side shows to keep us distracted from the reality that America, and the world for that matter are living on borrowed time. They'd rather keep your mind on made up scandals such as Russian collusions and other such nonsense.

No-bid government contracts and seemingly endless change orders are exactly what Rockefeller was talking about when he exclaimed *"competition is a sin!"* Multiply this business plan with thousands of differing cronyisms between government and corporates in nearly every industry, every single day, and you can see why government budgets are so out of control. Everyone remembers the joke about thousand-dollar toilets inside government-built airplanes. It's really true. When comes time to pay for all of the wasteful spending policies and programs throughout government, there never is enough dough. How are we to pay for all this waste and fluff? The next crime here is that the large banks and Wall Street obtain ultra-cheap money from our the unfederal reserve and government often for less than even one percent. Some of that money gets turned around to buy government bonds from the same U.S. government that just loaned it to them at a much higher interest rate, profiting from the "spread". More often, this near free money gets plowed into the stock market using sophisticated leveraging and electronic trades that can often times turn one million dollars into perhaps $10 million dollars in short order!

Unbelievably, banks turn around and use this near free money to issue credit cards at up to 25% annual interest to the millions of unrestrained or cash strapped retail consumers whom are used as suckers. Oh, the banks have dozens of way to expand their money exponentially. See how money flows to the top now? And it's legal. There used to be usury laws but no more. If it all goes bad, don't worry because the taxpayer is on the hooks since all the risk in on the back of the taxpayers, with Uncle Sam as the administrator. Great work if you can get it. There are hundreds of scams performed everyday by the big banks, the entire financial industries and so forth. Many of the scams are highly technical and you aren't supposed to understand it on purpose. For instance, with electronic trading thousands of transactions are automatically traded per second, making it much easier for professional traders to profit from the thousands of buys and sells per second. Can anyone truthfully say that this type of money is "earned?" For many of the banks and elites, this is how they earn a great living. Yes, off the backs of those of us helping the real economy fire on all 8 cylinders! The eventual world debt crash, soon to come, will hit American's and the world harder than ever before experienced. Later, I show how a world money is verifiably already in place and ready to take care of this next worldwide big bang to arrive from Europe!

Such trillion-dollar examples of thievery abound in the world of finance. Literally trillions of dollars every year get lost, stolen or wasted inside government programs including the military especially. Yet, the crony Washington elites can't seem to find money to feed, clothe or rehabilitate the homeless in America. Nor offer excellent free healthcare for all! Beginning in the 1970's, these financial games by the top .001% replaced a real economy that really made things…like cars and refrigerators.

This was the beginnings of the *"financialization of the American economy"*, and we have been witnessing this predominant style of income grab by elites for nearly 50 years now. While workers toil, sweat and worry about tomorrow due to falling real wages, shitty jobs and losses of security, the financial industry has seen the highest income growth just pushing money around and manipulating it as though it was free (which it often is when Uncle Sam is partnered in). Unlike years ago, when America and the top 1% actually made products, today's 1% often don't produce anything besides the unsustainable financial bubble economies of the last several decades. President Trump is making a heroic effort with some success at revitalizing American industry and helping the small guy to earn a living outside of a service economy.

You might ask yourself, why has banking and the financial sector been so favored by those in places of high level governmental policymaking? Banking indeed is one big laundering money laundering machine of epic proportions. This is old business folks! Think back to the oldest international bankers who were called the Knights Templars from the 1100 A.D. era. These lenders essentially owned Europe, the Catholic Church and most of that part of the world at that time by issuing widespread debts and the acquiring's of unmatched real estate and valuables such as the world had ever known before. through their shrewd, often shady lending practices.

The most successful bankster of all time was Amstel Rothschild. He famously said long ago; *"Give me control of a nations money, and I care not who makes the laws."* He knew that making loans and partnering up with lawmakers he could not be stopped! And nothing has really changed as far as how money is made for the last 200 + years since this creator of our modern money system said those words. America had begun adopting the Rothschild's banking scheme in America even before 1913 when the Federal Reserve was begun.

Now, the top 8 banks of the world together garner over half of the world's wealth. These are all intimately tied to the Federal Reserve and International Monetary Fund marriage with the Rothschilds. I say it is at your peril to not read the substantial offerings of proofs in this book. The rich really do run the world and we are their expendables. This is globalism, but they won't tell you that. They worry you about global warming, not the huge and real dangers that they themselves have created. Doesn't globalism sound great?

My hope to the reader is to help the process of making the connections, the how and why America has evolved into the big state, racing toward and into a big brother fascist/socialist state where the ideals of our Founding Fathers are ignored or disgraced by many. And why our culture, our morals, our love of country and its traditions are waning. Many are asking "Why would anyone want to ruin the most successful civilization the world has ever known?"

No, it's not conspiracy anymore. It is here in large part, and its real!

## .3

# CONTROLLED OPPOSITIONS!

**"The further a society drifts from the truth, the more it will hate those that speak it." George Orwell**

President Donald Trump, while trying to make his case of "Making America Great Again" has been faced with a daunting task in the face of all those whom are just fine in accepting the last 50 years of politics, or perhaps even want even more government interference in their lives. Besides his obviously "rough around the edges" demeanor, or perhaps because of it in part, he has an unenviable task similar to trying to lead a stubborn corral of horses to water. The man is not perfect, for sure. But I contend that the other half of the country who did not vote for him, too many had been brainwashed (literally) by the Lamestreet liberal medias for years. They have been slamming any conservative leaning candidate or agenda that peeks its head out into the light. Mainstream media news pundits are overwhelmingly in the league of "controlled opposition" when talking their views, be it liberal or conservative! These know their very professional survival is threatened if they reveal and awaken their listeners to the truth about what is really going on, even if they wanted to. The 6 major networks own ninety percent of the media we follow and are owned largely by globalist elites as proven further on. These make it very clear to their station managers that their very livelihood is endangered should they not follow the political tone, prompts, and the story lines imparted to them before the newscast is aired. Which isn't too hard to follow since most all of their hosts or guests are peer reviewed before even getting to the second interview for the job or interview. Leftist networks have become notorious for inviting a conservative to be a guest wherein they arrange a panel of five or six liberal guests to gang up and give little time to respond properly! Reminds me of a pack of wolves.

Even Fox News, who undeniably has earned a reputation of at least somewhat honest accounts on current events, (amongst cable mainstream news networks) they dare not expose the inner, sinister workings behind many of current events, especially events that might expose the real agenda behind a news item. So, they set limits as to how far a journalist can delve and divulge into particular truthing's. They always have to keep in mind the leanings of their networks expensive advertising clients and government regulators who represent the deep state's control over news they deem to not be favorable to be heard. This is the deep state silencing of truth.

Let's get real, O.K.? For instance, do they dare criticize big agriculture and their unhealthy farming practices, when one of their sponsors is owned by Monsanto? I don't think so. This is one reason why you seldom witness the airing of an intelligent program considering the pro's and cons of varying corporate practices or how some of their policies affects our lives, our health or any one of many other examples for instance.

Remember, the corporates are the ones who lavishly fund the news outlets very existence via huge ad budgets, and don't forget, the government owns their licensing's. Examples of news peoples and journalists who bucked the systems rules and got fired? Juan Williams is one, even though he is fairly liberal in leanings, NPR fired him for criticizing some Muslim's. Don Imus was also fired for using the word 'Nappy". Laura Schlesinger using the N word, even though it was in proper context. Even Helen Thomas, long time reporter for "The Hill" for remarks concerning Israel during a Presidential press conference, more further on. This goes on every day!

In 2013, Fox fired two reporters for not complying with the stations demand to drop an exposé on the large dangers that are presented when Monsanto's synthetic drug called Pisolac is injected into milking cows in order to increase the production of milk. Armed with reams of scientific materials backing their case, station corporates pulled the story. The two reporters filed lawsuits against Fox soon afterwards. Monsanto had put so much pressure to pull the story that they warned of dire consequences i.e. pulling many millions of dollars of advertising away from Fox's 22 stations around the world! This type of corporate muscle is played out every day on network news, stealing away the truth.

Dear reader, I don't take aim at only the liberals. You will notice that I will often criticize both sides of the political isle when I believe the shoe fits, for both parties are largely on the gravy train, looking out for their own personal interests including working for the globalist agenda. Each party has their own official set of politics, each supposedly believing in their own "fix" to the problems the country faces. Both sides are guilty of supporting big money whom fill their coffers while offering only scraps from the corporate banquet table. They both offer up phony official policy to fool the masses. Lie, cheat and steal is the norm in today's politics, so how can I possibly fully endorse either? Donald Trump is the upsetter for these types.

## OBAMA'S FRAMING OF DINESH D'SOUZA

Dinesh D'Souza, the famed creator of several pro-America movies was placed in jail for 9 months in 2015, ostensibly prompted by the hate from President Obama. His wildly successful conservative leaning movie dubbed "2016-Obamas America" had just been released. According to D'Souza and his story, this was an obvious political shakedown, coincidently just at the same time of this anti-Trump movie being released to widespread theaters. The official reason was for failing to report to the I.R.S political contributions of $20,000. Huff Post, 1/24/14 by Abby Ohlheiser. Mr. D'Souza is not a politician and likely had no idea as to the special reporting requirement most politicians are accustomed to! Seldom would any average person even be audited or worse yet be jailed! To be honest, he had criticized President Obama a few times, but isn't free speech alive? This was an obvious attack by Obama and his administration to teach someone who had two things immediately against him in the administrations eyes. Number 1, he's a Christian, and #2 his new film was patently against Obamas leftist, socialist one world agenda. His film instead espoused patriotic and traditional American values. Oh, what a terrible thing to espouse!

Pres. Obama was going to teach him a lesson for others to learn from! During D'Souza's detainment, the judge decided (with the blessings of Obama I am sure) that Mr. D'Souza was 'unstable', after witnessing his natural agitation following his arrest once he knew he was being framed and duped! Well, the government thought it was an opportune moment to force him to live in a half-way house for 8 months, plus regular weekly 'social engineering' sessions with a court ordered psychological counselor in order to help him mellow out his 'extreme views' about America! In addition, a surprise stipulation came later from his Manhattan Federal Court Judge Richard Berman, "clarifying" his sentence to require Dinesh to perform 8 hours per week for his entire 5-year probation period as well. That's 1600 hours! N.Y. Post/Josh Saul 7/13/2015. This was a surprise to say the least, pointing out how it's possible for Obama to use his powers to instruct ridiculous punishments for a selected few. This type of abuse of power seems to be common course these days. After I looked back at other cases of campaign law violations, there was absolutely none that had punishments nearly as serious as this one, even many with campaign violations in the hundreds of thousands of dollars! Coincidently perhaps, in the same period of his original court case, the IRS has made it far more difficult for conservative political groups to operate under newly placed rules inside any 501 (c)-4 corporation that many charitable or church organizations use. The founding fathers warned us how government could become the masters if we let them! Update: President Trump pardoned him in 2018!

*"In time of great deceit, telling the truth is a revolutionary act!"* George Orwell


## SHUTTING DOWN JUDGE NAPOLITANO

Perhaps one of the most clear and somewhat current examples of how the media elites try to hide the real agenda from the public in 2013. It was the last show before the cancellation of Judge Napolitano's show entitled "Freedom Watch" on the Fox News network. Napolitano got fired for airing a five-minute expose' of the real agenda of the political system in early 2012 at the end of his show. He obviously wanted the last moment of that days show to drive home a point after the airing. Obviously, they and their elite owners didn't like him calling out the actual ironies of our government, and the lies we are told about our supposedly fair and honest political system. This deception of an ethical media and government has been pounded into nearly all citizens regarding voting, political, economic and war policies as long as we can remember.

Some of the forbidden questions posed to the viewers in the last few minutes of the show by Judge Napolitano's were along these lines:

* Freedom of choice in elections: Does leaving you with just two viable choices imply freedom of choice?

* What if there were more than 2 platforms to take? What if both parties used up their time with illusory squabbling about smaller issues, but the big issues were obfuscated or ignored since they were bought and paid for, catering to their large corporate donators, (who are largely globalists).

* What if no matter who won the election, things remained the same?

* What if the heart of government remained the same no matter what the people want?

*What if George Bush waged an election of smaller government and non-interventionist policies, yet did the opposite?

*What if Obama ran on a platform of anti-war, pro civil rights, lower deficits, and proceeded to engage in senseless wars, assaulted rights that the Constitution is supposed to protect, divided the country even more on racial issues, and ran record deficits?

*What if the biggest difference between candidates wasn't substance, but style?

*What if the stylistic differences of candidates were packaged as substantive ones, no matter who ran?

*What if there were more than two sides to an issue, but the two parties wanted to box you into a corner seeing no other option?

*What if the two parties didn't really care about your concerns, but only their careers whom they owe to the top 1%? And more.

It's an amazing five minutes if you have the time to watch it on YouTube! This shows how real free speech is nearly dead, and we have limits on what the media can or can't say on public airwaves! Whether it's the truth being spoken is beside the point to these elites with their own hard driven agenda.

To these media elites, the truth isn't why they are in business. Unfortunately, since we can't depend on the mainstream media to convey much truth, the answer to finding the real news is to step away and find alternative news sites, not owned by these media giants. Instead, find news outlets that offer up more truth & meat on issues facing us all, and there are now plenty of them. We have unfortunately become a nation of non- civic minded citizens who wish to leave it to others to figure out the problems "out there".

Studies show that only 25% of Americans can pass a civics test, so take it from there. We unfortunately can't trust our "paid for" politicians, so we must rekindle the spirit of not taking freedom so for granted! It isn't and never has been free, yet most today do take this for granted. We have to share inequities with as many as we can, especially Washington. Understanding the real systemic problems of our country, and even the world, should be the real and urgent subject on television and internet.

The elites who run things don't want you to know or figure out the gargantuan manipulations most of us naturally buy into, especially as to the Federal Reserve. Glen Beck was another one whom was fired by Fox News when he fully exposed the Federal Reserve. His guest was Edward G. Griffin, the most respected expert on the real story behind the Federal Reserve. He is still the most read author of the most respected and read book on the Federal Reserve conspiracy, entitled Creature From Jeckyll Island. So much was exposed about the secret workings, dangers and the robbing's of the world behind this agency, well, this was to be Glenn Beck's last show on Fox! That show can now be easily watched in entirety on YouTube. It seems that even Fox has their limits as to how much can be spoken of the elite's secret, hidden agenda. The Deep State had finally said to Fox, "this is the last straw."

Hitler was famous for his quote *"If a lie is said enough times, people will eventually believe it. The bigger the lie, the better, for it will be more believable."* Think for a minute just how incredible and valuable this uncommon knowledge about our human behavior is! Knowing this This has been the backbone of a good propagandist strategy.

How liberating it is when you can read the truth and see why the large corporate owned & far leftist leaning Mainstreet outlets are lying to you. I am a fan of the really great, timeless quotes given by many of the world's greatest, most influential movers and shakers of history as you will notice. Such shows that real truths don't change. So, I hope you enjoy them and appreciate the relevance to the subject spoken of.

As this nation's citizenry, we have taken our eyes off the political football for decades, instead turning our attention to NFL Football, the NBA, Singing with the Stars, etc. Now it is clear that we must get serious, go back to American basics of freedom, liberty and justice for all and take our country back. We must regain control of our government by waking up, begin monitoring our politicians, the government actions or inactions, and read between the lies. Only by having a sense of disdain for much of what you hear on the big news outlets can you find the whole picture of what is really going on. The disinformation campaigns can often be exposed if enough citizens find other more honest sources of the news. Begin monitoring not just what the talking heads and politicians say, but what they actually do. That's what the politicians congressional voting records are for and are readily available online. We have lost sight of making politicians actually listen to their constituents, and making our words get back to Washington. Due to years and years of political laxness on the part of citizens, the politicians have been handed a green light to cow-tow and be bought out by the corporate, Wall Street and special interest groups that fund their huge war chests for reelections instead of their listening to their constituents.

## ELIMINATING BREITBART

Andrew Breitbart was only 43 years old when he died unexpectedly on 3/1/2012. He was an extremely talented, successful columnist and founder of the successful Breitbart Report. Often not liked by the left side of the isle, he spoke unabashedly about his conservative thoughts and criticisms of current events in his well-known online site. He was conservative, a friend of the Tea Party movement, and had gained a reputation of bringing forth new ammunition against the left, especially in respect to then President Obama. Many question the events and timings leading up to his extremely untimely and strange death circumstances that still stand unanswered.

On 2/12/2012, as a speaker at the 2012 CPAC convention, Breitbart claimed he that he obtained video(s) showing Obama back in his Harvard college days that would expose Obama in meetings with extremists, communists and much more to prove his Marxist ideology. Even showing Obama arguing with his college buddy Bill Ayers over their differences on how to overthrow America. Bill Ayres was the founder of the Weather Underground in the 1960's, a far-left anarchist bunch of communist terrorists. It was Bill Ayers whom blew up several Chicago Federal Buildings in Chicago, later writing the infamous pro-communist takeover book "Rules for Radicals"

During this taped speech at CPAC (available on YouTube), Breitbart claimed he would release the video on March 01, 2012 which would come to be his last day on earth! He claimed this video would crush Obama, exposing his long held true leanings as a radical anti-American Marxist during his college days and much more. Claimed was that Obama had made friends with several "silver pony tailed radicals in the 1980's, such as Bill and Bernardine Dorn, equally radical. The two were on the FBI's Most Wanted List at one time. These once said, "One day, were gonna gain the presidential residency while the country was asleep". That took money, BIG money. A working partnership between Ayers and Obama working on a large grant from the Chicago Annenberg Project made possible many millions of dollars to be funneled to the two and their leftist ideologues from the $170 million-dollar grant. Breitbart said that "racial division and class warfare was an integral part of Obama's "change we can believe in" mantra's.

As Breitbart walked outside of his regular watering hole in Brentwood, Calif. bar in the early hours of March 01, 2012 (just hours before he was to release his video to the press), he was 'claimed' to have suffered a sudden heart attack while standing on the corner outside the bar to have a smoke before going home. The bartender claimed he looked perfectly fine when he left the establishment. The only actual witness was a young man named Christopher Lassiter who said that Breitbart suddenly bent downward and fell to the curb. The young man also claimed that Breitbart turned very red when he collapsed. Doctors know that a person having a heart attack does not turn red. Some claim it was murder by use of the CIA's heart attack gun which employs a special frozen, poisoned dissolvable bullet sent by special compliments of Obama. All signs of the slight penetration into the skin are hardly visible at the time of impact but results in immediate death. Any residual signs of the chemicals of the projectile are completely worn off in 4 days, long before an autopsy is performed. Of course, there are many clever ways that the CIA and others can employ to stage a natural death. So, it gets more interesting. Usually an autopsy is performed within one week, but Breitbarts wasn't taken for at least three weeks. On March 21, the same day the autopsy report was to be released, his coroner Michael Cormier went to the hospital complaining of pain and vomiting. Cormier died from arsenic poisoning hours later.

Steve Bannon was made executive chairman of Breitbarts within days of Breitbart's death. Almost immediately he answered the questions of "when will we see the tapes?" Bannon promised that the tapes would be released within 3 weeks likely. Yet the tapes never surfaced. Many claim that the tapes were confiscated by the Obama cartel, likely the CIA. The video never showed up anywhere, zilch. Not long afterward his wife also died. A very strange tale of events, for sure. Perhaps he paid the ultimate price for being a patriot? Some call these types of happenings as "conspiracy", and perhaps in a technical sense that is true for such questionings are not provable. But when you see the same strange set of events happening over and over again to people who hold proofs that go against the official story, well, you might see what I mean. I could give the names of hundreds of names of similarly very questionable causes of death by people that had something the deep state didn't want to be let out. Part of this anomaly is explained in the next chapter!

"*Every thing secret degenerates, even the administration of Justice! Nothing is safe that does not show how it can bear discussion publicly.*" 1861, Published by Lord Action and his circle (1906).

# .4

# THE AGE OF DISINFORMATION

## ON EDWARD BERNAYS, MEDIA, SCHOOLS, "SHOCK-VERTISING", BOY-MEN, DOING THE TWIST AND OTHER INSIGHTS

*"Withholding information is the essence of tyranny. Control of the flow of information is the tool of a dictatorship."* Bruce Coville

Is it any wonder why the general public has been amazingly misled by our leaders, schools and our Mainstreet newspeak outlets leading this up to this travesty Most citizens just go along and get along, all the while they are being bred to be docile subjects who are willing to believe that the government is looking out for them?

How is it that President Trump's every move becomes a scandal? Why is it that nearly everything we hear today on the differing media outlets becomes suspect of political bent? Does ANY real journalism anymore?

Bill Whittle, respected journalist with PJTV exclaimed *"the news media is the most trusted scam in America."*

Is all this just a set of random events without preplanning? Think again. For proof that the state is very involved with this twisting of our minds and the truth, read the following shattering truth that most know nothing of!

Edward Bernays lived from 1891 until 1995. He worked in the highest echelons of intelligence and planning for the U.S. government much of his career as well as major American companies. Known as the father of propaganda, he was celebrated as one of America's chief manipulation experts whose work has become a part of our reality today.

As a member of the Creel Committee, he helped U.S. President Woodrow Wilson propagandize in support of allied war aims during World War I. He went on to be an architect of U.S. policies and planning. He went on to design PR campaigns for politicians and companies such as General Motors, Procter & Gamble and American Tobacco. Combining the ideas of Gustave Le Bon and Wilfred Trotter on crowd psychology, as well as the psychoanalytical ideas of his uncle Sigmund Freud, Bernays was one of the first to attempt to manipulate public opinion using the subconscious.

Bernays, with the explicit sanctions of our government, was instrumental in formulating mind control methods still employed by globalist central planners and used in our school systems to subliminally induce students to accept with glee whatever is purposely fed to them. Not to be confused, the timing of his works also coincided with the MK15 mind control project used by the American government to control many types of subjects of let's say 'special interest'. Bernays also pioneered the PR industry's use of psychology and other social sciences to design its public persuasion campaigns.

*"If we understand the mechanism and motives of the group mind," he wrote, "is it not possible to control and regiment the masses according to our will without their knowing about it? The recent practice of propaganda has proved that it is possible, at least up to a certain point and within certain limits." (Propaganda, 2005 ed., p. 71.) He famously called this ever important scientific technique of opinion-molding as the "engineering of consent."* This technique was to be used more heavily by the deep state mold makers in coming years.

Bernays' techniques of engineered consent no were not completely new. Marx and others had used the same techniques but was hardly advertised. This method of silent group control is still very alive and active inside the classrooms and auditoriums of our schools today. As a matter of fact, you will see just how prevalent this is. The big push of the entire agenda of the far left is based on this religion of sorts. The movement of global warming, population reduction, a global village and the use of politically correct language in particular. Bernays's list of accomplishment in the use of propaganda for the one world cause was, and still is legendary.

Unlike some other early public relations practitioners, Bernays advocated centralization and planning. For instance, inside his 1945 book *Take Your Place at the Peace Table* he makes a clear appeal for corporate socialism. It is no coincidence that he was highly admired by Hitler's Dr. Joseph Mengele known as the butcher of the Jews.

Furthermore, Bernays touted the idea that the "masses" are driven by factors outside their conscious understanding, and therefore that their minds can and should be manipulated by the capable few. "Intelligent men must realize that propaganda is the modern instrument by which they can fight for productive ends and help to bring order out of chaos." He felt this manipulation was necessary in society, which he regarded as irrational and dangerous as a result of the 'herd instinct' that Trotter had described. Adam Curtis's award-winning 2002 documentary for the BBC, *The Century of the Self*, pinpoints Bernays as the originator of modern public relations. Bernays was named one of the 100 most influential Americans of the 20th century by Life magazine.

One-way Bernays reconciled manipulation with liberalism was his claim that the human masses would inevitably succumb to manipulation—and therefore the good propagandists could compete with the evil, without incurring any marginal moral cost. In his view, "the minority which uses this power is increasingly intelligent and works more and more on behalf of ideas that are socially constructive." This IS the mindset of the globalist elites who truly believe that they are superior to mere mortals and only THEY are capable of directing the world.

Here is one of Bernays's famous quotes:

> '*The conscious and intelligent manipulation of the organized habits and opinions of the masses is an important element in democratic society. <u>Those who manipulate this unseen mechanism of society constitute an invisible government which is the true ruling power of our country.</u> ...We are governed, our minds are molded, our tastes formed, our ideas suggested, largely by men we have never heard of. This is a logical result of the way in which our democratic society is organized. Vast numbers of human beings must cooperate in this manner if they are to live together as a smoothly functioning society. ...In almost every act of our daily lives, whether in the sphere of politics or business, in our social conduct or our ethical thinking, we are dominated by the relatively small number of persons...who understand the mental processes and social patterns of the masses. It is they who pull the wires which control the public mind.*" *Propaganda* (1928) pp. 9–10

None of this is new. Beyond the booming Trump economy we are witnessing today (even though still benefitting only the top 10 percent and stock market in large part), does one not notice how very much that Americans, and peoples of the world for that matter, have either fallen for the globalist village lie, or are still included as part of those who question the entire premise altogether? In other words, the world seems to be divided on the issue.

I ask this: Are you not shocked that your government employs people like this to engineer our country and the world? The name Bernays has now been supplanted with thousands of other scholars, politicians, policy makers and the such inside of every institution of learning or substance. You shouldn't so surprised if you have not been tuned into this current history. Where you too busy? What happened to America the Beautiful, the Land of the Free? All the evidence that I have pieced together does in fact validate the idea that the overriding plannings of the elites has always been engineered and organized primarily for the elites, primarily the monied interests. In the worst sense, a magnification of what we now witness. Yes, a complete world corporate communism.

It should be clear beyond any doubt we are talking about global government run by the top .001 percent onboard elitists. That being the case, the free market economy will become nearly extinct except for a handful of multinationals whom will run what in essence will be a monopolistic economy. Today we see how companies like Google, Amazon and dozens of other goliaths also own, control and profit from a plethora of subsidiary or separate companies under their wings without 99% even realizing it! We only know the brand names, not who makes them after all. As this monopolization become more and more concentrated, it doesn't take a rocket scientist to see the writings on the wall, for this is the plan and always has been. Today's supranational corporations and banking elites will have succeeded in a worldwide monopoly over most or all products and services you buy. The ultra-wealthy thrive as much power as they can harness just for powers sake. The plans are for a one world army, economy, center of power, even a world religion of satanism disguised as something other!

You can see today how very concentrated wealth has drawn down to only a handful of corporate elites (which I cover extensively further on.) Skipping specifics, this plan has been slowly implemented with successes and failures beginning over a hundred years ago, but it is now extremely close to fruition unless it is fought back most valiantly. Their entire scheme has always been based on lies, deceptions, and whatever it takes to reach their aims. Socialism, communism always requires big lies. So, the big question is: How does one discern information correctly when being bombarded by disinformation agents everywhere you turn? For those with the time, true research is required!

## USEFUL IDIOTS:

The elites and their useful idiots have done a superb job of filling our minds with extraordinary blocs of time watching mindless entertainment television, rigged sports, the web, all the useless, and mindless entertainment they want us to watch or engage in. Watch a reality show. It celebrates manipulations, aggressiveness, deception, primacy of self over all others. The reward for being ruthless is to win the show, gain money and fame. The media's, owned by the elite capitalists, impose their reality, their agenda onto the rest of society. The globalist's success at "pulling the wool over our eyes" for the past 100 years has been done in order to enrich themselves through the disparagement of America's lower classes and disappearing middle class who are only receiving crumbs from their banquet table. These are the ones whom throughout history will dependably cry out for more and more government help, eventually accepting a growing socialism, becoming merely a property of the state.

The purposeful 'spin' that Joe/Jane citizen hears on their way home from work or in their living room forms an immediate opinion on the topic just received and the elites know it. Stressed for time or self-serving distractions, most citizens instantly create an ill-informed, mal educated opinions that gain support for their real self-serving agenda. It is obviously late in the game, but we must really take our thoughts out of the 'arrested development state.'

The elites don't want informed, well-educated citizens who can still think critically without the establishments blinders on. They want mal-educated's (my term) as can be seen by today's graduates who are no longer taught to really analyze, never step out of the P.C. crowd, and never question the official mantra of their schoolings. What used to be called a "liberal education" meant that the student learned several subjects such as the arts, literature and so forth. They were encouraged to read between lines, think for themselves, be critical. What far too many schools, or at least individual classes teach today is the opposite of critical thought. We are still carrying Fabian John Dewey's idea of education. Dewey was the original architect of American schooling going back to the 1920's. What the state-run educations system largely wants out of graduates hasn't changed much in 100 years. They want obedient workers just smart enough to produce or supply the basic needs of society within the workplace (that the .01% provides them) and dumbed down enough that they will passively accept the increasingly shitty jobs that no longer pay a decent wage, no longer have retirement benefits, and often only provide reduced part time status in order to push the cost of healthcare onto the state in the form of corporate welfare.

American schooling has been slickly, and until recently stealthily, been indoctrinated by Marxist/John Dewey/Edward Bernays styled methods for the last 90+ years to sell the socialist, secular lie in order to create their new world of compliant drones whom look at the state as their mommy and daddy. The thing to remember is that this entire reprogramming of society takes generations to succeed.

Most importantly, over and above all the above problems with education, America's education system since the 1940's has blindly bought into the ideology of anti-Western "Cultural Marxism" as I describe and document in the upcoming chapter entitled Frankfurt School. We are witnessing that 75 years of our state owned, top down, anti-Western education systems have become the breeding grounds for the disproven socialist ideologies they foster.

Universities across the globe have for years been indoctrinated with anti-Western ideology, especially Americas own. Today in large part they don't train students how to think critically, to examine and critique systems of power or cultural/political assumptions unless such allowance is directed toward the disparagement of Western values of course. Far too often students are not encouraged to ask broad questions of meaning and morality once sustained by the humanities. The universities have become breeding grounds for systems managers trained to serve the corporate state. Since the federal government has made college tuition as easy to obtain as fogging up a mirror, all that added cash has thrown the whole college system out of whack on several critical levels. The large corporates have inundated the universities with enormous amounts of endowments and corporate sponsored classes while showering the budgets of many departments with billions in corporate and government dollars. Ever since federal government began sponsoring federal college loans, tens of thousands of disappointed college grads have flooded into a new world of few jobs to qualify for. As such, many move back in with mom and dad for years after not finding a good job. Instead, many work at hamburger joints and such for years into the future. The delicate balance of needed jobs and the ability to offer the proper educations to match the times has been largely disrupted due to the political agenda driven by many of the college administrations who create the changes in today's college curriculum offered.

While college revenues skyrocket, we witness college presidents being increasingly paid hugely more than is justified, while offering no guarantee of any real career for these students. Who are these college career counselors who advise a young person to major toward a career in a losing and overcrowded field with low wages and little opportunity? Well, it seems there are plenty of them based on the results collected to gauge student success.

Yet, in 2014 it was reported that the average college presidents are making long term student success. $428.000.00 per year, three and one-half times more than the average full-time professor! Rodney Erickson Penn State president made $1.4 million in total salaries in 2014 as well. Orin Loftin, Texas A&M made $1.1 million dollars the same year. Although these are not typical, we must realize that since the fed's college loan programs have become hugely larger big money operations that puts affordable, excellent education as second fiddle. As such, skyrocketing tuition rates make it impossible for most to pay-as-they-go, such as prior generations enjoyed. Source: CNNMoney, U.S. article entitled: The Highest Paid Public University Presidents/article by Emily Jane Fox, 6/8/15.

The partnering of colleges and large corporate funded programs are further perpetuating the globalist mindset into the students. Of course, big corporate donors come with strings attached. As a result, college professors are seemingly told to remain silent toward their students when learning of the abuses of the globalist, corporate powers. Professors are too often encouraged at times to label anyone who questions the excesses of unfettered capitalism as being "politically motivated" in order to escape any real discussion of globalism and its false promises of equality for all. Deep questions as to why the same elitist powers who operate and own the largest conglomerates and banking interests in the world always seem to be behind the globalism bandwagon, pushing for fairness, equality of rights to all, et al. That's the problem with the far left's mindset often, for they haven't learned how to do their own subjective research. Even morality is taught as subjective, and knowledge is whatever you determine it to be. Cultural Marxism is rampant and has bred a nation of narcissistic followers. Source in part from book Death of the Liberal Class- Chris Hedges (excerpt pg. 11)

As a result, many of our "educateds" are in actuality maleducates. These classes of peoples have become unable to truly discern news, get beyond their entrenched liberal biases, separate truths from fictions, nor see beyond the headlines. Few have been introduced properly, if at all, to the many tyrants throughout recorded time whom had cleverly changed the perceptions of the realities brought down upon their citizens prior to their enslavements. The Marxist playbook asks, or forces, their naïve citizens to follow all the states requests for the public good, lest be labeled or worse. Values and attitudes toward the state can be changed through mass propaganda, lies and psychological conditioning upon the subjective civilians as most would suspect. History assuredly repeats with little twists here and there. The 50 years of mass propaganda Americans have witnessed on Mainstreet television has been successful in breeding re-educateds (my term), whom largely have been convinced to deny themselves of their own innate common senses. This also applies to political contests. Politicians often change the political narrative to feelings, rather than facts. It is so much more effective if done properly. We are beginning to see how the corporate culture vilifies all who do not speak in the language imparted to the public by corporations and state. We recognize this tactic as "politically correct."

For instance, during the Trump/Clinton Presidential campaign, Trump spoke words that touched a nerve in many, many young people, and they didn't like the sensation, to put it mildly. What he said seemed like a reference to individual freedom and responsibility and power—and that had the effect of a silver bullet traveling toward the heart of a vampire. Why? Who are these young people? What has been happening to them?" According to famed social writer John Rappaport:

# Planned Collapse of Americanism

*"The problem for social engineers: how to impose a top-down system of control on a population. The answer: prepare the young for that system by making it look like endless childhood."*

*"College students everywhere are now entitled infants. This is the rapidly expanding trend. As such, they are ripe for any 'philosophy' or program that justifies their endless needs. For them, government is more than mommy and daddy. Government is a non-judgmental truck that pulls up and delivers an endless stream of consumer items..."*

*"Many people on the receiving end of 'inner-child therapy' came to believe they contained an actual entity called the inner child. This belief tended to create a regression, in which they sought to find themselves in a happy early past and STAY THERE—then behaving like children."*

*"A false dichotomy is set up: a person is either a free, open, playful, blissfully ignorant, demanding child; or a cold, sterile, guarded, rigid adult. As if these were the only two possibilities."* All from the bright mind of John Rappaport!

It has been documented that many college students, after being purposely mal-educated (my term) for years by the leftist politically correct disinformation machine, have never learned how to employ actual critical analysis to examine both sides of issues or ideas. A traditional liberal education is avoided. Instead, many students are sneered at or embarrassed by their professors if they reject or question the lefts official mantra's and the deep-seated belief system that is a religion for the left. Critiquing leftist ideas on items like open borders, abortion, expansion of the state and high taxes, the state's wars on religion, gun ownership, home schooling or other Constitutional rights representing true freedoms and traditional ideas can lower your college scores! Such ideas are increasingly discouraged and labeled as archaic, dangerous ideas to truly argue about. This affects the young perhaps as well as college kids. By discouraging closely held beliefs, our state run/state indoctrinated "screwling system" has contributed to the sheep mentality amongst a huge cross section of American citizens!

*"We'll know our disinformation programs will be complete when everything the American public believes is false."* Quote by William Casey, CFR Member and former CIA Director from the first Staff Meeting in 1981.

A poignant quote from P.J. O'Rourke helps explain the ideology, the motivation, for a large section of the liberals out there looking upon government as a nanny-state. To wit;

*"At the core of liberalism is the spoiled child – miserable, as all spoiled children are, unsatisfied, demanding, ill disciplined, despotic, and useless. Liberalism is a philosophy of sniveling brats".*

Selfishness, greed, narcissism and self-gratification and feelings of entitlement are the results when cultural Marxism is bred into young people's lives. It is the anti-thesis of independence, freedom, self-responsibility, moral guidance and a unified nation. This ideology leaves one with the impression that everything is without moral compass, truth and morality is subjective according to circumstances. Bred into many of these human robots today is the idea that the "collective", the village, is to be nurtured for the common good, yet it offers no great or compelling reason for anyone outside of government to perform that function. This was, and still is, the Perhaps that is because few outside government can benefit monetarily from the collective lie. That is the idea!

Political correctness is the hallmark of a good and compliant citizen after all. Left with no higher, moralistic power I.e. (God), there is no downside to doing whatever one wants if he feels it is justified under his own set of subjectivities. Is it not such a surprise that we observe so much rudeness and crazy thought processes spewing out of so many of our young (and middle-agers) who have been unknowingly brought up in such a destructive, "screwling"/ disinformation network and oft confused secular world?

Interestingly, when it comes to the major media outlets that most of us get our news from, the same board members keep popping up over and over again inside the board rooms of all the six major alphabet news outlets! These wealthy elites are nearly always of a globalist mindset. I have done the homework of reviewing all of their bio's, political leanings, business histories and comments and I can tell you this is normally the fact but for a few. These leftist elite owners have long created newscasts that foster a false reality of the world which is aimed at citizens that agree with their liberal worldview, their biases and what drives profits of course. Their leftist anti conservative positions are finally beginning to kill their ratings for they have gone berserk, spewing out outlandish lies that the public is finally waking up to. By now, most of you reading this are already aware of my assertions I am quite sure. The alphabet news owners slickly and deceptively change the reasons, the motives and explanations for many of the news events covered. Often times simply by changing the narrative. Without saying one negative word, it can change the message slightly enough to engender a somewhat negative feeling towards particular groups not particularly friendly to their big government democratic party agenda i.e. Christians, patriots, conservatives and nearly anyone that doesn't follow the official lines of the left or the global elites. The same can accomplished with a positive message about news item that is in reality, terrible and not in the best interests of our American ideals. The American people are usually pretty honest, gullible people. The news outlets know this and have taken advantage of what they perceive as a weakness.

These knowingly push a socialist, degraded agenda, often promoting non-conventional and destructive social mores onto their airwaves. They can make Miley Cyrus or Katlyn Jenner look like role models. Shock advertising such as this eventually becomes accepted a normal and fine. **Hitler said: "If a lie is said enough times, it will come to be accepted as truth."**

# SHOCKVERTISING!

The real values of corporate capitalism are disseminated with popular culture. Often, the corporate prostitutes use the "shock" advertising technique. "Shockvertising" is an actual type of advertising that deliberately, rather than inadvertently, startles and offends its audience by violating norms for social values and personal ideals. It is the employment in advertising or public relations of "graphic imagery and blunt slogans to highlight" a public policy issue, goods, or services. Shock advertising is designed principally to break through the advertising "clutter" to capture attention and create buzz, and also to attract an audience to a certain brand, to place fear upon a political candidate or the prospect of a new law being considered, bring awareness to a certain public service issue, a health issue, or cause (e.g., urging drivers to use their seatbelts, promoting STD prevention, bringing awareness of racism and other injustices, or discouraging smoking among teens). In marketing their products, it can expose any taboo, typically showing an unnecessarily sexually suggestive image. Benetton Group has had several shocking ads of a priest and a nun kissing, a black woman breast-feeding a white baby, and death row inmates' thoughts. Near everyone is familiar with the many suggestive billboards put up by Legal advertising that employs "shockvertising" would depict or re-enact a car accident, which is now illegal in New York. One can imagine the many ways this technique could be abused upon the public to form opinions. This is one of the techniques out of the Tavistock arsenal of psychological methods to change people's minds. All this boils down to what has been called Predictive Programming. Below is an ad by Dolce & Gabbana an expensive clothing line. I don't believe I need to explain it.

This form of advertising is often controversial, disturbing, explicit and crass. It may entail bold and provocative political messages that challenge the public's conventional understanding of the social order. This form of advertising may not only offend but can also frighten as well, using scare tactics and elements of fear to sell a product or deliver a public service message, making a high impact. In the advertising business, this combination of frightening, gory and/or offensive advertising material is known as "shockvertising" and is often considered to have been pioneered by Benetton, the Italian clothing retailers which created the line *United Colors of Benetton*, and its advertisements in the late 1980s (see Benetton below). Source: WikiLeaks/shock advertising.

Above, we see an ad for Federici Gelato. Under the two obviously gay priests on the left is the caption "We Believe in Salivation. The pregnant nun caption says, "Immaculately Conceived." This is an obvious over-the-edge degradation and disrespect for the billions who are Catholic or who practice Christianity in particular! Shocking? Absolutely! THIS is today's culture, especially in large metropolitan cities like New York, Paris, San Francisco as examples.

## DUMBING DOWN IMPRESSIONABLES

The hugely impressionable young, living within the largely secular, narcissistically inclined corporate driven marketplace as we live amongst today are being constantly bombarded with every type of new, edgy product(s) even if it bends the limits of societal or moral compasses to be blindly ignored. Political and entertainment advertising is very convincingly sold to convince people to fall right into all their various, slicky marketed sales efforts. How can we explain the popularity of the Stephen Colbert types who verifiably lie and besmirtch the president of the United States every 10 minutes unto a politically deficient audience whom can't tell you who the Vice President is? Am I being a smartass? Well, Newsweek on 03/20/11 did a survey and found that 29 percent of Americans do not know that answer and over 50 percent do not know what the U.S. Constitution stands for! I thought the schools were supposed to teach that, but it seems not anymore. Such examples of dumbing down are not a mistake. Elites know that only a dumbed down society will fall for anything.

Efforts that are meant not only to sell a product but put the young and older alike into a trance of short lived contentment until the next "must have" fad comes around. Living within a dumbed down, visually driven world of consumers, the young in particular begin their lives with constant temptations to emulate, idolize whatever or whoever the consumer culture sells them as a necessary component to remain happy and content. The young and older alike are obviously pulled into this false matrix while chasing toward the rainbow of contentment. What is the next thing to think positive of, pedophilia? If those in Washington D.C. politics are any indication, we are in trouble. This instant gratification type of thinking has led hundreds of millions into unrealistic and narcissistic expectations of fast fixes to every problem. I contend that this is much to blame for kids who are diagnosed as ADHD so falsely. Outside the demands of schooling, nearly everything that comes at them is almost magically solved in their world of hyper speed internet, I-Phone, games, cartoons and puff entertainment.

Little known is that even Steve Jobs banned his own kids from using the I-phone and I- Pads. He knew that too much entertainment degrades and demoralizes in today's world. Article: Inquisitr, 9/11/14 entitled "Steve Jobs didn't let his kids use iPhone and iPad." Tim Butters

Within George Orwell's 1949 book entitled "1984" had a prediction about the soon to come society we see today. Let's remember, Orwell was a major Fabian Socialist, so he knew well the plans of the Fabian Socialists, what they had in mind, and how they intended to achieve their reversal of Americana. Orwell predicted that in the future, our government and news media would purposely attempt to dumb down the populace with distractions and misinformation on their airwaves in order to make them more pliable, distracted and compliant subjects. Today, six hours of television a day is the norm. For far too many young, reading is obsolete, unless it is about comic characters, Justin Bieber or another current idol. To appreciate this, remember this was in 1949!

Socialists have no need for a citizenry who thinks for themselves or know how to analyze things very deeply. Orwell theorized that young men in particular should easily be distracted, even to a point that most might develop into rather immature "boy-men" whom would naturally arrive very late into manhood. They would become removed or delayed from the traditional man's role of fast moving forward in developing his future plans, which usually included raising a family and being responsible for others. Faced with the easy lure of endless electronic games and sporting events within newly built impressive mega stadiums, he could play out his feelings of being a participant in these so called "manly" events, while escaping the responsibilities and confusion of growing up. Happily, distracted, the attendance and camaraderie of fellow men in this environment is sold by beer commercials as being "manly". In reality, such falsehood advertising has been a money-making scheme to sell "manliness" at a cost. Today, electronic devices abound, largely used for plain old entertainment. This has surpassed and been more successful than Orwell and the Fabian's could have even envisioned.

Another scheme by the Fabian styled elites has been to upset and blur the lines between men's roles and women's roles in raising a family and the proper roles of the opposite sexes. The immature "boy/man" young males we see today are very often discouraged and afraid of the confusing responsibilities and roles he might have to deal with in this new type of two incomes, shared responsibilities, complicated family unit. Especially within the ever-challenging economy we have seen since the 1970's. Besides, marriage failure is at 50%, so what gives? As a result, it is confirmed that America is experiencing record low marriage rates amongst the young. I mean, it takes two. There has been an upward trend in recent years with men who say that it is all just too much to deal with and therefore postpone or avoid marriage at all. The new economy is not the one his parents enjoyed, and the specter of providing well in such a world is overwhelming for many. It is easier to just stay in his fairy tale world of games and other types of entertainment, even pornography, pedophilia or worse. It is easier to just have non-binding friendships. As such, traditional nuclear, God loving family values with traditional roles have largely been replaced with broken non-families at a statistical divorce rate of well over 50% plus another 20+ percent whom live non-traditional relationships. Societies who have strayed to this extent have always collapsed.

The Rockefeller funded one world global elites and corporatists killed two birds with one stone just as George Orwell foretold. The elites have made literally trillions of dollars on sports, stadiums, beer, pornography, electronic games, Facebook and reality escape routes that rob precious years away from millions of young people, delaying their most productive years and fulfilling years, in most cases. We all know young men who are acting like juveniles even thought they might be in their thirty somethings. These just can't help but be overly attracted to the escapes, useless classes, internet gaming's, Facebook. The average young spend at least 10 hours a day on some type of electronic device according to 2016 surveys by the fast moving, sports, cars, etc. while still living at home with mom and dad and are helping to propel the mommy state instead of looking for a job perhaps, and that's the plan.

Doesn't it seem odd that we now enjoy abundant and instant news coverage as never before, yet peoples' actual knowledge of events is abysmally low? We all know that more information doesn't necessarily result into more actual knowledge. Why? Firstly, because most people today have been taught how not to critically analyze or think after attending the leftist PC "screwling system". Secondly, today's news is not simply reported, it is managed and massaged. And because the owners of the big 6 networks are globalist entities such as General Electric, Disney/ABC, Time Warner, Fox, Univision and Comcast for instance. With their agenda, they try their hardest that you never hear anything negative about any one of their huge conglomerate businesses if it can be helped. Any event that might hurt sales, or the reputation upon any of their holdings/brand names will surely be massaged or just dropped in nearly all cases! Just a few of G.E.s networks include NBC Television, which includes 13 stations covering 28% of households, as well as NBC and CNBC and their news networks. In part these include the Today Show, Nightly News, Meet the Press, Dateline NBC, NBC News at Sunrise. Put together, "this cartel of networks has enough influence to change politics and define social influence" Source: Ben Bagdikian, Pulitzer Prize author of the book "New Media Monopoly." Furthermore, Bagdikian says:

*"What we should be concerned about is the narrowing of choices, because that removes from voters the full spectrum of views and information with which to choose its government... a dangerous trend that threatens democracy itself."*

An example of how the rich purposely twist the news and our understanding of it in order to enrich themselves, let's look at the argument our politicians have framed over the idea of doing away with the estate tax. Little explained is that pretty much all of those that might be affected by the doing away of the tax are in the top 2% earning category whom are worth many millions. And half of the 2% will help the .01 percent the most. Yet, by omissions of facts, the corporate owned media changes the narrative to let us all think that it will apply to most! The idea is just a huge tax break for the really wealthy, again.

In 2015, a Fox News survey was recorded on the streets of New York asking everyday people about their thoughts on the Bill of Rights. Perhaps as no big surprise, a large percentage of the average Joe or Jane knew little or nothing of what the Bill of Rights contains in it. So, the interviewer explained to them a made up story that *"President Obama wants to throw away the Bill of Rights because it is out of date, restrictive and limits free choice in today's world, what do you think of that idea?"* Surprisingly, nearly 80% of average people on Manhattans New York City streets agreed with the premise of this made up story. They backed up Obama and were willing to do away with the Bill of Rights! This is how dumbed down we have become and it's on purpose. Sadly, much of the left in particular believes their Democratic leaders like sheeplings! It is like a religion. Perhaps you remember a bumper sticker around the 2008 Obama run that said, "I vote democrat; therefore, I don't have to think."

New York City is of course about 80% democratic voters so what does this say? Firstly, it is obvious that most don't know what the Bill of Rights even is, what it says nor much anything else of it! The failing liberal New York liberal school system has done its job well for the socialists. When Presidential candidate Ted Cruz criticized people within the Manhattan areas of New York as basically being consumed with money, Godless and narcissistic, he upset his opposition candidate Donald Trump, but I understand what he meant. He wasn't talking about New York's people in general, but rather talking about the attitudes on Wall Street, and the general attitude of many in the city.

Students on the liberal campus of George Washington University were in for surprise during a week in October 2017 when they expressed support for a tax plan they thought came from socialist Sen. Bernie Sanders, but in reality, belonged to President Donald Trump. In a round of recorded interviews on the liberal campus, CampusReform.org Media Director Cabot Phillips first asked students what they thought about the president's tax plan, identifying it as coming from Trump. Naturally, they told him it was not ideal for most Americans because it benefited the upper class and was "horrible" for the middle and lower classes. Phillips then asked students about an "alternative" — supposedly authored by Sanders — that included items such as increasing child care credits, eliminating the so-called "death tax" and lowering tax rates on smaller businesses. The students thought these ideas were positive for Americans. What Phillips didn't tell the students at first, however, was that the proposals were actually part of

**Trump's** tax plan! The looks on some of the students faces was incredulous! What does this say? Does it say that their news sources, their professors are communicating the truth? Or is it the sad truth that the young are saturated with temporal and empty-headed nonsense much of their days? Once you read the chapter on the Frankfurt School, you will understand.

Even though all the above statements are absolutely true, we must not forget that even the few left in the media whom don't have an inclination towards latching on to the misinformation campaign spewed out by both sides, the CIA is the enforcer of the State Department and deep states propaganda department. Whether it be the latest news on warring or anything of major significance, the CIA is communicating with the news networks and giving them the official version of a story and telling them to how run with it! If you have any doubts, consider the following honest quote from the top of the CIA:

*"The Central Intelligence Agency owns everyone of any significance in the major media."* William Colby, CIA Director

# .5

# MANUFACTURED REALITIES / BLACK LIVES MATTER

*"There is no such thing in America as an independent press… We are the tools & vessels for rich men behind the scenes. Our talents, our possibilities and our lives are all the property of other men. We are intellectual prostitutes".* John Swinton, Fmr. N.Y. Times Chief of Staff.

The world has been misled by our news sources on an extent never before seen. Unfortunately, our view of what's real out there in the world is largely shaped by the 6 major agenda driven news outlets, more specifically, Comcast, Walt Disney, 21st Century Fox, Times Warner, Viacom and CBS. And even though the CIA has their fingers on the media outlets, these wouldn't change their leftist, Illuminati stance even without the CIA's oversight. You see, these don't exist to offer objective news content to the American people, nor to the world. They exist to make money, monopolize and drive the one world corporate agenda of which they will remain and thrive in. They are not going to do or say anything that would threaten their relationships with their biggest advertisers either, particularly the behemoths such as pharmaceutical firms who spend billions in advertising every year as just one example. Do you think that the media or government is going to tell you that many of the foods, drugs or vaccines we ingest might kill you at some point in time?

Most of the foods we eat are sprayed with huge amounts of dangerous chemicals full of poisonous and cancer-causing ingredients? How about exposing poisons within our food supply like GMO's that the huge killing machine Monsanto (Now Bayer since its buyout) produces and laces our foods with? Many are concerned with the fact that most of these medias are virtually controlled by extensive cross-ownerships and corporate officers. As so, they try their hardest to block out inconvenient truths that goes against their liberal edicts and heavily funded advertising sponsors who pay their bills. In 1983, 90% of U.S. media was owned by 50 companies. Today these 6 companies have expanded to own 90% of the media world. Oddly enough, owners and managers of these big 6 are nearly exclusively made up of Jewish owners whom are nearly always on the far left.

These mainline networks work hand and hand with the elite globalist's strategy of using Hegelian tactics to whip up dissension and angst. Their scripts for the airwaves are carefully reviewed and approved by paid in-house censors who take their walking orders from the owner's policies prior to being handed over to their talking head newscasters. The intent of their programming is not to report the full, complete truth. If a news item just cannot be ignored (even though they would like to), it's their job to make sure that the story can be "massaged" if needed to spin the story, even leave out truthful facts that might bring to light some of the inconvenient truths that would expose the real and driving agenda behind the story. Their subliminal and purposeful deceiving messages often form automatic, predictable responses and opinions upon the busy worker bees (like most of us are). Instead of focusing on truly important news stories combined with that rare to find item called "real journalism", these mediums saturate the airwaves with Hollywood's latest divorce, Caitlyn Jenner's sex transformation and you know the rest. Such events are really irrelevant and don't do one thing to build up informed citizens, nor to provide good morals for the populace. **Hitler knew these techniques well. Inside his book Mein Kampf, he iterated "People's power of forgetting is enormous."** He used this to his great advantage.

Many of these newscasters are essentially drones that can't think much for themselves, nor are they paid to. They are paid to simply read the altered news as per the script given to them. Yet our controlled media calls these parrots 'journalists', or 'anchors'. Brian Williams was an example of a parrot reporter, and now he found a place on MSNBC, a socialist mainstay network. For those who don't know, NBC is run by NBC Universal, a leftist one world corporation whom also uses the all-seeing eye as their official logo. NBC also owns Univision, a huge leftist network throughout South America, often encouraging a one world, borderless world especially as pertains to the U.S. southern border!

As hard as it is for many citizens who are still in their "normalcy bias mode' or "suspended reality" that they find themselves, it is hard for them to believe that the media often manufactures their own version of reality and overplays it. But the globalists for years have been surprisingly successful at brainwashing the public.

Propaganda 101 states that if a lie is said enough times, and repeated often, it becomes fact within one's brain. Once it is accepted as a truth, no matter what hard evidence you might present, it is nearly impossible to convince otherwise. It's that strong of a technique. Good propaganda forms such a strong belief in one's mind, it is nearly impossible to change. Hitler claimed that the bigger the lie, the easier it was to believe! A famous Soviet propagandist once admitted that "The only way to change people's beliefs after being well propagandized on a subject is to introduce absolute shock", (like a revolution or a complete betrayal of long-held beliefs.) Now we see why both sides of the political spectrum are so hard headed!

In 2015, there were a total of 990 police killings, largely justified. Blacks were involved in around 200 of them of which most were also justified. Of the few that were not justified, purposely inflated numbers of black protests, rioting's and the numbers involved in them have mushroomed and grown in size. Before going to press, the horrible killings of 5 white police officers and wounding's of at least seven more took place in Dallas, TX. The primary shooter was black, disgruntled and atop rooftops with his rifle during a police protest. He took aim at white police officers whom were risking their lives while they kept peace down on the street. This man was obviously worked up to a fervor and misled by the Black Lives Matter organization, as well as the leftist medias as to the facts about black police killings. This killer was obviously led to believe that blacks are being unfairly killed by white officers at an astronomic, alarming and unfair rate, even though the facts don't bear this out.

Why do they report only blacks being attacked, or killed by white men or white police, even though studies show that the odds of the opposite happening are about 1000 times more likely? Black on black crimes dwarfs any other crime statistics. Part of their game is assuredly to stir up racial hatred. Play something enough times and it becomes reality in people's minds.

## THE PUPPETMASTER EXTRAORDINAIRE! GEORGE SOROS

Black on white racist group "Black Lives Matter" is verifiably funded by billionaire, one world communist lover George Soros in the many millions of dollars, as well as mega funder of over 100 other such leftist one world groups alike. These groups call out and encourage antiestablishment hate whitey radicalization coming out of the black culture, especially in large crime ridden cities across America. What about White Lives Matter. Better yet, don't Blue Lives Matter? I think we all agree that all lives matter.

The founder of the violent leftist group Antifa in Australia says he quit the movement after George Soros demanded they become more like terrorists than be the more peaceful action group he had begun. They succumbed to Soro's money, so he left the group. Founder Shayne Hunter says he established the Australian wing of the far-left organization but had to walk away after 4 years saying "Soros was using us to start a civil war in every country in the world". He said that he started the group as a way of protesting, but Soros invested money to set up violent training camps, teaching "soldiers" and to fight and use weapons. Now, after finally walking away from Antifa, he describes them as "a cult" that is brainwashing impressionable minds into creating instability from within, saying: "I wasted 4 years of my life." Furthermore, he asserted that *George Soros is destroying the fabric of society from the inside out to suit his own agenda* "

Through his Open Society Institute, Soros spends billions toward leftist anti-Constitutional socialist groups behind his efforts to cause civil and societal breakdown across the globe, especially in America. Of the many, here are just a few that he supports: Southern Poverty Law Center, Center for American Progress, Media Matters for America, MoveOn. Org, ProPublica and Center for Public Integrity, Black Lives Matter and the list goes on. A partial list is found on his Open Society website and includes at least 100 such groups whom he funds extremely generously. In mid-2017 Soros admitted that he released **$18 billion doll**ars to be allocated amongst his hundred plus leftist groups. Yes, that's with a big B! Such an amount is a record breaking dollar donation coming from a single man's cause! Is this what our founding fathers envisioned? Well, they did warn us, and they put reasonable safeguards in the Constitution of The United States to help prevent any one group from stamping out dissent to a particular agenda.

Briefly speaking, George Soros is a real piece of work! Perhaps one of the evilest men on earth many claim. George was born in Hungary as a Hungarian Jew. In a televised segment on the 60 Minutes American program, he admitted the following: At the age of fourteen, he left Hungary to avoid the German holocaust. In his need to avoid being labeled Jewish, his Jewish father Mr. Tivador Schwartz (a very wealthy businessman) paid a friendly attorney to forge papers where he swore to authorities that George was his cousin and a Christian. They let him go. Soon afterwards, he met up with certain Jewish mafia type contacts and joined them in helping them to confiscate Jewish properties and property that Hitler had moved in on. The fact that he was working against his own Jewish people was never considered as an important point. Soros admitted to 60 Minutes that it was just a business opportunity. He called this time the greatest time of his life! From that point on, it was evident that he was a psychopathic opportunist whom would always put money, self-interest and power far above human lives or suffering.

As a young adult, Soros attended the London School of Economics, a Fabian socialist, globalist school as described more elaborately further on. His history of plundering countries, economies, causing many deaths and suffering therefrom is now well known. In the interview on 60 minutes, he admitted he had no remorse at all for all the deaths, destruction, disasters and misfortunes that have followed him wherever he does his dealings. It is always just written off as a "business opportunity" according to Soros. His immense wealth has allowed him to control economies, cause countries to fail and worse. He is atheist, declares himself a messiah of humanity, a godhead and more illusions of grandeur.

He knows that over time, his dialectic of paid dissension rises to a boiling point. The history of nations shows just how successful the split and divide techniques, if employed on many different levels within a once civilized and stable country can work to tear a that country apart, often without the use of bombs or bullets.

## MEDIA WARS ON GUNS

As the above practices exponentially increase around the country, many in the black communities have bought into the entirely false narrative that nearly all black shootings are racist if a white police officer is involved. These are fodder for the socialist led bandwagon intent on creating chaos, split and divide. Meanwhile the leftist media's too often feed the lie to their listening base. Yet FBI statistics show that blacks are not unfairly targeted by police all things considered. In fact, as a percentage of the population, they are less likely to be arrested all things being the same. The leftist rhetoric is louder than the realities. Calls for gun control mainly affects honest citizens of course, for criminals could care less. Anti-gun advocates yell out on television that we need to outlaw guns, regardless of the fact that legal Caucasian gun owners are extremely unlikely to commit homicide. So why should these be targeted for gun control? In Chicago, near all homicides are black on black gang members using unregistered and/or stolen guns inside of their own neighborhoods with drugs being involved. Their cries for gun confiscation from honest citizens has no merit of course. In reality, it is a Marxist plan to confiscate all guns as Hitler did, and for the same reason, control.

Gun deaths in Chicago have gone off the charts even though Chicago has the strictest gun control laws besides New York City. For the entire year of 2015, Chicago's gunshot death total came to a horrific 447. Those shot and injured came to 2559, a total of 2996. Likewise, 2016 gunshot deaths rose to 720 deaths. A rise of 373 deaths in one year alone! Those shot and injured in 2016 came to 3689, for a total of 4379. The year 2017 stats are much, much worse so far as of this writing. Over 95% of the deaths are caused from gang and criminal activities from those whom don't care one bit about gun laws. And yet police "pull-overs" had decreased 80% during the same period. It seems police are becoming jaded and much less secure going into a war zone on a daily basis. We have asked police to become gestapo agents going into public war zones. What is next? National Guards or Swat raids in order to sweep out the bad ones?

**Gun murders of persons 10-19 years of age: Below are the cities with the highest gun murders for those 10-19 years old.**

1. Los Angeles...............................................251

2. Chicago...................................................213

3. New York.................................................203

4. Philadelphia.............................................124

5. Detroit.....................................................119

6. San Francisco........................................... 101

7. Houston................................................... 83

8. St. Louis..................................................82

9. Miami......................................................81

10. Washington..............................................76

Cities #1-6 and #8 (at least) are all longtime Democrat strongholds with some of the toughest guns laws in the country for many years. Sorry you on the left, but the facts are the facts.

For years, the one world elites have intentionally pitted individuals against each other through the media's sensational overplay of individual and unfortunate incidences. Guns are a perfect example. It takes just one lone, Caucasian, wing-nut job on psychotropic meds or holding a mental illness who proceeds to go out and kill several people in a movie theatre or a school, and all we hear for weeks on the Main Street media is how we should outlaw guns for everyone, law abiding or not. On drugs or not. Crazy or not! This is purposeful propaganda. This is Hegelian Dialectic. True and constructive debate on guns will seemingly never be solved by mutual dialogue.

The horrific Las Vegas shooting from the Mandalay Hotel on 10/01/17 wherein a crazed shooter killed nearly 100 people, injuring over 500 more, seemed that it almost surely was to bring about new tougher gun laws aimed at honest people in large part. It was the biggest such shooting in America's history after all. Does anyone within even one of the six networks mention that nearly every single one of these mass killings carried out by a lone gunman just happens to take place within a fully marked "GUN FREE ZONE?

Guns are a very sensitive subject, especially if you are one who has been directly and personally affected due to a gun accident or incident. Sadly, it is clear that the leftist fake media is intent on politicizing the gun issue to only look at their side. You know, the routine. Take away guns from the 99% of law abiding citizens instead of sensible procedures, laws that will actually cure much of the sometimes unpreventable shootings. There is a laundry list of sensible and highly effective answers to this problem that are hailed by police and other gun experts for instance. Instead of facing the real problem head-on, looking for real answers to the gun problem, the leftists, the Democrats plan is always to misinform the masses into giving up their guns rights and other freedoms "in the name of humanity". For decades, the far left and their paid media's have been largely successful with indoctrinating/occupying America's young mushy minds with various campaigns of disinformation, misinformation, and leftist propaganda using bleeding heart pleas.

California and other states have banned so-called "assault weapons", passed by lawmakers that obviously don't know the difference between a semi-auto assault style rifle and that of a semi-auto hunting rifle. All that differentiates the two types of guns is looks. Many politicians really don't know the difference and make decisions based on no knowledge of guns. Without actually taking guns away, they think this will be the next best thing for the meantime. It is apparent that our government is fine with the thugs and killers having guns, just not us! Gun control works! Just ask Hitler.

Silently, Obama and his minions silently passed law that confiscates all guns from Social Security and V.A. beneficiaries if they, or someone else such as a neighbor "claim" that the beneficiary isn't capable of handling his/her own bank account or some other minor matter. The Daily Beast reported that Pres. Obama and Hillary Clinton had been toying with the idea of a creating a civil war as a justification for the confiscation of every single gun, going so far as to even suspending the 2016 Presidential election in order to keep the Democrats in power. They would have used the oldest political trick in the deep states bag, call the Hegelian Dialectic tactic of "*Create a problem, offer a solution, fix the problem*", a long-used tactic to bring about change otherwise impossible. Thank goodness it never happened.

Pres. Obama and Hillary Clinton were totally frustrated with their failures to reverse our Second Amendment before leaving office. These two were seriously trying to achieve gun confiscation before being replaced. One must keep asking the logical question "why is it that they want our guns, not the drugged-out lawbreakers so much?" Many top experts who study gun issues, racial tensions, as well as the poverty and disparity on the streets of America, are increasing showing concern that America may be on the precipice of hugely larger street riots, even civil wars, around the country. The Second Amendment was installed exactly for this reason for goodness sake! Whether it be an out of control government or crazy rioters, citizens must be able to protect themselves against those who own stolen, unregistered guns and mean to cause harm.

Serious to consider is that just the act of government forced confiscation against those owning registered firearms could fuel the beginnings of a civil war in itself. And it won't be pretty once it spreads. This is a major reason why America has been blessed with President Trump.

# Planned Collapse of Americanism

Not often reported by the Mainstreet Press is that guns deaths have decreased back to levels before 1990. Why don't people realize this simple fact. It has fallen 63% since 1993. Nevertheless, eight out of ten U.S. citizens believe that it has gotten worse. Sandy Hook School and other such isolated, rare incident do in fact give the leftist medias and socialist gun objectors false ammunition to get public support. We must remember that the left panders to the hearts of the Americans, not the facts!

Gun violence since 2016 has edged up ever so slightly. Yet a Pew Research Center study said that *"Despite national attention to the issue of firearm violence, most Americans are unaware that gun crime is lower today than it was two decades ago,"* With all this talk of supposed increased gun violence, the Dept. of Justice and ATF reports yearly on gun sale application requests. In 2015, they indicated that there were over 12.6 million gun permits issued that year alone. The year 2016 indicates a jump to over 20 million. Yet in 2005 there were only 147, 484 requests. So, we are now witnessing a tenfold increase in a 10-year period!

So, it appears that the more guns sold, the better the numbers since most are sold to law abiding citizens! Which begs the question, is all this hysteria really justified? Sources;www.bloomberg.com/news/articles/2013-05-07/gun-deaths-dropped by...www.pewresearch.org/fact-tank/2015/10/21/gun-homicides-steady-aft www.nydailynews.com/new-york/gun-deaths-drop-2000-nyc-article-1.. Law Street Media article Analiese Mahoney, Crime in America-Safest and Most Dangerous Cities in the US. (no date).

When will sensible discourse on this serious subject take effect?

# .6

## JUST SNOOPING AROUND?

### NSA, DARPA, PRIVACY & THE FIRST AMENDMENT

The world today is not operating 'normal' if one uses pas history of the world as a reference. Anyone today over the age of perhaps 50 knows how 'normal' felt like in their earlier years. Privacy and free speech abounded.

With the exposure of Planned Parenthoods selling unborn baby parts to willing buyers, thru its partnered firm called 'Stem Express' (and worse yet no one is arrested), we know things have gone way downhill. When the White House holds a wild party specifically to celebrate gay marriage and puts up rainbow colored lights streaming upward along the entire front of the White House for several days, we know for sure. Especially disheartening was days later, in July of 2016, Obama refused to turn off the rainbow lighting to make way for blue lights in respect to all the police officers recently shot around the country by Black Lives Matter type thugs. For me, this was just one more proof of his anti-Americanism, cop hating deep seated views. How did America The Beautiful turn out this way? Perhaps eight years of bad policies in Washington.

The smart globalists have engineered a slow, Fabian styled change in attitudes as well as nearly everything around us. The goals of the globalist new world order have required them to be extremely patient in their goals of world government by means of the Fabian methods. That is, primarily using extremely slow, patient transition vs. communisms quick, violent means to accomplish their goals. The plan has been successful to date, turning many citizens into compliant sheeplings who believe all the official lines pumped out. This plan is far more difficult than just taking over an individual country by quick, brutal force, after all, we are talking about the entire world here. But fruition is finally very close in time, and it is being coordinated on a mass proportion never before attempted. The grid is almost entirely laid out for these power merchants. With every new regulation, law, mandate, tax, and complicated edict to follow, we have become less free than ever before.

According to the Patriot Act and its follow up revisions, if you the American citizen display any of the following beliefs, American government can consider you a suspected terrorist…

Speaking against any gov't policies, especially in public.

Talking against the Mainstream ideologies

Nationalistic beliefs and the Constitution of the United States

Belief in the 4th Amendment, which guarantees against unlawful search and seizure

Belief in the 2nd Amendment right to own private fire arms w/o government interference.

Belief that the Federal Reserve is not legitimate or part of some conspiracy.

Belief that traditional, personal and national ways of life are under attack.

Being anti-abortion / pro-life.

Being an active Christian, Jew or other faith.

Bumper stickers with things like: "Know your rights or lose them".

Be connected to conservative group(s) or publication(s) or website(s).

Hoarding some gold, silver or storing some food.

Being particularly respectful of the Founding Fathers and their principles.\

Taking pictures of police harassments or other government misdeeds.

Placing politically incorrect or anti-establishment thoughts on Facebook or another social media sites, blogs, phone calls, texts

Being against high taxations, too many regulations, big government, abusive executive orders, snooping's, etc.

The NSA is watching as we all know. And it's far worse than you could imagine likely. Edward Snowden let us know just how bad. If you demonstrate several of the above traits, you are at a higher risk of being more closely monitored by the NSA, or worse yet, arrested under the flimsiest circumstances. I guess the answer is to just be a nice, compliant wallflower, and you'll be left alone, (maybe).

## THE SURVEILLANCE STATE

Nearly everyone has heard of Edward Snowden, the infamous former NSA contractor who blew the lid off of their huge prying eyes in 2013. Snowden was an ex-CIA employee, American privacy activist, computer professional. What we found out is that our own government is performing millions upon millions of searches on you and me, all unconstitutional. Snowden is continuing to awaken Americans of all the lies and illegal actions that the U.S. government has been perpetrating against the American people. The deep state didn't like him for obvious reasons, so he is a fugitive criminal still in the eyes of the American law system, running from country to country for asylum.

Although NSA has at least six locations around the country, the main one located in Fort Meade, Maryland. The building is reported by WikiLeaks to be 5 million square feet, employees 20,000 people and has 10 acres below it. It is built on 350 acres, employs 18,000 parking spaces, and encompasses a three million sq. ft. building that equates to 68 acres of office space as well as 1300 buildings on the site. We now also have at least ten more facilities spread around the USA.

Another immense, record breaking data facility has been built in Bluffdale, Utah as of late. This place cost $1.7 billion dollars, holds nearly a million sq. ft. of space for technical support and administration. It also includes four building of 25,000 sq. ft. each (100,000 sq. ft.) specifically designed just to store the 10,000 racks of computer systems onsite. Each rack can store 1.2 petabytes of data. If that isn't impressive, just consider this mindblower…

It is estimated that to track every phone call made in the United States in one year requires around 272 petabytes. Amazingly, that would only take a little more than 200 of the 10,000 servers available! It can store data at a rate of 20 terabytes (equivalent to the entire Library of Congress) per minute according to William Binney. The place needs 65 megawatts of electricity that will cost around $70 million dollars a year to keep the computers cool enough to run well, requiring 1.2 million gallons of water per day. The two sites mentioned take up more seven time the space of the pentagon complex! Sources include: articles by DailyMail.com 7/20/16 by The Daily Reporter, The Guardian.com 6/14/13 by Rory Carrol, The Salt Lake Tribune 8/6/13 'NSA in Utah-Mining a Mountain of Data' by Tony Semerald.

William Binney was a senior NSA crypto-mathematician largely responsible for automating the agency's worldwide eavesdropping network. A tall man with strands of black hair across the front of his scalp dark, determined eyes behind thick-rimmed glasses, the 68-year-lawsold spent nearly four decades breaking codes and finding new ways to channel billions of private phone calls and email messages from around the world into the NSA's bulging databases. Acting as chief, as well as being one of the two cofounders of the agency's Signals Intelligence Automation Research Center, Binney and his team designed much of the infrastructure that's still likely used to intercept international and foreign communications

Binney left the NSA in late 2001, shortly after the agency launched its warrantless-wiretapping program, yet still has close contacts within the gargantuan, ever-growing agency. "They violated the Constitution setting it up," he says bluntly. "But they didn't care. They were going to do it anyway, and they were going to crucify anyone who stood in the way. When they started violating the Constitution, I couldn't stay."

Binney says Stellar Wind was far larger than has been publicly disclosed and included not just eavesdropping on domestic phone calls but the inspection of domestic email. At the outset the program recorded 320 million calls a day, he says, which represented about 73 to 80 percent of the total volume of the agency's worldwide intercepts. The haul only grew from there. According to Binney—who has maintained close contact with agency employees until a few years ago—the taps in the secret rooms dotting the country are actually powered by highly sophisticated software programs that conduct "deep packet inspection," examining Internet traffic as it passes through the 10-gigabit-per-second cables at the speed of light. In secret listening rooms nationwide, NSA software examines every email, phone call, and tweet as they zip by, as well as tracing bills, tickets, credit, etc.

The former NSA official held his thumb and forefinger close together: "We are that far from a turnkey totalitarian state." Right up to today, Binney is continuing hit fight.

The NSA believes it's on the verge of breaking a key encryption algorithm—opening up hordes of data. From article *of James **Bamford** (washwriter@gmail.com) author of **The Shadow Factory: The Ultra-Secret NSA from 9/11 to the Eavesdropping on America***

Obviously, I am not convinced one bit that our government has downsized the NSA at all. Quite the opposite. Our government will never stop expanding their snooping abilities or any other powers they have granted themselves without our permission, it's just not part of its DNA. The NSA uses the large majority of its capabilities on citizen spying, not defense.

The scope and size of Americas spying and snooping apparatus would be a pipe dream for Karl Marx, Adolph Hitler, Stalin and all past murderous tyrants and dictators. They could have done so much more! Many estimate that the NSA's database and spying ability is 10 thousand times more powerful than Hitlers program. Thank goodness, he didn't have this much capability. The hundreds of millions they killed would have been an even higher number, as hard as that is to believe. History shows that such overreach into people's lives is always a precursor to total control.

The U.S. agency called 'DARPA' (Defense Advanced Research Project Agency) is an agency that many citizens and experts are becoming very afraid of! Its official research was thought of to be working on high tech weapons systems for our nation's defense program.

But in recent years, verifiable information has come out that agencies increasing role has been to design and implement high technology has been used for nefarious reasons toward the public, and very little towards weapon systems. For instance, in 2013 Google executive Regina Dugan admitted they were working together with DARPA on "ingestible informational chips". Not just the run of the mill RFID chip that's been around for a while. The newest one is about 1/3 the size of a grain of white rice, intended for citizens who will soon be forced to have injected or ingest. Thereafter the government will track citizens of nearly everything. We already have similar abilities to place RFID chips into people and track an incredible amount of date about them. In recent days, credit card companies are contemplating the engaging of biometrics or face recognition technology when you attempt to use your credit card. Can RFID chips be far away?

DARPA has numerous other such project of all types and sizes that are designed to be used against society's freedoms and prosperity. Navy Seals and high value military peoples already have chips installed to track their possible disappearance and such.

This is all a part of the long talked of "technocracy government" that is tucked within a 1970 best-selling book written by one the top leaders of the one world movement, no other than Foreign Policy one world guru Zbigniew Brzezinski. Yes, the Former U.N. leader as well as a current globalist leader/member who is still within the top ranks of the CFR, the Trilateral Illuminist elites. Within his well-read book, entitled "Between Two Ages/Americas Role in the Technetronic Era", Brzezinski spoke of the era between the beginning of the 1970's and today.

Brzezinski quite accurately predicted the coming of an Orwellian world that would make it possible for government to monitor nearly everything about its subjects, using that information to make decisions upon differing groups of people whom did, or did not, live their lives according to the new world order's wishes! He claimed that the citizens would need to be convinced of the need for such an apparatus. Threats must be developed, or at least amplified in order to gain support for big government power.

The one world Illuminati styled plan has already been very busy placing many mandatory edicts upon their compliant, state serving citizens to follow. In this new world, the state can easily force people to follow the states prescribed actions and protocols in nearly all activities (under false pretenses like climate change, etc.) If there's a bright side, it normally won't take a gun to make people obey. Let's put it this way; once a chip, a trans-human device, or a bio-metric I.D. tracking device is implanted into a citizen, their very survival will be dependent on the states compassion, or not. With cash being a thing of the past, it would be natural for any sane person to follow along if they know that the state has the power to just push a button and disable their Earth card, denying any purchases. One could quickly find that they are all of a sudden not allowed food purchases, their vehicle could be electronically disabled, (which is already possible). Nearly anything the surveillance state wants from you it can obtain quite quickly under such terms of engagement. One-worlder Bill Gates has his own plan to help the cause. He proposes that every single person in the world have their vaccine, health records and phone number placed into a world database. Every person! Just another way to track you throughout your life perhaps.

My friend, the technologies are already here. The future world is the past, and today we are living in it! We will likely all soon be required to have an implanted RFID chip, or an even more advanced high tech insert or ingestible micro device, within 10 years many predict. This is eerily similar to what the Bible has long talked of in the final days in Revelations 13:16-18. *"He required everyone--small and great, rich and poor, free or slave- to be given a mark on the right hand or on the forehead. And no one could buy or sell anything without that mark, which was either the name of the beast or the number representing his name. Let the one with understanding solve of the meaning of the number of the beast, for it is the number of a man. His number is 666."* Marx, Stalin, Lenin, and such tyrants would have loved it!

In the 1970's many churches and naysayers took note of this Bible passage and many have failed in their exact predictions of when it would happen, while most others have just been waiting to see signs of its fruitions. Whether you the reader are inclined to take this passage seriously, believe in a God or not, surely one must admit this Bible passage (as well as many others if you are inclined) is awesomely prophetic to the age we are in, where such technology exists as a means of placing a mark or identification on (or in?) every person of the world, lest he be unable to buy or sell! This is all so relevant to today. Even 50 years ago we didn't have this technology. To give credence to the Bibles prophecy, it seems incredulous and naive to consider that anyone in 70 A.D. could have envisioned even the concept of any such technology coming forth, or even the possibility and necessity for a worldwide, interconnected and "computerized" (what is that?) network tied into a Master data file on every living person. A printing press was way over a thousand years away at that time. Who could have envisioned a system such as we have today nearly two thousand years ago as the above passage suggests? For me there only one possible answer: The infallible word of my Lord Jesus Christ.

While on the subject of religion, I'll keep it short. Whether you're Christian, Jewish, Catholic or something else, we all need to be aware of the war on faith going on today in the U.S. government at full speed. Pres. Obama shunned any consideration upon the thousands of Christians being killed in the Middle East, not wanting to say a word of the massacres going on over there. This was the first American president in our history to act so indifferent to Christians. He had called Christians as "Bible thumping, gun-toters" or something to that effect. To the leftist Marxist socialists (which he is), religion is an anathema to their ideology. Even though the Gallup polling organization estimates that about three quarters of the country identifies with the Christian religion, the president seems to be committed to the destruction of this same majority that has its faith rooted in God, to differing degrees of course!

Well, it's all beyond superstition today! The average American is in 200+ databases. Furthermore, we have around 10 million surveillance cameras equal to 1 camera for every 10 Americans. Technologies are a two-edged sword when it comes to maintaining a free country. And whatever technology the military officials tells us is the newest and best, is in fact at least 20 years' old. The real cutting-edge stuff is always kept out of site, not allowed out. The public is always the last to know, and for good reasons normally.

## .7

# THE SYSTEM IS THE PROBLEM

## *On Elections*

Professor Carroll Quigley, whom <u>Bill Clinton</u> famously called his favorite professor and mentor, had this to say in 1966 within the professors most famous book "Tragedy & Hope". Explaining the elites aims, Quigley had this to write...

*"The chief problem of America for a long time has been how to make the two Congressional parties more national and international at the same time" (neoliberalism)".*

*"The argument that the two parties should represent are opposed ideals and policies... Right and Left is a foolish idea, only acceptable to the doctrinaire & academic thinkers. Instead, the two parties should be almost identical, so the American people can 'throw out the rascals' at any political election without leading to any profound or extensive shifts in policy.* Source: Tragedy & Hope, pgs. 1247-1248, New York, The MacMillan Company.

The above quote is almost word for word what then-President Obama said in mid-2016 while being taped talking to a group of students in Venezuela! Should we wonder where Obama's true leanings fall? Such a belief undermines all that our democratic process offers!

Moving on, Quigley continued that "Instead, the two parties should be almost identical, so the American people can 'throw the rascals out' at any political election without leading to any profound or extensive shifts in policy." Source: Tragedy & Hope, pgs. 1247-1248, New York, the McMillan Co publisher.

So, I ask the reader the following...Up until the election of President Trump, does the above not exemplify the exact problem most voters had realized up until Trump? The globalists had gotten everything they wanted for 200 years! Finally, a new promise was presented! A true difference in substance!

Prof. Quigley had served professorships at prestigious Georgetown Univ., Yale and Princeton. For two years, Quigley belonged to the inner circle of the ultra-secretive globalist power group the Trilateral Group. He was entrusted to inspect its records in an advisory role. What he left there with was an arsenal of useful information about the clandestine organization. He was able to learn their true goals and secrets. He actually <u>was</u> a one worlder, yet privately disagreed with some of their tactics and ideas. Quigley believed that the public needed to know some of these facts regarding how the elites think, and their methods to carry out their one world plans. This book was his most famous, with over 1300 pages, largely intended for academia. The above is so telling. Doesn't it explain so succinctly and artfully how people just accept the growth of big government so easily, believing that this is what most people really prefer and expect to produce the best results? The establishment has created what is called "manufactured consent" that is scientifically proven to produce predictive programming. For years we have listened to what the media and politicians tell us, not realizing that much of the information we digest has the globalist spin on it in order for the elites to keep people's minds from thinking for themselves. The elite's propaganda machine keeps people in the matrix, believing that problems such our huge debt is caused by others, not the elites themselves. Such has created the vacuum that exists in the average person's knowledge base when it comes to what they perceive as political truthing.

To large degree, many feel that our voting process is completely rigged. Presidential candidate Bernie Sanders clearly should have won the Democratic nomination but for Crooked Hillary's immensely larger war chest and her huge political machine that was able to twist the process to serve her and her own socialist incumbents (not that either choice would have been desirable in my estimation.) And in each election, and whomever gets the grand prize, the process only serves as a hollowed-out form of public choice. But as I reiterate, Trump broke all the rules and pissed off the elites.

What should be the amazing thing about this whole election process is that over 50% of the populace is either employed by state or federal government, receive some type of assistance from the government, or belong to a union (of which nearly all are voting robots for the Democrats).

The black vote is beholden over 96% to the Democrat Party as well. But that is changing. With such a gigantic built boost in their democratic base, a democrat party win should be a "slam dunk" come every national election, would one not think? Yet, it is often a slug out event according to the official polls. This dependent demographic model is what the left, the socialists and the Dems in particular have worked so very hard for during the last 50+ years to attain, so why can they still not always win? One answer is that so very many of the establishment Republican Party leaders have become accustomed to leaving their conservative base in order to compete for the leftist corporate donors at times as well as short sighted special interest individuals and groups whom are always looking for what government can do for them, even doing so at the eventual cost of less freedoms, higher deficits and the loss of honesty within the isles of governance. This tends to further level the playing field downwards closer to the threat of a far leftist agenda that would change the direction of America forever perhaps. The other hand played is often the threat of war and the need for a strong military leader for which the Republicans usually have a handle on.

Populist candidates such as Donald Trump and Ronald Reagan were somewhat exceptions to the rule, and this seems to happen about 30 or 40 years once the corruptions, ballooning budgets and insane policies of the existing system hits a crescendo, finally creates a voter backlash against a self-serving statist agenda. New President Trump will surely risk his life if he attempts to operate too far outside the beltway statists and the deep state. His entire presidency should expect non-stop attacks at every turn, some extremely bold and unconventional.

How do the elites and the shadow government nearly always succeed at putting in "their boy", come election time? One way is to subvert the voting process, such as taking advantage of the newer, big money financed Citizens United Supreme Court decision that allows Super-PACS to now actively pursue nearly unlimited funds from billionaire donors under the name of the Pac instead of personally.

The Supreme Court decided that corporations are quasi-individuals, so the devolution of the voting process was forever amplified. Now, these Super-Pac's can raise virtually unlimited amounts in order to put their beholden candidates into power. The $5400-dollar limit on individual contributions still stands, but now all the monied interests can pool their money into these Super-PACS as far as to the moon and back in order to buy their prioritized favors from their bought off politician(s). This allows the wealthy elites to buy their politicians in absolute defiance of the Constitution and everything the Founding Fathers worked so hard to prevent. This is obviously against the wishes of our Founding Fathers.

The elites that run the election system know the electoral process is far from honest. For instance, around April 15, 2016, RNC Rules Committee Chairman Curley Hoagland was interviewed. During the discussion on the subject of the fairness of the current election process, Curley admitted that electoral college system is not fair. Nextly, the interviewer asked Curley, *"Why are they even holding primaries?* He responded, *"that's a good question."*

Unexpectedly, in the 2016 presidential elections, Donald Trump was the first presidential candidate in decades to seemingly run on policies that often bucked the establishment machine, speaking with a new breed of brash politico that the establishment had never encountered before. Trumps approach was unabashedly non-establishment, not a part of the politically correct sheepling candidates, nor did he need to be financially beholden to the Washington establishment and corporations due to his own wealth. The establishment was scared to death of his nationalistic tones which would take away a chunk of the obscene powers enjoyed by the elites, statists, crony's and so forth. Trump is a quick, yet plain talking populist with a truthful non-politically correct outsider tone that voters were starving for, especially middle Americans still reeling for the last 8 + years since the big crash. Some compare President Trump to Pres. Reagan on steroids. Of course, the establishment, and the left, mocked him for his unconventional New York street talk. Ronald Reagan had a bit of this un-electability in his early run. The GOP and the establishment didn't want Reagan either, but he too was that once or twice in a lifetime presidential personality that the people loved. Americans today are starving for outsiders who are not bought off and will actually do for their good, but the establishment and elites do not like such renegades normally and will do anything to rid them. Will Pres.Trump actually be allowed to pull off an honest presidency?

As in the 2016 race, the GOP tried everything in its bag to disqualify Donald Trump. (R.) John Kasich and (R)Ted Cruz were told to stay in the race even though they were clear losers. These were the GOP's official party line spoilers, part of the deep state, who were purposely kept in the race against Trump. Anybody except Trump, the anti-establishment candidate! The GOP's Super Delegates pushed hard to derail Donald Trump in the primaries. Republican Super Pac's with hundreds of millions of dollars tried to sway undecided delegates to change their votes by showering them with free first-class dinners, private jets, and whatever it took for them to cast against Trump. The threat of a brokered convention was thrown out there to consider by the GOP establishment who were in fact scared to death of losing their all-powerful mafia organization that had long been manipulating and profiting greatly off the carcasses of the nation's citizens for eon's. Even in the final laps of the Donald's primary and Presidential race, the establishment GOP leaders such as Mitch McConnell and House Leader Paul Ryan couldn't stand up to support the Donald to make his cases against Hillary's numerous "pay to play" and often illegal scams over the years. Instead, they stayed quiet, even distancing themselves.

What few realized is that the real powers, the shadow government consisting of the global elites (you know whom I am speaking of), told the establishment GOP it would be better to stay quiet and allow Hillary to win if possible in order to assure a continuance of the growing socialist agenda (which is their agenda). Yes, Obama had done quite well in his eight years in that respect, and Hillary would continue as his clone. She would eliminate the second Amendment in particular via the two or three new Supreme Court Justices whom will be retiring in the coming administrations. Hillary was always having a love affair with Wall Street, bankers, and she would've be done without their huge money. She would have overturned or created new laws while executing even more freedom robbing and un-American styled Executive Orders just as her ally Pres. Obama did. This can be compared to Hitler's rewriting the German Constitution while assuming power away from Pres. von Hindenburg (under a longer time frame).

Remember, nearly all recent U. S Presidents have verifiably been groomed ahead of time by the Bilderberg Group, the Trilaterals, and the CFR (notwithstanding Pres.Trump.) Upcoming constitutional and nationalistic candidates are often ignored by the major parties and the medias. Trump was often called "a clown" hundreds of times by the medias. You see, American patriots are summarily discredited as kooks, even comparing their nationalistic tendencies as Hitlerite. Which is like "the pot calling the kettle black!" These outsiders are not given any kudo's if they don't support the neo policies of the establishment, aren't members of the CFR, the Trilateral Commission and/or other hierarchy organizations such as the Bohemian Club or are just too honest to accept crony favors. They are then slammed by the paid-for press in order to discredit the candidate. Nextly, big money donors shun them. Ron Paul and Rand Paul are good examples. These two wouldn't join in on the "pay to play" game of that establishment. No, they operate by the Constitution and run against the elite neo-establishments primary concerns of money, money, profitable warring's and power. Therefore, both were made unelectable. Candidates who rally to end the Federal Reserve, support campaign reform, i.e. (eliminating Super-Pac's), detest corporate cronyisms and unwarranted warring's are deemed "unelectable. It is no doubt that the Donald broke all records. And the country was ready for it. It was amazing how so many of his political enemies came out of the woodwork, looking for a post inside his new cabinet!

Presidential hopefuls like Barack Obama, Hillary Clinton, Bill Clinton, Jimmy Carter and nearly every other president had been groomed by these groups and told not to bother running if they don't agree to take directions. This is why Trump had such a hard time running for and with the GOP! Even before the 2016 Republican Convention, the GOP warned that they might not throw anything towards Trump, even claiming they would spend their war chest on themselves if need be! These can also change their rules on a dime as well. Well, we know they changed their mind after Trump became an irreversible political sensation for their base.

And perhaps the most egregious abuser of American ideals is the Federal Reserve who is allowed to operate completely independent with no audits nor government control. Readers beware! I am known to ramble on and on repeatedly about the unfederal reserve! For I believe that once people connect all the dots, it IS the key to most of America's decline in one way or another. Moving on…

This single banking scam has enriched Wall Street traders, big bankers and the elites to the tune of many trillions of dollars of unearned income on the backs of American taxpayers. By some estimates this scam has created hundreds of trillions (yes, that's correct!) of dollars of scandalous favoritisms, transfers to and from, secret government waste and endless illegal misappropriations of funny money played out over many years! In fact, my follow up book will delve deep into this snowballing epidemic that threatens America as we know it.

Famous French historian Alexis de Tocqueville at the time of the birthing of America, had spent several years moving around and closely watching the young American landscape. Although much of his writings speak positively about the new country, he had this to write about the politicians he watched running our country, to wit;

*"There are many men of principle in both parties in America, but there is no party of principle."* **Alexis de Tocqueville**

## HOW NEO POLICIES FOREVER CHANGED AMERICA

This very short but important subchapter is super simplistic explanation of neo policies and the general direction that neo policies have taken American politics. It seems that true conservatives and true liberals as well, are becoming extinct. Although people equate the Republican Party and its followers as generally conservative, the party today has little semblance to true conservatism for which it tried to stay true to. The same can be said for the Democrat party as well, originally the party of true liberalism. Experts on the subject can go back and forth about who, when and what regarding neo policies and its evolvement. Few within the rank and files of typical Americans have any clue what neo policies even mean! And this is on purpose. As I explained already, your government doesn't want to advertise what their changes in policy mean, nor do they think you to really care or even think about it at the end of the day. Maybe that's true, but you really need to know this one!

Most have no idea that since the 1950's both parties unofficially grabbed onto neo policies. Traditional conservatism and liberalism went to the wayside. Take your choice, neoconservatives or neoliberals, both parties latched on to the change. The effects it has had on our lives and our children's lives is immense. The cold war, the Vietnam war and the anti-establishment period of the 1960's and 70's all had a large part to do with this change of official US policies. These were times of change. Both parties took on variations of the neo movement to fit their needs. One of the classic songs of this tumultuous period came from song group Peter, Paul and Mary, entitled "times they are a changing". Yes, they really were changing.

The entire neo movement has been a construct of the corporate globalist deep state operatives. This is <u>very</u> important to know. And, it goes to follow that the biggest thing to come out of that period was the ramping up of the highly expensive, highly profitable military machine and its use similarly. And the idea that America should take the lead in the world to spread democracy around the world. Yet we now many realize that this "democracy" claim is devoid of much truth in practice, for it has largely failed to succeed nearly anywhere we have trampled, Iraq being the most touted and biggest failure to achieve the goal. Instead, it is now acknowledged using simple math that most of our warrings since have been more about creating yearly war budgets in the near trillion-dollar range for the purpose of enriching many of our war contractors to the tune of tens of trillion of dollars over the years with this war economy Americans have inherited for their grandchildren. Of course, we need a defense budget, but it is bloated beyond recognition or the actual needs to defend the country. The other major gift(s) of the neo policies has been the official sanctioning of globalism and supposed free trade agreements. (another monopoly gift to the global pirates).

That being said, the left leaning, corporate controlled media is complicit in this plot, taking advantage of this misnomer they themselves have perpetuated, wrongly packaging and portraying most of today's Republican politicians as "conservatives." Yes, in order to give the impression that as long as they can gather enough "Republican" support, a great compromise has been accomplished insofar as the public knows. We've all heard the term for these moments, it's always called a "bipartisan effort", a play with words and truth. Both sides today are on the left side, just to differing degrees! Good old Senator Bob Dole and such types were always praised for "reaching across the aisle", coming to a "bipartisan effort"! The dog and pony show would go like this… Both parties would squabble publicly about seemingly important issues that affect everyday people, (and often do). But these are essentially peripheral issues in the big scheme of things. For once it is realized that the Constitution of our country is itself being ignored and not firmly interpreted or enforced, it becomes obvious why so many things are wrong across society! This is a great example of how socialism gradualism takes hold over the years!

Upholding the Constitution and protecting our nation against foreign enemies has always been the primary job of our leaders, especially from our president. Issues like race relations, welfare increases, inequalities, job insecurities, endless safety nets and so forth are the primary issues that take up time in Washington D.C. Why? Because politicians have failed to act in the best interests of common people until emergency measures are screamed out to be instituted by small groups of activists.

Today we see one scandal after another of some sort being used to take up much of the valuable time availed to Congress for solving the nation's problems, and the eventuality is always the same. The hidden and accepted number one rule in Congress is the following: Use up time in Congress to make mostly illusory improvements on smaller issues that will firstly and foremostly build up a bigger and bigger nanny state, expensive and often dysfunctional programs and perhaps most importantly provide more governmental control over our lives. Ah, the globalist elites dream to keep us dependent!

But don't dare touch real and fair banking or Wall Street reforms, revamping the unfederal reserve system, making our tax system more equitable. No, don't force big business influence in Washington politics to be scaled down! Stricter lobbying rules, even fines? Forget it! Revamping American tendencies to get involved in wars of other nations? As a note to that last one, we will one day realize that Trump will end our long-term involvements around the world. He will deal with strength and get nearly all he wants for America!

Real election reforms are always for next year's debate. No, these are off limits. As a result, what we wind up with year after year in a nutshell is the neo-policy. What we often wind up with are new or expanded laws that succeed in increasing governmental budgets across the board, increasing the war machine without true consideration of the cost/benefits involved or the need to stop meddling in all the world's problems.

Year after year, little if any discourse ever happens in Congress when it comes to discussing the neo-establishments primary goals of expanding or beginning new wars aimed at expanding America's role around the world. Not to be forgotten is the neo's dependency upon the unfederal Reserve for the endless money required to carry out the big state's wants. Anyone paying attention realizes that unnecessary warring's have increasing astronomically since WWII, with another "enemy" that is always on the horizon!

So, how did this start? Both political parties since the 1940's have quietly taken on the label "NEO" (new) in front of their Left or Right nameplates. It is impossible for either a neo-conservative or a neo-democrat to be anything else than what the name stands for. The terms "neo-liberal" and "neo-conservative" conveys so much in common that they are almost indistinguishable, yet for most typical Americans, both of these terms are summarily and vaguely thrown out there with no explanation of the actual ideology of these two. The term neo of course means "new". That is easy. Neo policies are best described as favoring a pro-war economy, pro-globalist, pro-corporatist agenda that is designed to favor the top 1% elites as long as possible, regardless of the inevitable economic and moral bankruptcy of America. We are now there.

The neo (new) type of American policy had been quietly introduced into American politics on both sides of the isle starting around WWII. The planners realized after that war that this war machine thing was extremely profitable for the multi-billion-dollar elite owned military machine. A war is always justified too because of the old saying "wars create jobs." The answer to the neo's military agenda success has been to keep looking for new enemies and keep developing sophisticated, extremely expensive weaponry while letting a few of your enemies come into possession of them. This would force ever more sophisticated weapons to stay ahead of the enemy of course! Of course, the globalist elites and Washington were happy with the immediate financial payoffs that come with building up a stronger and stronger military machine infinitum. There is perhaps no other business on earth that can generate the profits of war after all.

# Planned Collapse of Americanism

Nearly immediately after WWII, America went to war with Korea, Vietnam and a few smaller excursions. After the Korea conflict, CFR member and U.S. Secretary of State Dean Atchison admitted:

*"The only reason I told the President to fight in Korea was to validate NATO".*

The United Nations called it a "police action", even though 5 million young men were killed. Both were failures, unpopular, a neo-conservative war exercise assumedly carried out to ensure that the military industrial complex kept well-oiled and funded.

*"Never before has this nation been engaged in mortal combat with a hostile power without military objective, without policy other than restrictions governing operations, or indeed without even formally recognizing a state of war.'"* - General Douglas MacArthur

Before retiring, President, General Dwight D. Eisenhower, a traditional liberal, made his most famous speech, warning America's military against employing this newly built gigantic war machine for nation building, hegemony or other such expansionary efforts. He warned American government to use wise judgement before using it again. Since then we've had near nonstop warring's, justified or not. Eisenhower held much distaste for any type of American hegemony, and it was expressed in this exact quote: *"We must guard against the acquisition of unwarranted influence, whether sought or unsought, by the military complex."* Dwight D. Eisenhower, 1961.

Yet the neo war hawks, profiteers would not listen. President Trump appears from all evidence that he intends to avoid war through strength, instead of limp wristed negotiations such as we witnessed under Obama.

# .8
# AMERICAN FABIANISM!

Many wonder who '**they**' really are? Who are those in America and around the civilized world whom are behind its very slow decline using progressivism (a slow walk into full state control). Who are those who are so hard at work indoctrinating politicians of both parties to ween us away from our traditional way of life, our family bonds, change our religious beliefs, our schooling methods, our independent nature, our entire culture while creating a dependency of a welfare state to suck upon like a mother's nipples?

Besides the Deep State itself, wouldn't you want to know perhaps the primary group that has been the most successful political force behind the slow creep into socialism we Americans have witnessed for at least a hundred years? You may tend to think that any such group coming out of the U.K. in the very late 1800's could certainly not still be effective, probably having lost their 'window of opportunity' to influence future generations. You would be 100% wrong. This is one of those things that only history can teach, and Americas schooling is devoid of teaching anything of this group nor the huge 'behind the scenes' workings that it still has behind the world's leftist political agendas. Yes, those that infiltrate the media misinformation machine, the dumbing down agenda in our schools, the destruction of beautiful music with rap, hip hop and worse. These are the purveyors of liberal accretion who have sold out young stars coming out of Hollywood that know little if anything of history, yet preach to the world to fall for anything they and their mushy brained leftist friends have been fed. Would you expect a state financed, state-controlled education system to expose the real plans for America? Academia leaders are 100% dependent on the state for their jobs and generous retirement benefits, most looking at socialism as a great thing, yet most not knowing how seriously flawed their gullible belief systems are going to take them in the end game of the globalists. I contend it's on purpose.

The official mascot of Fabianism is a picture of an upset turtle whom yells *"When I strike, I strike hard"*. In other words, we will work our ways much like the frog relaxing in the heating pot, then strike hard when we are ready! America today is about to witness a hard strike on our modus-operandi.

To learn more on the essence of the Fabian Doctrines beyond this book, read Sydney Webb's "Theory of the Continuity of Development from Capitalism to Socialism" writings. America today is about to witness a hard strike on the American modus-operandi if the globalist elites of which near all are Fabians in ideology, get their way. If not for President Trump's swift actions against the globalists plans, we would already be there.

Perhaps not one person in a hundred has heard of the Fabian Socialist Society. Even fewer know of the Frankfurt School's teachings or the many other schools of psychological thought disorder such as the anti-Western Cultural Marxism that is widely taught in public schools across much of the civilized (liberalized) world. Even fewer know what these represent and teach, or the deceptive and slick techniques they have used for so very long in order to change America and the rest of the world into believing that there is a utopian vision better than what we see. Yes, their dreams of one world utopia run by elites whom they believe can manage us all better than we can ourselves. Understand that Fabians are just one important part of a larger network of one world communist revolutionaries turned mainstream. They work inside of the US Government offices across the land, especially in Washington D.C. This ideology they carry with them works stealthily to push legislation that is anti-American, anti-nationalistic while often times being under wraps to public scrutiny.

The Fabian Society was founded in 1884 by husband and wife team Beatrice and Sydney Webb. Beatrice taught Fabianism at Oxford working for railroad magnate Cecil Rhodes of Rhodes Scholars fame and program. The Fabians also founded the London School of Economics, a globalist one world leaning university in London of which many famous leftist leaders of finance and politics have attended. Of these, many are American socialist politicians, banking heads and elites such as Federal Reserve heads.

Major original monetary contributors to the Fabians are/were in large part of the same suspects that nearly always show up to fund all one world programs. Major original contributors were the Rothschild's banking empire which includes J.P. Morgan plus the Rockefellers, Carnegie and these types most glaringly. The infamous socialist writer and playwright George Bernard Shaw as well as the famous writer H.G. Wells were two of the most important founding leaders of the Fabian Socialist movement besides its founders Sydney and Beatrice. Large numbers of known influential leaders, writers, actors were followers as well.

The Fabian Society derives its name from the Roman general Quintus Fabius, known as Cunctator from his strategy of delaying his attacks on the invading Carthaginians until the right moment. The name Fabian Society was explained in the first Fabian pamphlet which carried the note. *"For the right moment you must wait, as Fabius did most patiently, when warring against Hannibal, though many censured his delays; but when the time comes you must strike hard, as Fabius did, or your waiting will be in vain, and fruitless."*

This tactic is used in guerilla warfare or terrorism, (attack and hide). Does the Korean War, Vietnam War, ISIS or the Taliban come to mind? Examples in history where this tactic was used includes George Washington in the first half of the American Revolution, Sam Houston in aftermath of the Alamo, the Hundred Year War against England, Napoleon's Grande Armee as well as more modern warfare when one side holds far less firepower than the other and must wait for the right moment, using just the right sneaky methods to carry out a fatal attack. The Fabian strategy has been used in American wars and politics for 100+ years. Fabians know that the world, the American people, will never accept full world socialism in one fell swoop. Instead, Fabian incrementalism has been a huge part of the globalists long running plan bring about socialism without bloody conflict if possible.

Major original monetary contributors to the Fabians are/were part of the same suspects that nearly always show up to fund all one world programs. Major contributors were, and still are, the Rothschild's banking empire, Rockefellers, Carnegie, J.P. Morgan, George Soros, and these types most glaringly. The infamous socialist writers George Bernard Shaw and H.G. Wells were perhaps the two most important founding leaders of the Fabian Socialist movement besides its founders Sydney and Beatrice. Many, many well-known's have and are members as well.

The Fabian philosophy has required much political patience amongst the very top leaders of the world's top politico, bankers, finance, prime ministers and such types. Don't ever think that this organization is passé and just history! It is very alive in Washington and around the world, but under sheets, as will be revealed as you read through the book.

Fabianism differs from communism tactics mostly on one point. They believe in "evolution rather than revolution", i.e. slow incremental change within the existing system instead of quick, brutal overthrow. Much like the parable of the frog who gets inside a warm pan of water, and as it gets hotter, he hardly notices the increase in temperature. He becomes lazily relaxed and acquires an acceptance and numbness to it. Only when the warm pan is fully bubbling that the frog realizes that it's too late. This is the Fabian's strategy and it has taken over a hundred years, but they appear very close to that goal. But the goal of an eventual world communist government still is the final goal. It is a war of accretion. The global capitalists and elites love the movement for it is a hidden force that make like a wind to their backs. The worlds bankers will control it all by owning all the governments through secret trade treaties and the endless debt they loaned to most world bodies for many years. The elites have master-minded this plan. With the largest bankers now owning nearly all the largest corporations and financial entities around the world as well, today they virtually have everything under their thumbs!

In 1900, the Fabians founded the liberal English Labour Party within Parliament. Every Labour Prime Minister, from Ramsay MacDonald to Gordon Brown, has been a member of the Society. Today, well over 200 members of parliament are members, and the Fabian Society continues to be at the heart of the Labour movement! This is comparable to the Democrats in America. The main reason Britain has become so very socialist (outside of Margaret Thatcher's conservative terms) has been the influence of the Fabians' Labour Party. The U.K.s leap into liberalism, multiculturalism, welcoming unvetted and dangerous Muslim extremists into the country, has been spearheaded by the liberal policies of the Labour Party. Thanks Fabians!

In its infancy, the party called for a special English healthcare system for the "breeding of even a moderately Imperial Race", claiming that this "would be more productive and could provide a militarily superior force rather than the stunted, anemic and demoralized citizens of our great cities". They believed that Britain's upper crust was the superior race of the world, the lower classes were just too dumb and needed to be held down & oppressed. It was truly a feudalistic system where the neo-elites ran the show & split people into different class groups, mostly into the poor group. This party evolved out of the British Monarchy system of oligarchy of the late 1800's. Even after the Revolutionary War of which England lost, the King and Queen still harbored a deep wish to somehow control the new America in the same feudalistic, government dependent fashion they created back home. And, as you read earlier, these early globalists have indeed captured our country financially from behind the scenes in many ways, especially with our un-Federal Reserve!

While Fabian liberal Prime Minister Tony Blair was hosting the Fabian Societies 100th anniversary of which he is a lifelong member, he was photographed with a large smile, displaying the historic official stained-glass window pane of the Fabian Society. Tony Blair was a Chairman of the Fabian Society in 1997 before being Prime Minister! Such devotees of the Fabian Society doctrines, the Frankfurt School (below), London School of Economics, Marxist globalist teachings and all those trapping are well, oh so patient, always making slow yet constant progress.

Brexit of course, means "Britain Exit" from the E.U. Prime Minister Cameron lost his position of after its passage in 2016! Brexit was a win for the one world globalist elites, taking the U.K. into a one world agency operating out of Brussels. Yes, Britain has lost local control. All major decisions now come from a world body in Brussels! A precursor to America? Take note that the European Union was always intended to be a first run at consolidating power into few hands. Now with Brexit accomplished it has begun.

The Fabians are the Labour Party in Britain and nearly run politics in the UK outside of the Brexit controls they must now follow. They were the driving force to keep Britain inside the E.U, for of course they knew they would lose their grip should Brexit take shape. The Fabians agenda and its reach has expanded across the globe. Today, New Zealand's far left socialist trend of outlawing guns and socialized everything is verifiably driven by the Fabians as well.

Today, one can look on their website and see that the group has over 60 local Fabian chapters across just the U.K. In recent years the Young Fabian group, founded in 1960, has become an important networking and discussion organization for the younger (under 31) socialist activists. These played a huge role in the 1994 election of Tony Blair as Labour Leader, as well as follow up prime ministers Gordon Brown and David Cameron (whom lyingly calls himself a conservative) yet belongs to the Fabian Labour Party!

Today there is also an active Fabian Women's Network and Scottish and Welsh Fabian groups. On 21 April 2009 the Society's website stated that it had 6,286 members: Fabian national membership now stands at a 35 year high: it is over 20% higher than when the Labour Party came to office in May 1997. It is now double what it was when Clement Attlee left office in 1951. The most recent membership figure on its website at May 2016 showed 6975 members in June 2015. This exploding growth pattern of Fabianism has similarly applied to much of the world and its leaders!

Since its beginnings, the Fabian's socialist agenda has been the driving ideology behind many or most major governments and their leaders around the world, including the U.S.A! Yet the word Fabian is rarely spoken besides in Britain and more recently New Zealand wherein it is more visible and in power.

On June 24, 2016 with slim margin, Britain's peoples voted to leave the European Union and join in with Brexit. Little do most people realize the reality of what they have sown. No more will the Brit's be able to return to remain autonomous, independent, and making its own decisions on how to run the country. On the bright side though, there is talk by the Fabian British Parliamentarians of rescinding the Brexit! Such is entirely possible for the deep state gets always get what they want in time.

This is all bad news for the global elites and bankers, the Ruling Families. It offers up some hope that the world is beginning to see that the E.U. has never been much more just one more step toward attaining a world state run by the world's richest bankers, corporates and you know the rest. Yes, a consolidation of power that winds up in the hands of the Rothschild's, the Ruling Families and the oligarchs to do as they wish. And of course, these dearly wish for one world government. Since joining the E.U. the British Parliament had been left nearly impotent to make major decisions for itself. It was held hostage by the E.U. whom imposed higher taxes, unelected faceless bureaucrats issuing new laws and regulations without any vote or public debate. They failed the people of the U.K. just as any such system is destined to. Hopefully, the millions of American's who witnessed the Brexit on the news will take the cue from Britain's populace that any such "union" of corporate globalists is only created in order to enrich the elites, billionaires and the Deep State, furthering their hold over free nations. Perhaps they are beginning to see the writings on the wall and reject Washington's growing and out of control centralized government that is failing Americas peoples on so many levels.

## FABIANISM HITS AMERICA AND NOTHING IS THE SAME

Before talking more about this quiet revolution any more, let's go backward a bit. In the first half of the 1900s, Fabianism/socialism was openly quite popular in Europe. In 1900 the Fabian Society joined with the trade unions and founded the Fabian Labour Party within British Parliament. As such, Fabianism **is** the doctrine from which the dominant Labor Party of Britain still operates under. Founder Sidney Webb substantially wrote both the party's 1918 Constitution (including the original Clause IV), and its programme Labour and the New Social Order. In the first half of the 1900's Fabianism had silently moved behind the scenes into politics in America politics as well, even on the ground level. Fabian rallies, writings, speeches were quite commonplace. Coming out of the Great Depression, some Americans wondered that if Hitler's growing economy using Fascism (socialism) was working well, perhaps we should leave capitalism. Germany was rebuilding itself quite well, with little unemployment. By 1946 the American Fabians group had 8400 official members in 80 local chapters in the U.S! Lenin and Marx were seemingly being successful with Communism, at least for a while, (or so said the paid media). During and after the Great Depression, socialism looked especially attractive to those blaming capitalism for the great depression.

Pres. Franklin D. Roosevelt was a Fabian, and has to take credit for really jump starting a Fabian fascist socialism in America. It is well known that he had deep leanings toward Fabianism, even reading and making good friends with H.G. Wells and George Bernard Shaw. Wells described FDR as *"the most effective transmitting instrument possible for the coming of the new world order.... He is continuously revolutionary in the new way without ever provoking a stark revolutionary crisis"*...Sounds like Fabian tactic to me! FDR also knew very well that a democracy is the most dangerous political system, realizing that it is democracy that is the easiest form of politico to fall prey to socialism. Particularly when the time come for the 51% to vote itself whatever it wants!

Roger Baldwin (Harvard 1905) during this same period outlined a Fabian device of capturing power by stealth and deception. In an advisory letter to a socialist agitator he wrote in part:

*"Do steer away from making it look like a Socialist enterprise... We want also to look patriots in everything we do. We want to get a good lot of flags, talk a good deal about the Constitution and what our forefathers wanted to make of this country, and to show that we are really the folks that really stand for the spirit of our institutions."*

I just had to highlight the above. The above quote has been the primary long time Fabian agenda technique apparatus. It has allowed the far le Fabians to operate without being open about their agenda. They can blend in with either party affiliation and nobody will notice. You see, it's a slow race for them and persistence is the tactic to eventually change ideas through the use of caring, fairness, justice and other such platitudes in their rhetoric. The U.S. Congress and all of Washington are top notch pro's at carrying out the above deceptions upon the American peoples!! As a Marxist inspired socialist, President Barack Obama was oh so good at this technique! Karl Marx, Engels, Stalin and nearly all communists of past have actually used the Fabian method as a big part of their schemes to achieve power. The dates of these quotes may be from an earlier time, but the Fabian method has been so successful that it is still the primary method used by socialist one world leaders.

Young people ask me, why do I give such old quotes, speeches and examples of these anti-American groups throughout the book? The reason should be obvious to those of us a bit older, for nothing really changes much about this centuries old dream of these one world order devotees! Thankfully, during the earlier days of this movement there were ample recorded examples of the true motivations and ways that the far left operates. Likewise, I give ample examples of more current proofing's, quotes to prove the danger is alive and at our doorsteps. You shall discover the "New World Order I.e. the "One World Order" plan is <u>really</u> the "Old World Plan" for it is the same plan just being constantly updated and refined into what we see happening today. Globalism is the path. Yet today, the world is at the closest point to no return as we have ever seen. If the anti-American coup` we are experiencing across the world continues to mushroom as it has since the Trump election, true liberty and freedom could be a thing of the past.

"When we get ready to take the United States, we will not take it under the label of communism; we will not take it under the label of socialism. These labels are unpleasant to the American people, and have been speared too much. We will take the United States under labels we have made very lovable; we will take it under liberalism, under progressivism, under democracy. But, take it, we will."

—Quote from Alexander Trachtenberg (1885-1966) at the National Convention of Communist Parties, Madison Square Garden, 1944

Source: Bella Dodd (1904-1966)

Above, Communist leader Alexander Trachtenberg of course was primarily referring to the Democratic party as being the American Communists mouthpiece. He says "we will take it under liberalism, under progressivism, under DEMOCRACY!" The Communists have always used democracy as the primary means towards communism. Does not the above quote sound like the methods of the Democratic Party in particular over the last many decades? They have always used those three terms above to describe what they stand for! They are code words as many millions have realized! Although most liberals will deny this statement, we can see that it goes back to the Communist tactics as exemplified by Alexander Trachtenberg in the caption shown above! Come on libs, let's stop playing around. When we constantly hear the democrats constantly referring to so many problems around our country as being "un-democratic", we must take pause and consider where they are really coming from! After all, using the singular word "democracy" to explain America's system of government, the above quote fits exactly. And even though this was said in 1944, the tactics, the goals and ways for the communists is the same. This time, if successful to its end, the word communism is to be replaced with the words "New World Order". It's really about a new globalist world order.

Another such example of how the Democratic Party and Communist are birds of a feather, follows:

Alfred Smith, former U.S. Presidential candidate and Mayor of New York City delivered a speech in January of 1936 in Washington, D.C., entitled, "Betrayal of the Democratic Party." He had supported FDR in 1932, but in later days, he stated the new strategy of the Communist party in America:

*"Just get the platform of the Democratic Party, and get the platform of the Socialist Party, and lay them down on your dining room table, side by side, and get a heavy lead pencil and scratch out the word 'Democrat', and scratch out the word 'Socialist,' and let the two platforms lay there. Then study the record of the present administration up to date. After you have done that, make your mind up to pick up the platform that more nearly squares with the record, and you will put your hand on the Socialist platform."*

Perhaps that that says it all right there! The above strategy is perhaps the biggest long time secret that the Democratic party has in their arsenal. FDR had verifiably changed the real agenda and long-term aims of the Democratic party from true conventional liberalism (a true peoples party) unto socialism under the name of democracy and Democrat. Now do you know the real agenda of the Democratic Party in particular? Is this not an indictment of how the leaders of the Democratic Party operate? Always promoting more and more government dependencies, promoting what amounts to anti-republican policies, the agenda is clear... steer the U.S. into a state of complete socialism turned one world government. Unfortunately, the Republican Party has followed suit. The Democrats drive the welfare state agenda while the Republicans push the corporate ownership of the state although both are guilty vice-versa. Is it no mistake that the five states with the lowest economic stability and performance are Connecticut, California, Illinois, New Jersey and Massachusetts? What do they all share? They are all Democrat controlled state governments. And what about their public pension plans and labor union activism rate? The most generous in the nation. Cronyism inside of a Democratic state always produces the worst results for the majority of people in those states!

The "New Deal" was the new title chosen for FDR's socialist and fascist agenda. Yet Curtis Dall, FDR's son-in-law cast his doubt's that FDR was the originator of this vast "recovery" effort.

In his book, *FDR: My Exploited Father-in-Law* (1967) Dall stated, *"For a long time I felt that FDR had developed many thoughts and ideas that were his own to benefit this country, the USA. But he didn't. Most of his thoughts, his political 'ammunition,' as it were, was carefully manufactured for him in advance by the <u>CFR-One World Money Group</u>".*

Take note: The CFR (Council on Foreign Relations) has always been the globalist corporate one world order mouthpiece. It is a "power behind the throne" so to speak, to assist in the carrying out of wars, corporatist favored trades, and Fabianism has been the religion or social doctrine of that inner circle of power, with world domination and full control its consummate objective. FDR was not only acquainted with the works of famed Fabian socialist, author H.G. Wells, as Rexford Tugwell wrote on, but he was on friendly terms with good old Mr. Wells as well.

Leading up to the New Deal, the Fabian Socialists as they had been called, smartly decided to drop the word 'socialist' from their nameplate in order to hide their agenda from plain site. This tactic allowed even mainline, respectable people within communities to hide their socialist leanings and still remain a member.

It was leading member/famous writer Robert Shaw who said of the Fabian Society: *"the Society made it possible for respectable citizens to support socialism without suspicion of lawlessness to overturn the existing order"*. Does this sound like so many of our double talk politicians who perpetually keep voting for big government and endless entitlements while pushing the socialist agenda? And the shame of it is they pretend to be a conservative or a middle roader come election time?

## SCHOOLS OF NEW WORLD ORDER INDOCTRINATION

We will now delve into more of the differing and importantly connected reasons for our nation's historic decline. As is often the case, the direction a country takes is often tied to the style of political and social teachings it imparts inside its highest schools of teachings. And in each case, whatever prevalence of thought is fostered inside the education system of a country does not just happen by happenstance. America's liberal teachings arrived here from the British in large part. Historically, the Brits essentially owned the schools of higher thought in nearly every category before America came to be. They were the think tank of the world. Should it be no surprise that America's highest rated colleges have been greatly influenced by the liberal ideology that came here from Britain? This is where America's gradualism towards the one world agenda has come from! What if we could trace the primary influences that have guided much of our higher levels of learning in America over the last 200 plus years?

# Planned Collapse of Americanism

As you will see, the Rhodes Scholar Program and London School of Economics have been at the forefront of indoctrinating some of the world's top leaders with the globalist one world ideology, as well as how to work within the corporate elite system that often puts profit above people or anything else. Of course, Marxist American Ivy league schools of one world disinformation exist across the world, especially in America and the U.K. wherein they have operated for over 150 years! Harvard, Yale, Columbia, Princeton, Berkeley, Brandeis are just a few prime examples. As iterated further along, the Marxist teachings out of the Frankfurt School came to New York's Columbia University in 1934 and set up roots inside a new class surreptitiously named as the "Institute for Social Research" in order to hide the true Marxist agenda they had brought with them from Frankfurt Germany For the last 70 years this ideology has been taught in the above schools and other universities across the country to an extent that it is hard to fathom. (next chapter).

But even these esteemed schools of disinformation are outdone by two British Universities who are even more elite and offer a much higher level of new world order, globalist brainwashing's for the many who enroll and graduate before their entry into the world of influence.

As covered, the Fabian Socialists grew out of Great Britain. With the right elitist connections, they planted themselves into London's political power base and the Labour movement. The founders of the Fabians were the husband and wife team of Cecil and Beatrice Webb. During these beginnings, both taught Fabianism and Illuminati doctrines at Oxford University in England, working within the infamous Rhodes Scholarship Program. Yes, I said Illuminati! They worked closely with infamous Sir John Ruskin and multi-millionaire Cecil Rhodes (major railroad entrepreneur). When Rhodes died, his will left to perhaps the richest man in the world, English banker Nathan Rothschild, as trustee to set up the Rhodes Scholarship Program. Cecil and Beatrice Webb were left in charge of the Fabian Socialism program. Ruskin continued to teach the Rhodes Program to indoctrinate and teach the secrets of the wealthy. For any aspiring, smart student wishing to reach the highest echelons of business or politics, it is of equal importance to attend the one world, socialist leaning London School of Economics, or Oxford Univ. which is also equally important to the elites! The Webb's also founded the London School of Economics one year later, a quasi-branch of the University of London. It still is a one world socialist leaning university with a one world styled school that pushes globalism and socialist styles of economic instruction such as Keynesian economics. This school the Oxford University's socialistic Rhode Scholar Program have perhaps been the primary one world, economic and Fabian inspired schools in the world, operating right up till today, and they have close ties with each other from the outset. To identify Rhode's one world philosophy that has bled over into many of the leaders of today's world, let's look at his final wishes before his death.

According to Frank Aydelotte, a founding member of the Council on Foreign Relations and the American Secretary to the Rhodes Trustee's wrote in his book 'American Rhodes Scholarships' that in Rhodes first will, he stated his forward looking aims more specifically, to wit:

*'The extension of British rule throughout the world...the foundation of so great a power as to render wars impossible and promote the interests of humanity."*

In other words, make the British Rule the law of the world. Much of the platform would be patterned after Plato's "New Republic", i.e. an English speaking one world order using atheistic Darwinism. This lends credence to those whom claim that Britain had actually started the Revolutionary War in order put in place their usurious Rothschild's money system that would create our money and control it as well. So, even though they lost the Revolutionary War as our history books tell us, they walked away only after making a deal that would essentially guarantee to them the control of America's banking system. Soon we saw the Rothschilds controlling more and more of our new banking system, eventually in 1913 creating and controlling the Federal Reserve Bank from behind the scenes in London!

Within Cecil Rhodes' will, his goals in creating the Rhodes Scholarships was to promote global and civic-minded leaders among his graduates. With these scholarships, he "aimed at making Oxford University the educational center of the English-speaking race". Since its creation, controversy has surrounded both its former exclusion of women (thus leading to the establishment of the co-educational Marshall Scholarship), and the Rhodes' white supremacist beliefs and legacy of colonialism.

Rhodes wasn't shy about his goals of teaching students to be young colonialists, bringing the world under British control "for the recovery of the United States" (as a one world partnership), i.e. an English speaking, white, and male dominated society. In other words, he wanted to keep alive a British monarchy to rule not just England, India and Ireland, but America as well!

Traditional colonialism had begun to fade and morphed into the neo-colonialism we have today. This is part of what Rhodes' dream world consisted of, and I think we can see how successful his dream has become. Today, the two nations share immense shared ideals, a goal of a one world government that both can share in. The longtime marriage of America and the U.K. have together have accomplished the goals of Cecil Rhodes. A world assembled to benefit the few, made possible by the smart workings of the Royals!

America today has neocolonialism maximus with the Brit's, Rothschild's and the banking globalists quietly owning much of America as explained elsewhere. In place of colonialism as the main instrument of imperialism, we have today neo-colonialism . . . [which] like colonialism, is an attempt to export the social conflicts of the capitalist countries. According to its description in Wikipedia, the result of neo-colonialism is (here it comes!) that foreign capital is used for the exploitation rather than for the development of the less developed parts of the world. Investment, under neo-colonialism, increases, rather than decreases, the gap between the rich and the poor countries of the world. Likewise, the struggle against neo-colonialism is not aimed at excluding the capital of the developed world from operating in less developed countries. It is aimed at preventing the financial power of those countries being used in such a way as to impoverish the less developed. So, this is the Mr. Rhodes of the infamous Rhodes Scholar Program that so many of our liberal, globalist politicians have attended as part of their entrance into politics, big business and more. A quote from the oh so noble Mr. Rhodes (ha!) follows:

*"We must find new lands from which we can easily obtain raw materials and at the same time exploit the cheap slave labor that is available from the natives of the colonies. The colonies would also provide a dumping ground for the surplus goods produced in our factories."*    **Cecil Rhodes**

Lenin, just as with Marx, witnessed notes of this in 1917.  Lenin, in the pamphlet Imperialism, the Highest Stage of Capitalism (1917), he framed 19th-century imperialism as the logical extension of geopolitical power, to meet the financial investment needs of the political economy of capitalism.    From *Neo-Colonialism, the Last Stage of Imperialism*, Kwame Nkrumah.

As stated, today's geopolitical might was created in large part not only for the purposes of national security but more often than not, to provide great opportunities for the elites, the banks, and the connected corporations wishing to remain healthy and growing, no matter what the costs.  Has anything changed since 1917?  The obvious answer is no, it has become more pronounced and extended than even Lenin could have imagined.  Anyways, this is what Rhodes scholars are taught to admire, going out into the world's highest positions with that very belief system.

Washington and the U.S. Defense Department are full of Rhodes scholars running the decisions of life and death of our world.  This lends even more credence to the theory that the U.S. has a built-in bias towards the one world goals via use of world hegemony, neo-colonialism and so forth.  Here is a short list of major names of high profile insiders whom are Rhodes Graduates that are or have been inside our government, making huge decisions that affect where America is headed... Pres. Bill Clinton. Susan Rice FMR. National Security advisor, Wesley Clark Ex U.S. Army General and Supreme Commander of NATO, Ashton Carter, current U.S. Secretary of Defense, Robert Reich, FMR. U.S. Secretary of Labor, Richard Haas, current crooked President of the CFR, James Woolsey, FMR. Director of the CIA, core member of Progress for the New American Century (PNAC) a neo-con think tank, and Bernard Rogers, Ex General, Supreme Allied Commander. As for news personalities, include Rachel Maddow, Naomi Wolf (writer), George Stephanopoulos and several more leftists that have graduated out of the Rhodes program, and all seem to lean toward the one world idea.

# THE LONDON SCHOOL OF "RECKONOMICS"

The importance of the London School of Economics cannot be overlooked one bit. Many of the worlds Presidents, Prime Ministers, world leaders, business tycoons, central planners, economic professors as well as many economic gurus have attended this liberal university that espouses a distinct liberal, internationalist agenda behind it.  Such is also an extension of the University of London. But how much do we know about the history of either school?  You ask yourself, why is this silly English university even important to this subject in this book? How is is important at all to what is happening in America today?

Four Fabian founders, primarily the communist duo Beatrice and Sidney Webb, founded the London School of Economics with the money left to their Fabian Society by millionaire Henry Hutchinson. Supposedly the decision was made at a breakfast party on August 4th, 1894. The founders are depicted in the Fabian Window designed by George Bernard Shaw. To remember is that this group of elites of this period were the wealthiest people on earth essentially. Beatrice Webb was a wealthy socialite who grew up in high circles. To remember is that she had very close personal communications, often over tea, with names such as Rothschilds, DuPont and near all the very upper crust of England especially during this time. She was a communist in her bleeding heart and never denied it. This is important, as it drives home the fact that near all these types are communists at least in one big part of their world agenda. The schools Oxford and Rhodes Scholars programme, London School of Economics,

Perhaps the most infamous economic guru who completed the infamous LSE economics course was the man mainly responsible for America's loose monetary policies since the 1930's, and still being used right up till today... John Maynard Keynes. Keynes economic policies of micro-managing the economy, controlling interest rates and money supply to control the economy is right out of the pro-federal reserve, pro-globalist policies of employing unrestrained fiat money that to juice up the economy when sound economic policies have been ignored by policy and lawmakers in order to greatly profit the bankers.

Federal Reserve Chairman Ben Bernanke and Paul Volker also attended the LSE as well. Famed Nobel winning, liberal economist Paul Krugman (also a Keynes fan) attended, and still is often a practicing professor there, even earning the Centennial award from the university. Krugman was famously criticized after the 2008 stock market crash for his opinion that the US government had spent far, far more on the bailout, America could have exited from the recession permanently! Yeah, that sounds like a one world socialist! It should not be so surprising how these same graduates of socialist, Fabian one world education systems have taken the world's economies slowly off a cliff. These pickings aren't just policy mistakes or mistaken appointments. These appointments are made by the real powers.

Federal Reserve Chairwoman Janet Yellen is another graduate of LSE. Both she and recent Chairman Ben Bernanke are both puppets of the un-federal reserves "real owners" whom offered up trick economic "solutions" that of course wind up profiting only the insider banks and financial giants with free money, free bailouts and record breaking financial favors to the real powers of the world. They serve their un-federal reserve private owners such as the Rothschild's.

Many of Goldman Sachs upper-crust employees have attended LSE, for it is almost a requirement. For instance, Robert Rubin, Fmr. Secretary of the Treasury under Clinton was just one example, serving under the Clinton regime He directed the loosening of financial industry underwriting guidelines. Easier said, he got rid of the 1930's Glass-Steagall Act. Remember that one? Yeah, that was the Act that would have prevented the crash of 2008 if it had been left in place! This is just one example of perhaps hundreds of corrupted decisions and collusions coming from these types of financial industry and globalist leaning employees whom often have come out of LSE and/or such types of one world universities.

Leaders all around the world whom have attended these types of schools are largely of the same outlook on world policies. Perhaps it is no coincidence that many of the attendees of these globalist/corporatist leaning universities wind up being members in at least one, or several, of the one-world private steering organizations such as the World Bank, United Nations, Council on Foreign Relations, the Trilateral Commission, the Illuminati's, the Bilderberg Group and / or holding influential high-powered posts of other elite clubs of the connected, whom never seem to just go away. Perhaps not so surprisingly, one worlder George Soros attended L.S.E. as well. Remember, he is known as "The Man Who Broke the Bank of England" because of his intentionally deceptive short sale of US $10 billion worth of Pound sterling. His clever move created a panic in the markets, making him a profit of $1 billion during the 1992 Black Wednesday UK currency crisis. It nearly cost the Bank of England $3.5 billion dollars and reportedly did in fact cost them at least $1 billion dollars. And being that the Bank of England has been a Rothschild/Britain partnership from its inception, it is suspected that Soros used this ploy perhaps as some sort of payback or rivalry scheme upon Rothschild. This technique was also used by Rothschild's at the end of the Napoleon War as fact, providing the financial springboard for the firm. When Rothschild was made aware of Napoleon's defeat by his messenger a day before anyone else, Rothschild shorted the markets and caused a selling frenzy. Most investors were under the assumption that Napoleon was sure to win but that didn't happen. At the end of the day, Rothschild re-entered the markets and bought huge positions at a small fraction of what they were worth in that morning. Such indiscriminate abusers of their fellow man and nations near always seem to gravitate toward the supporting of radical far left causes AND far right causes just so long as they could work the system of the elites within either of the so-called establishment systems available at any given time. They realize that this is where the real money and power is found for them and their ilk!

In 1999, economist Paul Krugman was critical of Soros's effect on financial markets. *"Nobody who has read a business magazine in the last few years can be unaware that these days there really are investors who not only move money in anticipation of a currency crisis, but actually do their best to trigger that crisis for fun and profit. These new actors on the scene do not yet have a standard name; my proposed term is 'Soroi'.*

# .9

# THE FRANKFURT SCHOOL

## IMPORTING THE MARXIST ONE WORLD AGENDA INTO OUR SCHOOLS

### THE ARCHITECTS OF MORAL DECAY

It was none other than a group of fleeing Jewish intellectuals who fled from the Bolshevik Revolution and then gathered to create a cultural Marxist school in Frankfurt, Germany that is largely to be blamed for the anti-Western criticisms that bloomed in the early 1950's and forward inside of American colleges. Especially the ivy league types. Don't make the mistake of disregarding this story! The CIA and the deep state were fully aware of this group, their real presence and communist influence inside the classrooms of our universities, and protest marches. The Frankfurt school existed prior to Hitler's rise, then they had to flee before he caught up with them. If you attended an American university during these years, you probably encountered at least some of this ideology from one or more of your professors or even high school teacher unfortunately.

Without a doubt much of America's cultural decay and anti-Western far left values has been cultivated out of the Frankfurt School of Weimar Republic, (later becoming Germany when Hitler came to power.) It was founded in 1923 yet the school closed during Hitler's war against Jews. It was borne out of the Bolshevik Revolution where most of the school's teachers and leaders emanated from before the revolution ended. Frankfurt School was a Marxist/Leninist inspired university, combined with Sigmund Freud's inputs (also a devotee). While the Frankfurt School pushed their stealth brand of Marxism onto America via slow and peaceful change, the Fabians also took the road using accretion means, for the two had much in common. The propagations of the two ideologies across America for the last 60 plus years has been a monumental success, at least in the eyes of its instigators and followers. The negative cumulative effects after decades of anti-Western bashings inside American classroom has been, and still is, responsible for a large part of the degenerative declines across America. I am talking of our declines in morals, values, trains of thought, and so much more.

The Frankfurt School largely invented and taught the ideologies of Cultural Marxism and Critical Theory. **One student had called the two theories:** *"The destructive criticisms of Western Culture including Christianity, capitalism, authority, family, patriarchy, hierarchy, morality, tradition, sexual restraint, loyalty, patriotism, nationalism, heredity, ethnocentrism, convention, and conservatism".*

The Frankfurt School's studies combined Marxist analysis with Freudian psychoanalysis to form the basis of what became known as "Critical Theory", still widely studied and critiqued in many university classrooms. The two ideologies strayed a bit from straight Marxism for they believed that Marxism was too rigid and would never work in America as it did in with Marx or Lenin. Americans were too independent and would never accept communism in one fell swoop. Being critical of capitalism and

Marxism–Leninism as philosophically inflexible systems, the School's critical theory research indicated alternative paths to realizing the social development of a nation. Instead, they believed, quite rightly, that the two ideologies, when merged together as part of the bigger picture, could be successful at slowly destroying America from within without hardly a soul realizing the slick plan. While the nation was worried about communism in the 1960's, it was the immediate threat of nuclear war that was at the forefront of most people's fears. Certainly not this type of silent, stealth attack.

Most of these academia's fled to Switzerland for a short time after fleeing Hitler, then immigrated to America. Wasting no time, this ideology was brought into York City's Columbia University firstly. Just as in Germany, the program was called The Institute for Social Research. For many observers, it was originally dubbed the Institute for Marxism. These never just come out and call themselves for what they are! Soon afterwards, they migrated to other major leftist U.S. universities such as Princeton, Brandeis, Yale, and California at Berkeley as examples. But how can we be sure that the 'causes' of the breakdown in our schools, our universities and the fiber of our culture has largely been a product of a tiny group of intellectuals who immigrated from Germany in 1933? Let's see the evidence.

The Frankfurt School borrowed from Marxism and perpetuated what we call "Political Correctness". I believe strongly that political correctness is the at the top of the list for WHY Americans, especially after attending the public-school systems, have accepted the corruptions and upside-down values that have flooded America. They designed the idea of deprecating other ideas, using personal attacks such as being called out as a 'racist', 'homophobe', 'male chauvinist' and other such epithets in order to take the conversation away from too much inquiry into the facts of the matter, since they had no facts to back up their fantasy land, disproven Marxist ideas! Sound familiar? Political Correctness is in fact Marxism in a different set of clothes. The Frankfurt School did for Western civilization what Karl Marx couldn't. Out of Critical Theory was born the destructive criticisms of Western Culture including Christianity, capitalism, authority, family, patriarchy, hierarchy, morality, tradition, sexual restraint, loyalty, patriotism, nationalism, heredity, ethnocentrism, convention, and conservatism".

The Frankfurt strategy to destroy America from within owes itself in large part from the writings of unemployed Italian Communist Antonio Gramsci. Gramsci wrote his ideas while he was serving time in one of Mussolini's prisons. He died in 1937 at the age of 46. Gramsci wrote of a 'quiet revolution' that could be diffused throughout a culture – over a period of time—to destroy it from within. Gramsci was the first to suggest the application of psychology to break the traditions, beliefs, morals, and wills of a nations people. And it could be accomplished quietly, without the possibility of resistance if slowly introduced over generations if need be. Gramsci insisted that alliances with non-Communist leftist groups would be essential to Communist victory. Gramsci definitely used the Fabian game plan. With this plan, one can chummy up to whatever party or platform they wish to without letting loose of their real agenda yet still fit in. In our times, the left has far more options than in Gramsci's time. Under identity politics, cultural politics and the such, lefties now have many groups on both sides of the isle to conspire with without the others noticing. Such groups might include any combination of extremist environmentalist groups, international and global minded groups, civil rights groups, university professors, unions, liberal / new age church denominations, as well as large factions from both sides of the political machinery!

For this idea to work, Theodore Adorno claimed that Critical Theory had to contain a strongly imaginative, even utopian strain, which transcends the limits of reality. Its tenets would never be subject to experimental evidence. The pure logic of their thoughts would be incontrovertible. As a precursor to today's 'postmodernism' in the intellectual academic community, it recognized that disinterested scientific research was impossible in a society in which men were themselves not yet autonomous...the researcher was always part of the social object he was attempting to study." This, of course, is the concept which led to the current fetish for the rewriting of history, and the vogue for our universities' law, English literature, and humanities disciplines -- deconstruction.

Critical Theory equals Cultural Pessimism, such as we've seen metastasize in our American universities since the 1960's when this cancer began to metastasize our society. Under Critical Theory, anything emanating from the West is to be libeled and attacked over and over again, while at the same time, anything emerging from a "progressive" (communist) country or group is to be applauded. All blame for societal and economic ills are to be shifted to the West, especially towards white men who are living the American dream. A wife, kids, family, good job, a church to attend, a nice house, car, etc. Oh yeah, and the eradication of the assumption that the man would be considered the head of the household. In those days, such was not a novel idea (and still isn't in many households). By promoting the dialectic of 'negative' criticism, that is, pointing out the rational contradictions in a society's belief system, the Frankfurt Schools 'revolutionaries' dreamed of a utopian vision ala Karl Marx.

Critical theory also rejects the ideal of Western Civilization in the age of modern science, that is, the verification or falsifying of theory by experimental evidence. Only the superior mind was able to fashion the 'truths' from observation of the evidence. There would be no need to test these hypotheses against everyday experience. This utopia would be a product of their imagination, a product not susceptible to criticism on the basis of the examination of evidence. This 'revolution' would be accomplished by fomenting a very quiet, subtle and slowly spreading 'cultural Marxism' which would apply to culture the principles of Karl Marx bolstered by the modern psychological tools of Sigmund Freud. Thus, cultural Marxism, a marriage of Marx and Freud, aimed at producing a 'quiet' revolution in the United States of America. This 'quiet' revolution has occurred in America over the past 30 years. While America slept!

Radical liberal activists emanating from liberal universities were often devotees of the Frankfurt theories on berating Americanism. These and other malcontents play a very large part in providing the fuel for the explosions of love-ins, mind bending drugs, anti-establishment mentalities, new hippie 'communes', open sex with no restrictions, love the earth religions, a general attitude of "do your own thing", "make love, not war", etc. These narcissistic ideas were just too tempting for many of the young to resist. Known American college communist activist types such as the Abby Hoffman, Pete Seeger, Jerry Rubin and similarly devotees of the New Left sprung up anywhere a political protest took place, even helping with the planning's. Unfortunately, not all of these protestors were in favor of communism, often just wanting to be involved in politics and change. Many didn't have a clue that the organizers of many of the protests were from one or more of the hundred plus communist front groups operating in America.

In 1950, the charismatic founder of the Frankfurt School, Theodore Odorno wrote, The Authoritarian Personality, an infamous critique on Westernism that quickly circulated into the classrooms and campuses of colleges around the country. American political journalist James Buchanan asserts this book as "the altarpiece of the Frankfurt School". Adorno has been studied, critiqued, and looked at from all angles by thousands of academia's and their circles for many years. Adorno was a German social psychologist, psychoanalyst, sociologist, humanistic philosopher, and democratic socialist. And he was a very charismatic con man like so many other leaders of false ideologies are. The book is essentially a guidebook on how ruin a free country without the reader realizing its intent, for it has parts that sounded just so liberating with fun experimentations to 'do your own thing'. The ideology contained within Adorno's famous book of the time was, and still is, Marxist Cultural Marxism.

His theory blames the makeup of the Western man, the authoritarian personality, was a large part in the stifling's of true happiness and self-fulfillment. freedoms. His idea of the fix of course included communism, but he would never let that cat out of the bag. And it was aimed at America, especially towards young adults who could become the pawns of the movement and blindly carry it forward. The basis of the book was that the male authoritarian model needed to be done away with and replaced with his own ideas of a new social order. By the way, Engels and Marx also both denounced the 'Authoritarian Personality' as a product of the patriarchal family, instead promoting matriarchy (women led households and the demoting of the man's role). This is where Gloria Steinem was likely influenced enough to start her own pro feminist movement greatly degrading man's roles, disparaging the man's worth in family and society. Should we wonder why for so many years, Hollywood socialist lefties have aired so many sitcoms depicting a dunce husband with a smart wife? Some may be funny to watch, that is until you realize the sub plot and the political bent of the producers.

Adorno's thesis is that anyone who is imbued with middle class, conservative or Christian values is a racist and a fascist. It seems that such a libelous indictment against the American people is to be compared to Adolph Hitler's indictment of the Jews of Europe. The white, authoritarian male was a scourge to be dealt with in Adorno's eyes, likewise blacks, Hispanics, feminist women, homosexuals, and most minority groups are to be lauded as not just equal, but virtuous. We see this continuously in America today, where minority groups have built up a power base far larger than their numbers and demographics would indicate. Some critics point out that too often, far leftist's and minorities are able to do what the constitution doesn't provide them. Yes, things like new laws and edicts that might be unpopular with a large percentage of voters. This is where special interest groups petition the courts using various different tactics (usually involving bribes and favors) enough to get what they want. There is a term, a saying, that the far left, the socialist and Communists in America use too often to get their unpopular agenda accomplished through the court systems. And here it is; *"Use the power of the law to change the law"*. Quite simple but very effective!

What it intended to accomplish, and indeed did to great extent in America, was the subsequent emasculation & warfare against the masculine gender, especially white males. Adorno's old colleagues from the Frankfurt School, particularly Marcuse, Eric Fromm, Max Horkheimer perpetuated the guise of 'women's liberation', the Sexual Revolution, the anti-war movement, the New Left movement and many other such movements in the 1960's. Frankfurt devotees believed in 'personal evolution of transcendence of both masculinity and femininity to general humanness.' But there is much more involved than simple equality of the sexes hidden behind the veil. The psychological babble, the mantra of 'equality' between the sexes, was indeed meant to do more than the nameplate suggests. The real, hidden agenda behind the supposed equality of sexes was to slowly break down and destroy the traditional American family through deprecating the man's traditional role in marriage, especially white men. The raising of the traditional family unit was to be discouraged, taking "mom" out of the house and into the workplace, and, while giving her a sense of more independence, the home, kids and husband often would become her secondary concern.

The plan (which worked quite well) did its part in bringing about the problems kids with little parental supervision when mom was working, producing latch-key kids with little direction, large increases in divorces, broken homes, increases in money stress, welfare costs, abortions, narcissistic attitudes and so forth. A whole new set of problems for many families had taken hold, tearing down the traditional, healthy family unit.

Gender roles became endlessly confusing especially for men. Is it any wonder that young men are waiting so long to get married today, while at the same time fewer and fewer are just not interested in marriage whatsoever, sometimes delaying it indefinitely? This movement brought a whole new set of problems that many of today's men don't want to deal with. Systematic tearing down of traditional values across all sections of society is the communist tactic of "Deconstruction before Reconstruction." Tear it down before you rebuild it into your own vision.

Herbert Marcuse was another infamous, original Frankfurt School founder whom after coming to America joined the movement with his Frankfurt comrades. The convincingly and charismatically got busy spreading the attractive sounding, deceptive socialist/commy mantras on college campuses around the country during the 1960's, even coining the term "*Make love, not war.*" During this time, he took much time to train Angela Davis, the infamous and controversial communist professor at the University of Los Angeles who got fired for her communist ties, admitting she was a member of the Black Panthers and the U.S. Communist Party. She had met Adorno at Brandeis University while they both studied philosophy. When she had finished college, Marcuse of course sent her to West-Germany to study at the (reopened) "Institute for Social Research" in Frankfurt. In 1967, Davis came back to America and continued her studies, with Marcuse as her doctoral adviser. She is now teaching at the University of California in San Diego. Just the kind of teacher our young don't need to associate with let alone be taught by! Marcuse was a huge cult figure on college campuses, calling for "Repressive Intolerance". Using the name "repressive", he slickly made the term sound like it was against intolerance on all counts. Quite the opposite, it is verified that it meant intolerance of movement from the right, yet toleration of movements from the left. When the left speaks of tolerance, this is what they mean! We see this tactic so clearly today! The 2016 riots at Berkeley University was a prime example of this technique being used by the far left when confronted with the possibility of a conservative speaking getting on stage! And it goes on all the time across the country.

Marcuse wrote the 'Dialectic of Enlightenment' with his Frankfurt colleague Max Horkheimer. A creepy look into his ideas of reverse happiness. The essence of the book used Critical Theory as its basis. The use of the Hegelian Dialectic is a primary focus of the book, a brilliant technique long used by nearly all governments and others to steer events and policy (of which I write about further on.)   The real truth of the Frankfurt bunch and Fabians is that they are at the bone quasi communists. They don't want people independently happy as they pretended. In typical communist fashion they want power for the elites of the new state they envision. These are nearly always lovers of Satanism. Studies of the most dangerous leaders of the past nearly always can make a connection to back up this statement. Their core makeup usually consists of nihilistic self-hate, pro-evil, psychopathic personalities that deep-down cares nothing of individuals. They hate people who are happy, hate property rights, the family unit, individual self-sufficiency or a belief in God. These knowingly encourage and push hundreds of sick, immoral anti-human laws and rights through the states courts systems. Using "human rights" as a false backboard for their supposedly caring agenda, they have shown how they can attract the democratic party's members to impulsively just pull the D lever come election time when a politician or a party claims to own the term "human rights", regardless of what the term really encompasses.

Any type of sexism is encouraged, irregardless of how anti-human or anti-good for a healthy civilization is still praised. Schools tell children that there are 20 different sexual identities, and all are acceptable, even encouraged if that is what feels good! At an early age, schools now encourage students from the age of 6 and up to decide where they think they fit into the sex equation and how they identify themselves. How can a six-year-old, let alone a 16-year-old really be sure of his sexual leanings? And even if once in a while a particular kid can, is it the schools job to discuss it? Condone it? Jimmy say that he feels like a woman this week, so he is now allowed to use the female bathrooms today in many schools. This is an Antonio Gramsci technique working at full speed.  This is Cultural Marxism folks, the degradation of a stable society that slowly opens a gateway to communism/one world order. And it goes on everyday outside of the home.   Cultural Marxism's long running disinformation campaign has lulled large sections of Americans into their own sick matrix that loathes Americanism and endorses the idea of a society that rejects the past and is self-serving.

Yesterdays morals have been replaced with what is now called "SITUATIONAL ETHICS".   For 50 years, the far left has been largely successful at indoctrinating a new American society, especially its youngest. This ideology praises self-gratifications and self-happiness above all else. That is, if it fits with the conformity that comes with the adult world they are entering.

Everything is relative, so who should decide? This is the new rule of the day for billions of peoples across the world. They care of, and know nothing of, what it takes to sustain a civil, growing and happy society, and could care less. That job is for others to worry about. They are the deserved's whom are only on the lookout for themselves. Schools, family, society have been infiltrated with this concept of entitlement and self-narcissism. Furthermore, today's Cultural Marxist leaning schoolings are creating mal-educateds whom know little of their countries historical lessons, irregardless of which glowing "degree" they received from their school of mal-education. By winning 'cultural hegemony,' Antonio Gramsci pointed out that they could control the deepest wellsprings of human thought – through the medium of mass psychology. Indeed, men could be made to "love their servitude"' without even realizing they were helping the enemies of freedom. A bit like the Stockholm Theory in fact. Critical Theory's change agents and their revolutionaries have led recent generation to declare their intent to restructure America. Their activities are directed towards the disintegration of the traditional white power structure. In terms of the gospel of the Frankfurt School, resistance to 'Cultural Marxism' could be completely negated by placing the resister in what could only be called a 'psychic iron cage'. The tools of mass psychology could be applied to produce this result.

Antonio Gramsci's strategy is reflected in a 1990s book by the American Boomer author, Charles C. Reich, entitled 'The Greening of America'. According the Reich;

*"There is a revolution coming. It will not be like revolutions of the past. It will originate with the individual and the culture, and it will change the political structure as its final aft. It will not require violence to succeed. This is the revolution of the New Generation."*

Much of Reich's ideas stem from his belief that the "GREEN MOVEMENT" will be the primary tool by the one world globalists to bring the world into a united consciousness, a completely false realization that the survival of the world is upon imminent collapse soon! The fix? Nothing less than a world government is needed to solve all of the world's problems. And what could be a bigger problem than global warming if it was real I ask? Oh, if only it was real and simply not a long-term anomaly. With a crisis, no bombs are often required, only willing compliance is needed. Sound familiar to today's green movement chants? Knowing this, the Frankfurt new age prophets have long used the repeated manta 'Have the Courage to Change" for many years. OH OUCH! That rings so loudly, so much akin to Obama's oft-repeated mantra during his 2008 election, when he owned the phrase, "Change You Can Believe In" as his primary slogan. Don't we know that these and other such mantras of change have been used over and over again during revolutionary elections throughout history? We see such similar terms and phrases everywhere we look today if one knows what he is looking for. For the Frankfurt School conspirators, the worst lie sold is that each individual is gifted with sovereign reason, which enables each to determine what is right and wrong for the whole society aka "subjectivism." We know this to not always be true. This is the Cultural Marxism's attempt to convince groups and individuals to "empower' themselves" to hell with the rest of society or how destructive that motive becomes.

Black Lives Matter is today's perfect example of this deceptive ruse. This group is verifiably a George Soros funded group who escapades as working toward true black equality, and stopping white on black police abuses, etc. For the largely uneducated street thugs whom carry out cowardly crimes against whites, conservatives and the such without good justifications. In fact, these are useful idiots working for George Soros and his communist new world order accomplices. Uneducated and/or agenda driven devotees of such groups are often more interested in the money offered, ridding the white power structure and tearing down the existing state. This is a perfect Frankfurt tactic. Newly indoctrinated professors, using Adorno's tactics of teaching primarily single-factor histories of America and discouraging real debate, spread across college campuses, especially California, New York and other hubs of already left leaning towns. By constantly berating Western values in university classrooms around the country, this large scaled dis-information campaign has/had accomplished incredible success at inspiring and indoctrinating teachers to question much of America's roots and policies. It is well understood that most of the organizing and promoting's behind the hippie movement were heavily promoted by these various socialist/communist oriented groups and billionaires such as the Rockefellers.

Often times, the American Communist Society and other such groups has reliably been the culprit behind the funding and organization of many American anti-war or anti-establishment types of rallies or events. In the world of the far left, it doesn't matter how the job gets done. They knew the buttons to push in order to breed a new type of anti-establishment generation(s) that would continue on and carry at least some of the basic premises of the leftist mindsets into their adult life and forward. This "prevalence of postmodern reconstruction" of the history of western civilization in our universities for the last 50+ years has its roots in the Critical Theory of the Frankfurt School. This rewriting of history by postmodern scholars in America has come under attack. Keith Windschuttle, in his book, 'Killing of History,' has severely criticized the rush to 'relativism' by historiographers. What is truly astonishing though is that 'relativism' has largely supplanted the pursuit of truth as a goal in historical study. A noteworthy reference backing this up are included in George G. Iggers book "Historiography in the Twentieth Century: From Scientific Objectivity to the Postmodern Challenge.

As a testament to the quiet effectiveness of Fabianism and Frankfurt School's being so readily accepted during the 1960's and 70's and onto today on college America's campuses, such is explained very well by professor/author Gertrude Himmelfarb...

*"In the 1960's when the Cold War was going on and most academia were focused on just that, these techniques slipped right past the eyes of traditional academics, almost unobserved until it was too late. It occurred so 'quietly' that when they 'looked up', postmodernism was upon them with a vengeance." They were surrounded by tidal wave of faddish multicultural subjects such as radical feminism, deconstructed relativism as history and other courses which undermine the perpetuation of Western Civilization. Indeed, this tidal wave slipped by just as Antonio Gramsci*

*and the Frankfurt School had envisioned... A 'quiet' revolution, one that could not be resisted by force".* **And here we are.**

Now, the elite boomers and generation X'ers are in positions of power in the United States. Many have brought with them a revolutionary attitude toward Westernism to one extent or the other. For it is nearly impossible for those who grew up around the age of Aquarius and the New Left movement to not carry around their own share of this anti-establishment attitude of the 69's. Anyone attending a university in the last 40 years has known a few professors or alumni's that it was obvious that they still carried a bit of this attitude around. The worst of these are still working at destroying 240 years of American history. Too often their aim is to destroy any vestige of the Anglo-American path taken by Western Civilization in forming the unique American culture.

# .10
# HEGELIANISM / ORDER OUT OF CHAOS

*"The powerful elite families, consisting of bankers, a few powerful businessmen, and second-level politicians, have an end goal of a unified Statist society. They operate through a chain of influence and a number of closed-door organizations to impose their ideas on society by controlling key positions of power. Using the dialectic method of <u>Hegel</u>, Marx, Fichte and Engels, they foment conflict by funding and arming antithetical organizations to create a synthetic unity, as seen in the EU. This process will continue – thesis, antithesis, synthesis – on greater scales until a one world Statist system is established, or they are stopped."* Written by the late Carrol Quigley, Professor of History, Georgetown University within his famous expose` book "Tragedy and Hope".

*A side note:* Professor Quigley was verifiably President Bill Clintons favorite professor. At one time Bill called him his favorite mentor of all time, as well. I am quite sure Bill was amply impressed with Professor Quigleys research, learning quite a lot about the very plans of the elites he was about to be engaged with upon his rise to becoming the American President. It is likely here that he learned one of the most important and most oft used instruments to create a new world through psychological sabotage. Hegelian Dialectic!

Georg Wilhelm Friedrich Hegel (1770-1831) was a famed 19th century German philosopher and theologist, who wrote 'The Science of Logic' in 1812. As the above says, Hegelian Dialectic was used by the worst tyrants of the past several hundred years. Hegelian-Marxist Dialectic is an all too common tactic used to guide history in the directions that the highest powers wish to pursue. And it is very, very successful, albeit evil.

## ACTUALIZATION THROUGH CONTRADICTION

This tactic is most commonly referred to as "Actualization through Contradiction" The information I uncovered is a very exciting one for me personally, for it goes a long ways into explaining the nucleus behind nearly every major crisis we witness across the world. This is what explains how and why so many of the official stories, excuses and policies across our governmental actions seem so unbelievable or unlikely to be the entire story.

Before we go further, and in order for the reader to understand much of the claims made in this book, as well as my takes on the reasons for this "Upside-Down" world we live in today, one must understand Hegelian Dialect, for it is so fanatically enlightening. It is used every day by the spin masters in the media, our politicians, our schools, our colleges, military and more. Basically, you will see it being used all over the place if you can recognize it. Watch our political infighting and the created reasons handed out to the media as to how this and that happened and what needs to be done about it. Once you know how it works, you too will be ever suspect of what they say. So often these talking heads have their own agenda which often follows the agenda of the establishment elites or particular agenda to be driven. Perhaps most importantly perhaps, it is used to frame a debate and get the end results wanted, even if that result is totally illogical to someone with a good common-sense aptitude. The Hegelian scheme is to bring about forced change without the public even realizing they have been duped.

The course of history and the map of the world would look quite different if this tactic being explained had not been the foremost method of achieving major changes across the entire world by its leaders. Hegelian tactics have been used throughout much of history, at least as far back as Rome's fall. It just didn't have a name for it back then. Virtually every nation on earth uses this technique to achieve what it wants, even in small ways. The plan is secretly used daily by world elites in order to get what they desire most...power over others. America is not alone in their scheme today. The following information is known primarily by only a few who are heavily involved in the study of this un-politically correct and largely hidden history. Yet it is in fact 100% correct history. Both socialist and so-called conservatives who part of the status quo in today politics don't want you to know about Hegel's theory and how it is used, especially in today's world. That's for good reason as you'll see. The elites really control future directions, manipulate world events towards their end goals, and control what you hear on the largest news networks. And now you'll understand how they always get what they want!

The Hegelian dialectic reduced to its simplest form could be summed up as *problem, reaction, solution.* The *"agent of change"* employing the strategy creates the problem or crisis, foments the reaction *(tension)*, then attempt to control the outcome by providing the solution *(resolution)*. The interesting and powerful feature of the Hegelian dialectic is once the circular argument has reached synthesis, a new thesis can be created and the process begins anew, incrementally and progressively moving forward toward the next predetermined outcome—a sort of *dialectic helix*.

Applying the Hegelian strategy can be accomplished through a process of *tension and resolution.* A good way to illustrate the concept of tension and resolution used in a repetitive and incremental fashion is music.

# Planned Collapse of Americanism

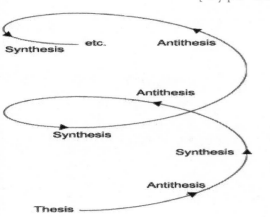

Hegelianism is the formula the elitists, the scientific community of world planning always refer to when tasked with the job of creating change not otherwise easy to achieve across society. This is the framework for guiding our thoughts and actions into conflicts that lead us to a predetermined outcome. If we do not understand how the Hegelian Dialect shapes our perceptions of the world, then we do not know how we are actually helping to implement the plan. In the Hegelian system, conflict is essential." The more conflict the better actually! As a matter fact, many wars, policy decisions, new laws and more are actually kick-started using Hegelianism tactics, and the ensuing "Planned Chaos". Here is the essence of Hegelianism.

Firstly, develop a thesis (create or exacerbate a problem, with anticipated reaction. Secondly, publicize it, even run it on airwaves repeatedly for weeks if need be. Thirdly, create an antithesis (generate large opposition to the problem, often using fear, panic.) Lastly, create a "synthesis" (offer a predetermined, self-serving solution to a problem created by number 1).

If the instigator doesn't get all he wants the first time, the process repeats itself again and again if need be until the end result is accomplished. Here is the catch: The "solution" isn't and never was intended to solve the original "problem." No, it is often meant to serve as a basis for a new problem, or exacerbate the existing one, eventually leading to their desired synthesis. Sometimes the process must repeat in a circular process, again and again if need be, until the final synthesis is achieved. The final goal of the instigator may come quite fastly or take dozens or hundreds of times to achieve. Soros verifiably funded and inflamed the demonstrations in the Ferguson and Milwaukee riots, as well as dozens more over the years, in order to build up tensions, create unwarranted degrees of racism, hate across America.

With Hegelianism, the bigger the "perceived and/or created problem is, all the better, for the bigger the more immediate the calls for a fix become, the greater the force larger compromises on the opposing side. False flag events are samples of this idea. In Nazi

Germany, we had Hitler's henchmen starting the Reichstag Fire whereby he falsely, boldly blamed it on his rival party, the Communists. That trick got rid of them (even with popular consent), which gave him dictatorial powers. Hitler's right-hand man admitted during the Nuremburg trials that Hitler had set up the incident as a false flag. He used the Hegelian Dialectic. And today we have ISIS, an outgrowth of Al Qaida, both of which were originally insignificant groups that, upon meeting up with America and a few of our allies, the groups expanded exponentially. They both have been aided by those whom are supposed to be their enemies as the Western newspapers and politico report! They have been funded, trained and supplied by America and its allies such as Saudi Arabia, Qatar and others. A plethora of news sources have responsibly reported such. The whole Middle East situation stinks of Hegelianism. Every major move over there seems orchestrated to create non- ending and perpetually permanent conflicts and emergencies requiring men and equipment to quell the created incidents.

In line with Hegel's thesis, we have quietly supported the ISIS terrorists whom have displaced millions of Syrian refugees spilling over into Germany, America, and many more countries all around the world, thereby providing tens of thousands of radical Islamic radicals/terrorists to spread even more violence around the globe, providing worldwide instabilities and stresses, a primary method to accomplish hegemonic wins for the US and its private war contractors set to make billions more dollars for the global corporate elites We can expect more and more conflicts while the planners are moving towards the final synthesis they desire. It seems the desired, or planned synthesis could very well come about by creating total breakdowns across regions of that part of the world who aren't playing ball or are set to become a part of a new and larger super state that will supplant the globalists goal of reducing the world down to just a handful of super regions, i.e. "a synthesis." Millions could die as part of this big plan. But so did so many other wars and conflicts in history. For these, "the means justify the ends." This would bring them one step closer, but not completely, to the one world government. This process is likely to repeat and repeat until the final synthesis is accomplished. When people are scared and intimidated by the possibility of war, they will react to, and accept, very large and quick government actions that are offered up as a solution, even though they give up many rights unknowingly or without choice.

The small possibility or prospects of North Korea, Iran, ISIS or some other group(s) nuking and/or attacking America in some way is already giving plausible reasons for the Deep State to further intrude on our privacies and such. Many other threats are to come upon America soon, and most have been long planned to happen with full knowledge and planning of the American and globalist one world leaders. Soon, it will assuredly call out for an even larger U.S. surveillance/police state, even a military state. Large disruption(s) on American soils will at some point automatically move into place many more restrictions American's freedoms of movement, put limits on free speech and liberties, engage more NSA spying. The global movement will mushroom. Civil wars on Americas streets are another inevitability that many believe is coming. The trick is to make people believe they have some say-so in the synthesis process, even though in the end, they don't. The decisions will always be decided ahead of time by the Hegelian Dialectics.

The globalist master planners, the CFR and Trilateral have a unified call to eventually destroy the existing American state with an entirely different paradigm. Karl Marx called this process as "planned deconstruction, before reconstruction". This is all part of the plans of the long running, super exclusive 'Hierarchy' structure that Madame Blavatsky of the Lucis Trust had eluded to over a hundred years ago. The Hierarchy structure consists of less than 50 top families around the world. These are the top controlling elites that repeat and repeat their closely guarded secrets to maintaining power. Applying the deadly duo of gradualism and Hegelianism is perhaps the most used and effective secret. The Bush dynasty is just one of many within the Hierarchy and the Illuminati. You will see how these elites throughout history have used this very process to condition a nation's peoples to the point that takeover is quite easy.

As Rahm Emmanuel, (Pres. Clinton's right-hand man) said: *"Never let a crisis go to waste"*. He knew of Hegel quite well. This is the long-awaited moment when leaders know they can politicize a situation, change the narrative, change attitudes towards a problem, and use it to call for more state involvement and a growing the state.

You hopefully will see that so very much of what happens in the news is in fact articulated and planned by government toward a predetermined outcome, a "synthesis." Changing the narrative is the first step when politicians want to change the publics perceptions. Electronic media brainwashing is used to form predictable responses to whatever happens.

## ANTONY SUTTON'S IMPORTANCE

Antony Sutton (1925-2012), was a well-respected, no-nonsense establishment scholar who made it his job to figure out what motivated the power elites, how they get their results. He studied the differing secret groups within the power elites and found out as much as was possible about the groups and their goals. He wrote eye opening works on Hegelianism. He was a long-time research Fellow of the Hoover Institution at Stanford as well as other elite schools, as well as a professor of economics. His career was unexceptional except were it not for two particular quirks: he chose to research the elite, and he was brazenly honest. Sutton wrote over a dozen scholarly books on how the real world works.

And more than that, he was exceedingly careful. He did not make accusations lightly, did not let his ideological views cloud his careful research methods, and was never afraid to say he didn't know the answers when he lacked the resources to support a claim. In some ways, he is a "founding father" of the modern anti-statist movement.

All of this made him non grata to the establishment, who admonished him frequently to back off lest his career suffer. He chose to leave the Hoover Institution in 1973, to continue his work unmolested, and published a number of books on the actions of elite families that sold quite well.

And what was the drive behind this? Was it blind power for power's sake? If Sutton and others can say definitively that these elite families and organizations i.e. the Rothschild and Rockefellers for instance, do not act based upon a left or right-wing ideology, then how could it be anything beyond self-interest? Sutton had an answer to this, and here it is...

"Left" and "right" are artificial devices to bring about change, and the extremes of political left and political right are vital elements in a process of controlled change. The answer to this seeming political puzzle lies in Hegelian logic. Remember that both Marx and Hitler, the extremes of "left" and "right" presented as textbook enemies, evolved out of the same philosophical system, Hegelianism.

The Trilateral Commission and CFR's stated policy goals of "managing conflicts" (as it does extensively in its own literature) simply implies "managed use of conflicts" for long, predetermined ends. Not for the mere random exercise for manipulative control to solve a problem. The dialectic takes the Trilateral "managed conflict" process one step further. From this axiom, it follows that controlled conflict can create a predetermined history. Sutton understood this process well. As a matter of fact, here are words out of Sutton's mouth:

*"World War II was the culmination of the dialectic process created in the 1920s and 1930s. The clash between "left" and "right," the Soviet Union and Nazi Germany, led to the creation of a synthesis – notably the United Nations, and a start towards regional groupings in the Common Market i.e. COMECON, NATO, UNESCO, Warsaw Pact, SEATO, CENTO, and then the Trilateral Commission. A start towards New World Order."*

Again, George Hegel's most basic premise used was "thesis – antithesis- synthesis" or in simpler terms we could just say "Problem-Reaction-Solution" as most say it. Consider the terrible 9/11 event. Although you may be one who doubts the conspiracy about 9/11, think for a minute what came out of it in terms of governing and the handing over of nearly unlimited power to the state in all its forms. Out of that event came the Patriot Act and dozens of amazingly powerful agencies, and rulings, who now wield unprecedented powers over the citizens of America. The NSA and many dozens of such agencies now have hundreds of thousands of hires who are in place to watch, monitor, report information to other governmental spy agencies of what you and I are up to, yet the NSA has yet to officially find but one terrorist since 2001! It wasn't put in place to find terrorists so much as it was to track citizens in preparation for the growing state. When America gets hit with an attack, a false flag event, or whatever may come (and they know it's coming), the domestic state already has the power and forces to make even the Nazi's SS look like a "J.V. Team", a term President Obama coined. Whether that power is used unconstitutionally to jail or abuse citizen's rights, freedoms, liberties during such unrest is not even questioned by many of these who are psychopaths dogmatically focused on power.

Moral absolutes to them do not exist unless it can be used as an excuse to justify corrupt actions. To the elites, the inevitable course of history is a final synthesis of all contradicting political ideas: freedom and tyranny, individualism and collectivism, freedom and slavery, and so on. It is in their view neither of these things. The final society *transcends* these things.

What's sad is that a portion of America falls for it. Entertainment often wins out in this new America of dumbed down, sound bite preferring populaces. Years of employing this technique has helped change the political landscape in America. So much so, that today, peoples who had once been considered middle of the road 'moderates' in the 1970s finds themselves to be considered belonging to the far right! Everything has moved farther to the left with each passing year. If you belonged on the 'right' back then, and still do, well, today you might be considered to be put on the government's 'watch list for right wing radicals!'

For years the groups behind the socialist agenda in America have been behind this slow leftward shift via Hegelian methods, allowing more government invasions into our lives, often without citizens even realizing it. It is a technique to sway politicians into voting for unconstitutional or Cultural Marxist legislations they wouldn't have considered in the past. Hegelianism in politics has long been busy over-sensationalizing and over-representing the cries of minority groups who represent perhaps 1 or 2 % of the populace. By overplaying some of these groups supposed plights, the typical groups who fit this bill are those who want open borders and mass immigration with the same benefits that citizens enjoy without having to pay for it. Other such groups appeal for special free benefits towards minority races or groups as some type of reparations, an ever larger welfare state, free college and scores of wrongly targeted favoritisms or special 'rights" not availed to the rest of society.

The people behind many of these much overplayed agendas are usually far left socialist groups operating on huge contributions from wealthy donors who are also socialist one world leaning types such as George Soros, the Rockefellers and that ilk. People love promises of more freebies and expanding government to "serve them". Libs always run on a ticket of more programs to supposedly help this group and that group for instance. Come election time, leftist candidates will offer more candy and 'rights' that aren't even in the Constitution. Leftists come from both major parties to no surprise. The conservative candidate will be made to look as uncaring if he doesn't appease special interest groups whom already have the Democratic side pulling for them anyways. Year after year, over and over again, this plays out over all elections, each year tilting more and more to leftist, socialistic positions. Today we see little difference between both parties. You may just call that politics, but let's look a bit deeper.

The real values of corporate capitalism are disseminated with popular culture. Watch a reality show. It celebrates manipulations, aggressiveness, deception, primacy of self over all others. The reward for being ruthless is to win the show, gain money and fame. The media's, owned by the elite capitalists, impose their reality, their agenda onto the rest of society. This is normal in their sick minds. Such types of marketing could be compared to President Obamas presidential runs. What he and his liberal news media sold to the public was not a brand, but an experience like Calvin Klein. Hitler had many blind followers as well. Nearly all the sheep lings believed in Obama's charismatic choice of words and body language, blindly believing nearly anything he said much like a religion! The same can be said of most dangerous would be leaders and dictators throughout history. People have a hard time looking past the hypes, promises and good looks. It seems that you have to unlearn much of what you learn in universities in order to become a moral human being.

## ARE YOU PART OF THE MATRIX?

Before we can even seriously consider what is true and what isn't true today, or even real for that matter in our agenda driven world, we must realize that most of us have been fed a steady diet of slanted news since as far back as we can remember. People by & large have fallen into the new world orders purposely created reality, we could call it their own learned matrix. By matrix, I mean "false reality" created by an outside force. The media's incessant use of altered, deleted and slanted news, day after day, typically forms immediate, unknowingly false views of the news events conveyed to their audiences. Yes, false realities as to the real why's, how's and actual reasons for any event covered.

Most have just accepted the created, fairytale mainline world view that blames nearly all of America's troubles on those outdated, intolerant, pesky Republicans and/or conservatives for just about every problem. Fortunately for America, Pres. Trump has shifted the blame the other way. The socialist set proclaim that anything conservative is actually holding back real "progress", as in the word "progressive", (a term traditionally used to describe communism.) As though everything would be wonderful if we could just trust the liberal ideology as sacrosanct, as well as believe the corporate media, the college academia's, the corporate advertisers and prevailing sentiments to be our guides to truth.

For years, the public had accepted the official propaganda machine of the corporate owned major media's, but finally an awakening is taking place. Finally, a recent Gallup poll indicated that 57% have little or no trust in the media, an all-time high. Today, the constant barrages of terrible news events in America and around the world is forcing many citizens to reassess their long held biases they formed through years of disinformation. The liberal utopia has not materialized and is now being exposed with decline on every front. The long-term results of the constant barrages of slanted, agenda driven news has finally reached an eminent tipping point for the new world order globalists plans, and the elites are now frantically having to speed up their plans in order to avoid failure. Many are growing disillusioned and realizing it must have been a huge lie. For 50 years, this has all been a growing "new normal' that the top .01% have created for you, your kids, and grandkids as well. But with most being very busy in their daily lives, it is obvious and unfortunate that many are just 'tuning out'. Just what they hope for!

*"All effective propaganda must be limited to a very few points and must harp on these in slogans until the last member of the public understands what you want him to understand."* Adolph Hitler

# Planned Collapse of Americanism

I want to ask a few questions relating to the America we now live in...

Do you believe that the constant, perpetual economic ups and downs every 7-8 years, almost like clockwork are just part of normal business cycles as claimed, or something else more sinister?

What is the reason that your buying power get smaller and smaller, especially since the 1970s into today, and why does inflation just never stop?

What is the reason that the top 1% incomes and worth have skyrocketed in recent years beyond comprehension?

Do you believe the official government statistics, especially as to the unemployment rate, inflation rate and economic reports in general?

Do you believe that the wars America engages in are always justifiable and moral?

Do you believe that these wars are actually being fought for the reasons given by your government such as for our national interests or security?

Do you think we have a fair, honest, unbiased Main Street media who tells the truth nearly always?

Do you think that we can trust at least most of what the Washington establishment says?

Do you believe that Wall Street and big banks are an industry that generally has your best financial interests at heart? Or are they the problem?

Do you believe that both politicians and Wall Street really have you in mind as to the countries survival, its sovereignty, its freedoms?

Do you think that the collusion of politics, business and banking is overblown?

Do you believe that the reason most are suffering financially is because they are just lazy?

Do you think that our government really hasn't really encroached much on any of the freedoms we expect, yet the have added rights that are damaging the existence of our country?

Do you criticize government and newstream policies of condoning ANY lifestyle without restraint?

Do you strongly detest the steady growth and media condonation of pedophilia?

How you answer these questions may soon be dangerous to your well being. In fact, some of these questions already are dangerous to answer to authority! And by now you must realize that the real answers to some of these questions may be far deeper and sinister than you probably would believe at first glance. Far too many Americans have fallen into a brainwashed construct put in place by those I have pointed at. We know that the left has tried valiantly for years to allow to believe that many things are rights that are automatic. Many people now come to accept many slickly marketed "rights" as were never put into the Constitution. As a result, too many have dangerously redrawn the line as to what mantras of equality, freedom of expression, and various "rights" pushed hard by far leftists really are in fact rights at all! This is just one more trouble sign for those who don't know or respect the Constitution of The United States! Without such basic understandings about America, how can the young preserve sanity in the greatest nation on earth?

Now, imagine some high powered clandestine men in a closed room speaking about the basis of their program(s) they have worked hard at for many years. They finally have mastered the mind of the individual.

*"We can frame the boundaries of manufactured reality. We can stage events and actual happenings. But we also have to infiltrate SUBJECTIVE PERCEPTION and fold it into the overall setup---not that we actually produce every single private thought or image or idea, but we insert seeds that bloom inside the mind, and then when they come to fruition, they appear to be OBJECTIVE EVENTS."* John Rappaport

These groups do in fact exist in the highest realms of government and corporatism, and they have been at work at least since WWII.

What we are witnessing is not something totally new and unfamiliar if one delves into the history books of failed nations. Historians have seen the methods and madness of powerful, greedy rulers and elites all around the world for centuries. As just one glaring example is the English Royals, have a representative parliamentary system similar in some ways to America's, yet the Royals became trillionaires as England became the powerhouse of the world through conquests and wars with help from the Rothschild banking, inflicting death and devastation to millions, all the while taking the riches that came from it all.

Washington D.C. and even the states of course, have many unethical or morally bankrupt agenda makers who hold the powers to push their agenda onto the rest of us. With their honest and caring sounding platforms on global warming, outlawing guns, bailouts, equality, safety, fairness, common core schools, as well as bigger and better government programs, they always promise wonderful benefits for nearly anyone who can fog up a mirror. They make claim that it is all morally justified for the "greater good". The promises are always to help the downtrodden, to protect rights, to 'protect' everything sacred in the nanny states eyes! These types are like drug pushers and enablers, and they aren't even elected officials. The elites have it figured out before it starts, since they plan it.

*"Everyone wants to live at the expense of the state. They forget that the state lives at the expense of everyone."* Frederic Bastiat, French philosopher, 1780

# .11

# BOOM BUST REPEATS

Shortly after each economic crash, the ultra rich and elites always arrive to scoop up deals, chasing after 'blood running in the streets', a term used many times by numerous robber barons of past. I can't blame those who take advantage of these situations as long as they aren't one of those whom helped engineered a collapse, yet sadly they often are, on some level at least! We do in fact still have some semblance of capitalism after all. But the fact remains that in the short time of 8 years after the 2008 crash, the banks are immensely richer than before their bailout.

The six largest financial institutions in this country today hold assets equal to about 60% of the nation's gross domestic product. These six banks issue more than two-thirds of all credit cards and over 35% of all mortgages. They control 95% of all derivatives and hold more than 40% of all bank deposits in the United States.

Americas leaders must break up the "too-big-to-fail" financial institutions for they are at too much risk to the country. Those institutions received a $700 billion bailout from the US taxpayer, plus more than $16 trillion in virtually zero interest loans from the Federal Reserve. Despite that, financial institutions made over $152 billion in profit in 2014 – the most profitable year on record, and three of the four largest financial institutions are 80% bigger today than they were before we bailed them out. We are now in 2017 and they are now even wealthier! Because of the bailout, thousands of smaller banks were unnecessarily shut down as a result of the harsh terms delivered to the small banks, not the big ones. Who took ownership of most of those closed local banks? The big six of course. Same as in the 1929 Great Depression, eliminating much of their competition in banking!

Unfortunately, the Federal Reserve is not audited as you may know. As such, it is widely accepted that the total amount of the bailout was many times larger than the $700 billion dollars they reported.

As such, the big banks, the un-federal reserve and the globalists (whom together, largely make up the rules) have the power to direct their economic marionettes, creating the booms, the busts, even starting and ending wars to profit from. They use their combined powers to manipulate the directions of the world. These often-evil men have no compassion for mankind, thinking of themselves as the chosen, the elite, often being their own Godhead, just as their blood families have operated for centuries.

*"All profits to the bankers, all debt to the taxpayers", again!*

As we know, after the 2008 crash the banks and Wall Street were showered with literally trillions of dollars of U.S. government dollars and guarantees, thereafter allowing the banks to once again take even larger and riskier bets than in 2008 albeit often in 'different investments' than in 2008! Even though the big banks have repaid their loans by now, don't forget they had at least four years to use all that money to make more! When they fail again, and they will, the un-Federal Reserve won't accept more debt to be extended according to a new bylaw that they passed in 2015. This nearly unknown rule from the un-Federal Reserve would seem to have more reason behind it than for it. This means that worker bees will in one way or the other be forced to come to the rescue with what is called a "bail-in". With a "bail-in" the government will just take a set percentage of your savings, a 401K, retirement account or likely whatever accounts you hold in order to repay the banks and/or make the financial system solvent again. Much like a thief in the night. We must all remember; the banks are always protected one way or the other. The IMF (International Monetary Fund) approved the bail-in strategy if time comes. As a matter of fact, they got every single banking institution in the world to sign off and agree with the bail-in plan when the time comes! Did you hear any of this on the dumbed down medias? It was the IMF headed by Christine LeGarde who, in 2016, codified the upcoming bail-ins that the IMF knows to be coming. Now it is a requirement for <u>all</u> banks inside the central banking system cartel across the globe to be signed up and bound to the IMF bailout regulations when the day comes! By 2016 all had signed on. So, that nice manager at your bank is definitely not going to be able to help you on the banking day of panic.

Technically speaking, the banks have pulled a real dinger for you readers! Because of the precarious and dangerous future they see ahead for the world monetary system, they have set up their business model so that when you deposit your money into their bank, they log it in as a bank ASSET! You have no rights to it once they have it should they go defunct once the FDIC has exhausted its small resources in an attempt to save the entire system in order to save you. You no longer have title to it in other words. In such a dire case for the economy, the bank has your money and it was never yours in the first place. The IMF has signified and ratified their plans for such a problem. They are ready now to enact a colossal countrywide, or worldwide, bail-in. Yes, a major raiding right out of citizen's savings accounts. Right? Many theorize that it makes sense that the banking system would close the bank on Friday after everyone deposits their paychecks. They would then call for either a bank holiday or claim that the banking computer systems have been hacked and that they need days to correct the problem. By then, the entire bail-in will be in effect. Will you follow your instructions given by the deep state i.e just keep your head down and work harder!

## AMERICA'S UNPUNISHED THIEVES

AMERICANS MUST WAKE UP TO THE OLD GAME OF THE ROTHSCHILD BANKERS AND WALL STREET CRIMINALS WHY NOT DEMAND THEY GO TO JAIL FOR A LONG TIME? CERTAINLY, THAT LITTLE COUNTRY CALLED ICELAND PLAYS TOUGHER THAN OUR OWN AMERICA JUSTICE CENTER WHEN FACED WITH BANK LOOTING. ACCORDINGLY, AFTER

THE 2008 CRASH, ICELAND SENTENCED OVER 26 CORRUPT BANKERS TO 74 YEARS IN PRISON AND STILL COUNTING!

14.02.2016

## Maurice Bedard

On Feb. 14, 2016 Iceland had just sentenced their 26th banker to prison for his part in the 2008 economic collapse with others to follow. The charges ranged from breach of fiduciary duties to market manipulation to embezzlement.

Iceland's President, when asked how the country recovered so fast from the 2008 economic crash answered with this statement:

*"The government bailed out the people and imprisoned the banksters -the opposite of what America and the rest of Europe did."* When Iceland's President Olafur Ragnar Grimmson was asked whether or not other countries - Europe in particular - would succeed with Iceland's "let the banks fail" policy, he stated the following:

*"WHY ARE THE BANKS CONSIDERED TO BE THE HOLY CHURCHES OF THE MODERN ECONOMY? WHY ARE PRIVATE BANKS NOT LIKE AIRLINES AND TELECOMMUNICATION COMPANIES AND ALLOWED TO GO BANKRUPT IF THEY HAVE BEEN RUN IN AN IRRESPONSIBLE WAY? THE THEORY THAT YOU HAVE TO BAIL OUT BANKS IS A THEORY THAT YOU ALLOW BANKERS ENJOY FOR THEIR OWN PROFIT, THEIR SUCCESS, AND THEN LET ORDINARY PEOPLE BEAR THEIR FAILURE THROUGH TAXES AND AUSTERITY. PEOPLE IN ENLIGHTENED DEMOCRACIES ARE NOT GOING TO ACCEPT THAT IN THE LONG RUN."*

NOT SO SURPRISINGLY, THE ECONOMY REBOUNDED FASTER THAN ANYBODY COULD BELIEVE! ICELAND IS THE ONLY NATION THAT PUT TOP FINANCE EXECUTIVES BEHIND BARS AFTER THE 2008 CRISIS! ECONOMIC CRONYISM CAME TO A NEAR SCREECHING HALT. OH, WHAT A BEAUTIFUL DAY IT WOULD BE FOR AMERICA IF THE WORST OF ITS BANKERS WERE WATCHED MUCH MORE CLOSELY AND WENT TO JAIL WHEN CAUGHT!

# RIGGED INEQUALITIES FOR THE 90%

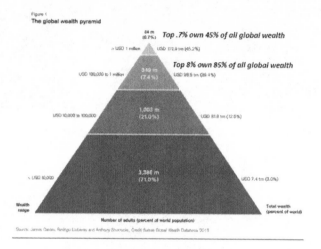

Figure 1
The global wealth pyramid

Top .7% own 45% of all global wealth

Top 8% own 85% of all global wealth

Source: James Davies, Rodrigo Lluberas and Anthony Shorrocks, Credit Suisse Global Wealth Databook 2015

*"If there's been a class warfare in the country, my class won"*

*Warren Buffett*

Income inequality is one of the biggest moral issues of our times. For instance, consider the following:

1. The money elite are doing extremely well, but the velocity of money index indicates money has not been moving around as it should (velocity of money) in the economy. People are holding on to whatever they have saved. The extent is so severe that in 2015 the money index was at the 1929 level immediately prior to the Great Depression. When money doesn't move around and get used, it's telling us that money isn't being spent, indicating a very weak real and actual economy on Main Street, U.S.A.

2. Famed economist Jim Rickards says the Feds own numbers reveal the fact that in 2014 the Federal Reserve's own balance sheet shows its own debt to leverage ratio

ballooned from 22 to 1 in 1913, into a wild ratio of 77 to 1 by 2015. The Federal Reserve's capital account is $56.2 billion dollars. It sounds like an impressive amount of money, right? Not when you look at the FR liabilities of a gigantic $4.3 Trillion! This has never been done before anywhere on the face of the world, let alone on a nation of over 320 million occupants. It cannot go on forever, and due to its sheer size, no one has a fix. Fed Chairman Ben Bernanke even admitted "We are in unchartered territory."

3. Today, the F.R. has to generate $30.00 of debt in order to create $1.00 of economic growth per top economist Jim Richards. That is anemic, counterproductive, the lowest ever.

4. The ratio between stocks and the % of GDP in 1929 was 87% just prior to the big crash. In 2014 that number had risen to an astounding 203% of GDP. Many mainstream economics agree that the real value of stocks are overpriced by 50-60% according to standard historical standards, methods of valuation.

5. Post WWII (the 1950s-60s) one dollar generated $ 2.41 of real stimulus. In 2014 that dollar created only 3 cents worth! Our stimulus dollars obviously don't have any wind left to give, at least it doesn't wind up where the public can benefit anymore.

6. The so-called Misery Index measures unemployment and inflation. It is now worse than the Great Depression, regardless of what the "official numbers" say. Our real unemployment rate is nearly as high as in the depression when including those officially out of the workforce and unemployment, for lack of work. Part-timers are officially counted as "employed", often at a greatly reduced pay rate from their old job. Those who have just "given up looking" and moved into a family members home are not included in the unemployment figure either. Millions who have completed an expensive college degree can't find work, etc. These are all either underemployed due to no fault of their own or have just been 'dropped' off the official number crunchers rear view mirror. There just aren't enough jobs, let alone good blue collar ones!

7. The bank debt vs GDP ratio in 2008-2012 averaged 0-5 times. From 2012-2014 it has skyrocketed to 30 times. Obviously, banks have loaded on the debt to unseen dangerous levels.

8. Total actual U.S. debt since 2009 in the U.S exploded. From 2009 to 2014 has swelled to over 60 trillion dollars. It stands at 350% of GDP. That number alone spells doom.

9. There is an added $200 trillion of unfunded liabilities U.S. politicians have promised taxpayers in the next few decades.

10. Large corporations are sitting atop a ton of money, not knowing what to do with it in this risky environment that they themselves have largely created. Purchases of new factories, equipment and long term costly investments into their business still residing here in the U.S. have mostly been put on hold or rebuilt overseas to produce products cheaper over there. Left with few options as to what to do with their stockpile of cash, many CEO and top management have been manipulating and buying up their company's stock and performing other tricks in order to boost their pay scale, bonuses and the bottom line without actually producing more real profits. We have an environment that

fosters corporate hogging's of money due to such a scary business environment that has been created by this alliance.

11. Consumer credit has ballooned to new heights reaching $3.2 trillion in 2014, led in part by little talked about is the record amounts of today's sub –prime auto loans. Many big bond fund managers are preparing for that bubble to burst in 2017 or 2018. Banks and auto dealers realize that it is increasingly hard to find a buyer with a good credit score and/or a solid job, and that is a recipe for disaster. Many can remember that in the 1980's boom they had a good job and could easily buy a new car under a short three-year contract. This is a recipe for disaster and can't be fixed until people can regain their purchasing power and good jobs. Look at the skyrocketing of consumer credit since the 1950's. Notice that since the last recession in 2008, household debt has also skyrocketed. Much of this run up in credit, debt is orchestrated by the banking/government cabal whom together have engineered purposeful inflation (loss of purchasing power), causing people to work ever harder to try and stay ahead or even. Notice how the graph shows what happened in 1971 when Nixon took us off the gold standard in the early 1970! Consumer credit went to the stars.

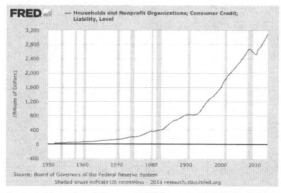

Again, with a phased in new publicly controlled Federal Reserve and gold-backed money system, the U.S. dollar might have been salvageable in the past, but no more. While all these numbers may be hard to digest, suffice to say that the global elites are purposely engineering an American, even global depression before 2018 very likely.

What price do we really, honestly pay for all the low paid, the unemployed, underemployed and destitute that are now dependent on government handouts? If you live outside the boundaries of healthy local economies, you really truly see it for yourself. FED charts have shown for several years now that at least ninety million citizens are out of full time work. Many of these have lost much of their dignity, lost the right to significantly contribute and provide for their families or themselves. Many young ones have turned to 'career-college', living at home with mom and dad, some even selling or doing drugs or doing crime to stay afloat or escape from the hopelessness they feel.

Largely as a result of money strife, the world's citizens are witnessing a spike in divorces, and the loss of two adult families. This is globalism in all its wonder!

According to a 2015 Credit Suisse Global Wealth Report, the U.S. middle class has fallen to 21st place behind nearly every major nation of the world. No one can doubt that the country is in dire straits, and only a fool would convince himself that this is the America we remember, and the middle class are beginning to rebel. Notice how the U.S. is at the bottom of the list of income equality. By 2017 it has improved a bit, but most of the money is going to the top 10 percenters.

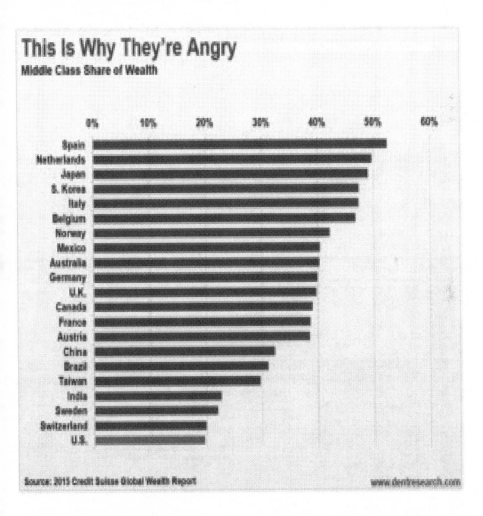

What the following real statistics show is that America is not at all the country we grew up in, especially if you're over 40 yrs. old. If this is starting to make you depressed, know that's not why I wrote this book. But in order to get the readers out of their "normalcy mode", we must be honest with ourselves, so we can at least work on a plan to overturn many of our governments failed policies. Sadly, with all the talk that the U.S. is still the strongest in everything, here are the facts that show we are fastly going downhill. Although these figures are for 2013, little if anything has gotten better. So, for all of you still in your own 'normalcy mode', still believing that the U.S. is tops in nearly everything, look at these sobering stats:

(Much of the following stats are derived from a variety of sources such as theeconomiccollapse.org, Russel Sage Foundation, University of Michigan report).

Note; Even with President Trump's accomplishment, the stats below have hardly nudged.


**On the world stage, the U.S. has fallen to:**


12th in freedom

27th in middle class wealth

91st in income distribution! Let's get real America, something is terribly wrong!!

America has a disappearing middle class, most wealth and nearly all income gains going to the top 1%.

America is now the greatest debtor nation in the world. In 1970, we were the greatest creditor nation. Today the U.S.A. is:

51st in infant mortality and/or life expectancy

Moved from 1st down to 13th in the worlds college systems ratings

25th in education scores

37th in healthcare quality, yet twice the cost of all other nations.

1st place in murders as a percentage of those in prison

25th in infrastructure

21st in railroads

The U.S. hasn't built a large commercial ship in 30 years. Most ships are now built in EU, even though their wages are double ours and are unionized.

The U.S. has not built a new dam in many years, and Pres. Obama claims there will be no more built, period (thanks to the Marxist environmentalists like himself). Not even environmentally friendly hydro dams!

Nearly every railroad contract in America is now given over to the Chinese to build.

50% loss of high tech in last 10 years

80% loss of manufacturing jobs since NAFTA (North American Free Trade Agreement), with more in the works

# Planned Collapse of Americanism

61$^{st}$ in unionization

14$^{th}$ in electrical grid

31$^{st}$ in internet speed

The list goes on. As you read the differing statistics provided, we can see that America has far more systemic problems than pre-Nazi Germany had! Germany just needed one big event (the Great Depression) to turn it on its head and give Hitler the beginnings of his ascent to power. America has far more systemic problems than Hitler ever had. It seems like our leaders and elites have the wind to their backs when it comes to justifying all the change they want to achieve with the overwhelming powers given to them by our great, yet too trusting people! Essentially, America in large part doesn't make things anymore, it doesn't save, it doesn't hardly produce or reproduce, to wit:

As of 2014-15, here are the official figures that show our losses in living standards for the 90%, and nothing has gotten better. Even the Chinese save a larger percentage of their income than the U.S., yet they only make $9,800 per yr. average.

1. The top 1% make the largest share of national income by large margin.
2. The middle class is being destroyed and hit hardest by their tax loads. Since 2007 the top 5% earners had 16.5 times as much wealth as the average household overall. By 2015, the wages for the same group had risen to 24 times as much income as the average household. As reported by the University of Michigan Report.
3. One out of 6 men in their prime working years (25-54) do not have a job of any type, even part time. Blacks fair far worse.
4. According to one survey, 76% of all workers are living "paycheck to paycheck". Most cannot come up with $400 for an emergency. Median family income is 7% less than in the year 2000, after adjusting for inflation.
5. 40% of all households in the US are experiencing financial stress right now.
6. One out of 5 households are now on food stamps
9. Doug Short, at Advisors Perspectives found that on a chained dollar adjusted basis (not counting sales taxes, property taxes, fees, home prices, etc., which we know are now much higher) real average hourly earnings are back to a level not seen since 1968.
10. Our labor participation rate at a 36-year low. If you count all the people that are considered to be "in the labor force" but are underemployed, part time, stopped looking, etc. there are over 100 million people out of work. Perhaps some have some type of part-time "under the radar" jobs, but that doesn't move the chart much.
11. As of 2014 average age of the typical car is now 11.4 years old, an all-time high. 13,
12. Just 10% of American households own 80% of stocks. By RT News
13. 47% of the unemployed have totally "given up" looking for a job.
14. More than one out of every 5 children in America is living in poverty. One out of five households have no one that works.

15. In terms of median wealth per adult, the United States is now at 19th place in the world. After the eventual coming economic crash, these numbers will sink even lower.

## Total public debt by month

In trillions of 2014 dollars. Non-adjusted dollar figures indicated with dashed lines.

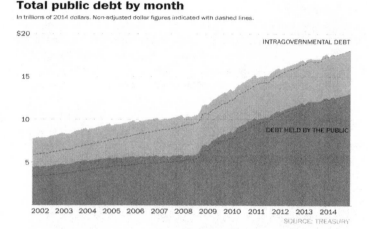

SOURCE: TREASURY

In the graph above we see the explosion of personal debt as well as government debt and how much it has exploded. For all the hoopla that America is back on its feet, things are never better, why are people so in debt with no end in sight? Obviously, people are living the illusion of getting ahead, but they aren't as a whole. We are a debt-based economy! Many of you can feel that just when you look at your paycheck! This is where the inequality quotient comes into play. For most, this is not a good deal. We have an economy that can't sustain itself without creating more and more debt of all types! How you say? First off, savings accounts are abysmal, and people just don't have enough cash to buy big ticket items, especially new automobiles. Credit cards are maxed out for most. Is this the signs of a strong economy when most are struggling to pay their bills even when they have full time work? What about saving for retirement? A 4-year college for Johnny? A real family vacation? You get the idea.

The entire way that the banker elites have raped nearly all the wealth out of the real American economy in the past is a crime upon humanity, worse than in the 1929 Great Depression on many counts, but it seems that nobody can connect the dots?

Robert Reich, Former Labor Secretary for Pres. Bill Clinton as well as Ford and Carter. Mr. Reich has written much on income inequality, producing highly read books on the subject, even producing his hit movie "Inequality for All." Even with all his accolades, I don't agree on many of his fixes to economics. Like so many things that comes out of liberals mouths, he too believes that big government can fix nearly everything. But he also believes in the free market to a large extent. In the case of wage inequality, I like some of his ideas often, as you cannot find workable answers to big political problems by following lock step with just one particular ideology. After all, they've all failed on many fronts throughout history when held to strict absolutes or run by crooked leaders.

So, why do the neediest suffer the most? His big take is that the poor don't have anyone to talk for them in Washington. The unemployed are politically invisible. They don't make major political contributions. They don't lobby Congress. They have no "National Association of Unemployed People" to represent them. Reich says... *"You couldn't find a class of people with less political clout."* Many of the unemployed were from good occupations, good positions and gainfully employed with benefits, but due to the new economy, most are now often unable to find work outside of perhaps a part time job at Walmart or such. Many have given up. Much within this group are often considered "employed" as far as the state is concerned, yet still depend on food stamps and healthcare from the government in order to get by on subsistence levels. In 2016 one out of five people are on food stamps. This is a crime in the wealthiest country in the world. Wealthy for who you may ask.

America's life support social system is spending more than ever before, yet a hugely disproportionate share of the welfare money is unfortunately going to the somewhat better-off families rather than the very poorest, due again in large part to the government derived formula used. These following figures are even worse today than when they were arrived at just a few years ago. Oddly, benefits for many of the better-off families rose more than 74% in inflation adjusted dollars since 1975. But for the 2.5 million single parent families with the absolute lowest levels of earnings, benefits dropped 35% between 1983 and 2004 in inflated terms. That means that in 2014, a family earning $11,925.00 a year likely got less than a same sized family earning $47,700.00 according to Robert A. Moffitt, professor of economics at John Hopkins University who is president of the Population Association of America. It seems that from their angle, the poor class are already poor, they already fit into the dependent class. I find it interesting that instead of Obama helping this class, he still had the money to hand out 20 million free Obama-phones.

The middle class has been raped by the top 1% earners since at least 1980, spiraling the inequality theme into a spiraling abyss. Since this time, American has turned into what has become known as the new "financialization economy". By the time Obama took the rein, 95% of the top 1% of earners in our economy made over $400,000.00 yearly, a level without precedent in modern history. Under Clinton, the equivalent figure was 45%, under Bush, it was 65%. A large majority of these "earners" are involved working on Wall Street, hedge funds and/or work in some type of financial service pushing paper around. President Trump has said that *"the hedge fund guys are getting away with murder"*. Time will tell if he can muster the courage to buck his friends on Wall Street. I wouldn't bet on that one!

These guys working on Wall Street have an average income of over half a million dollars, 10 times higher than the average family. Total Wall Street bonuses in 2014 came to $29 billion.

The graph below shows that since 1982 America has fallen away from anything resembling a real, actual economy where opportunities abound for anyone wanting to work hard. No, things have changed. 1982 was about the time factories were leaving America. The writing was on the wall already for those with mega bucks. What were they to do with all their money? Where were the millions of those out of work going to work? Well, some of those with some aptitude went into one of the hundreds of financial specialty fields, some of them even being invented for the times. That was where the action was beginning to boom. The American economy was transitioning from a manufacturing economy unto a financial one beginning around 1982. This was the "financialization of the American economy."

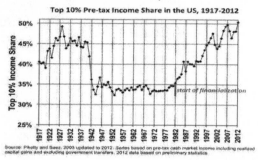

Top 10% Pre-tax Income Share in the US, 1917-2012

Source: Piketty and Saez. 2003 updated to 2012. Series based on pre-tax cash market income including realized capital gains and excluding government transfers. 2012 data based on preliminary statistics.

As you can see above, the top 10 percenters began their run-up in wages and left the rest of the other 90 percent to suffer without a real pay raise since this time. But a silver cloud always has its problems. Well, our economy still has not recovered the real jobs that left America from 1970 to present. Yes, the stock markets are hitting record highs in 2018. Thanks to President Trump's smart moves and cost cutting have offered up rays of hope for millions of people trying to get ahead for a short time.

In 1900, 90 percent of citizens were self subsistent, living in rural America, while asking nothing of the government! Today the numbers have reversed, with 95% being dependent on government and a string of other requirements that this demographic spells out. Today, what would happen if the American economy took a huge hit, a huge depression? This is what the elites are suspected of planning before long, thereafter sinking the Trump economy and presidency.

## THE "TRICKLE UP" MISNOMER

Deficits are surely intergenerational theft! Shockingly and disparagingly, for those in the bottom 25% in income, their real wages from 1984 thru 2013 actually fell 50%! How can anyone not see that this lower bracket of people has not suffered the most? With all the caring words from the Democrats, and Republicans, where have they really helped the poor attain an across the board improvement in jobs and opportunities after trillions of dollars in support payments? Where are the good lower and middle-class jobs for them? Most of these lower level jobs were shipped off to China, Bangladesh, India, Pakistan or any number of other 'stans'. These 3rd world nations pay starvation wages, typically no more than 25 cents per hour instead of the 10 dollars back here in the U.S. Although the U.S. does export a small amount of high tech items, it is miniscule. During this same time period from 1984 to 2013, most Americans median wage fell by 20%, while the upper median increased by about 30%, and the top 5% incomes nearly doubled as reported by the Russell Sage Foundation and government statistics. Why has this happened really? There are many reasons I explain throughout the book, but what's behind the reasons? What and who are the "shadow government?"

It is now reported by mainstream economists that the top CEOs salaries in America have risen an astounding 870% since 1979! It now takes a typical worker 1 month's pay to match what the top CEO's makes in 1 hour! I think that one figure says it all. So where did all that money go, and how? Keep reading.

Don't miss this one! The same FED charts show that the top CEO's typically make 380 times what the average worker makes, an all-time record even surpassing the disparities of the Great Depression. In 2014 the top 1% had grown so much so that they owned over 40% of the American wealth. The top 0.7% own 80% of American wealth. The top 8% of the world now owns 85% of all global wealth. The bottom 80% of American earners own only 24% of all the wealth in the U.S. That is how concentrated wealth in the U.S. and the world has become, and we wonder why it just seems so darn hard to get ahead for most of us.

Highly regarded systems theorist James B. Glattfelder made an intense study of the influences that the top internationalists have, and even he was surprised. The following was derived from an article in The New Scientist…

From a massive database of 37 million companies, Glattfelder pulled out the 43,060 transnational corporations (companies that operate in more than one country) that are all connected by their shareholders. Digging further, he constructed a model that actually displays just how connected these companies are to one another through ownership of shares and their corresponding operating revenues. According to his data, Glattfelder found that the top 730 shareholders control a whopping 80% of the entire revenue of transnational corporations.

And — surprise, surprise! — they are mostly financial institutions in the United States and the United Kingdom. That is a *hugely dangerous* amount of concentrated control held within a small number of hands...

Here are the top ten transnational companies that hold the most control over the global economy. If you are one of the millions that are convinced Big Banks run the world, you should get a creeping sense of validation from this list:

1. Barclays PLC

2. Capital Group Companies Inc.

3. FMR. Corporation

4. AXA

5. State Street Corporation

6. JPMorgan Chase & Co.

7. Legal & General Group PLC

8. Vanguard Group Inc.

9. UBS AG

10. Merrill Lynch & Co Inc.

Some of the other usual suspects rounding out the prominent top 25 are Morgan Stanley, Credit Suisse, and Goldman Sachs. Notice that these are all financial firms, banks.

What you *won't* find within the top are ExxonMobil, Microsoft, or General Electric, which I found shocking. Actual producers of goods are way down the list. In fact, you have to scroll all the way down to China Petrochemical Group Company at number 50 to find a company that actually ***creates*** something.

To no surprise perhaps, the top 49 corporations are financial institutions, banks, and insurance companies — with the exception of Wal-Mart, which ranks at number 15... The rest essentially just push money around to one another. Here's a fact about the number one player... Barclays Bank:

Barclays was a main player in the LIBOR manipulation scandal and was found to have committed fraud and collusion with other interconnected big banks. It was fined $200 million by the Commodity Futures Trading Commission, $160 million by the United States Department of Justice, and £59.5 million by the Financial Services Authority for "attempted manipulation" of the LIBOR and Euribor rates.

Despite its crimes, Barclays still paid $3.9 billion in bonuses in their last year, including a whopping $27,371,750 to investment banking head Marc Rich. That's 27 million! And yes, that's actually his real name. From Newscientist.com. Yeah, that's the controversial Mr. Marc Rich that President Clinton let out of prison on his last day in office at the insistence of his wife, whom reminded her husband that good old Marc had given $450,000 to the Clinton Foundation, $100,000 to the democratic party, and $100,000 to Hillary's campaign. Rich was worth over $1 billion dollars made nearly entirely from shady Wall Street deals and banking corruptions. He was indicted in 1983 for tax evasion, racketeering, and trading with Iran during the oil trade embargo. Reportedly, his sentence could have been 300 years! He fled to Switzerland and hid out to avoid the law for years. Later, Mr. Rich pled guilty to 35 counts of tax evasion and finally paid $90 million, the largest tax fraud up to that time. For years he was on the FBI's top ten most wanted!

These are the guys who run the world and we wonder why we have wealth inequalities? Their immense powers have manipulated the system to funnel upwards these obscene amounts of world wealth into just a few hands, even buying themselves out of jail. Did most of these types actually produce this much money? Of course not. More often than not most of it comes from the slick moving's around of money within the financial economy i.e. money that has been shifted upwards out of the regular economy for the last 25 years. These do not produce much of anything besides corrupting the legal and moral basis of business.

This is why I have doubts that even the Trump economy will cause income inequalities to significantly move upward but for the upper ten percenters. This is just not the way that the elites have wanted the American economy to behave, going all the way back to the 1970's!

## ON THE MINIMUM WAGE

More social programs only feed dependency, but Washington knows this much but up until the installation of President Trump into the White House, little had really been done to give entry level and mid level workers the number of jobs and opportunities to fill the needs. Now America has the lowest unemployment rate perhaps ever in our lifetimes! The jobs created are the largest providers of lower to mid waged jobs in the new America. That's great, but the minimum wage has fallen far behind inflation since 1970! According to many studies, if the minimum wage had kept up with overall income inflation since 1968, the minimum wage would now be over $21.16 per hr. The movement to raise the minimum wage to $15.00 is well justified, but the corporate raiders have left the lower and middle classes unable to earn fair wages that at the very, very least keep up with inflation! How many know that in 1960, the minimum wage was set high enough that a single mother with 2 kids could meagerly support her family! If adjusted for actual inflation since 1968, the minimum wage would be $21.16 according to most reputable sources. Based on the Economic Policy Institute, a family of four needs to make $63,367 a year to cover basic necessities. USA today analyzed the same scenario, claiming that the number needs to be $130,000 if you include the costs of owning a home, a car, retirement and school. From the book 'The Economics of Revolution' D. DeGraw -washingtonsblog.com/2014 inequality-01-impoverishment-society.html As a matter of fact, as of 2016, the last time the American economy had such bad labor statistics was WWI!

Source: Unemployment figure second highest since WWI: http://finance.yahoo.com/new/whatrecovery-unemployment-apf-5632122944.html

Now, let's take a look at how bad the non-retired workers are faring today.

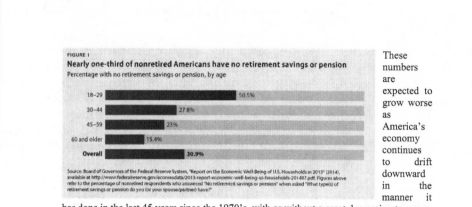

FIGURE 1
**Nearly one-third of nonretired Americans have no retirement savings or pension**
Percentage with no retirement savings or pension, by age

| Age | Percentage |
|---|---|
| 18–29 | 50.5% |
| 30–44 | 27.8% |
| 45–59 | 23% |
| 60 and older | 15.4% |
| **Overall** | 30.9% |

Source: Board of Governors of the Federal Reserve System, "Report on the Economic Well-Being of U.S. Households in 2013" (2014), available at http://www.federalreserve.gov/econresdata/2013-report-economic-well-being-us-households-201407.pdf. Figures above refer to the percentage of nonretired respondents who answered "No retirement savings or pension" when asked "What type(s) of retirement savings or pension do you (or your spouse/partner) have?"

These numbers are expected to grow worse as America's economy continues to drift downward in the manner it has done in the last 45 years since the 1970's, with or without a great depression to come.

Inflation has destroyed that standard. Why inflation? The banker owned Federal Reserve has for many years robbed America's working class with purposeful inflation that quietly steals purchasing power while it rewards the ultra wealthy. We will cover more on that whole subject further on though. Oh, how the corporate global elites have overhauled the American system to benefit themselves! President Trump is overhauling as much as one man can though!

## IT PAYS TO KNOW PEOPLE!

As if the stealing's of our money wasn't enough, D.C. politicians also have a grip on Wall Street. It often seems the heads of Washington D.C. know exactly when to get IN, as well as OUT of the markets often times. For examples, prior and during the 2008 stock market crash, it is confirmed that some key D.C. politicians did in fact greatly profit from inside trading, which is legal in that great city on the hill!

According to Peter J. Swiezer's book entitled "Throw Them All Out", during the 2008 crash, Senator John Kerry was tipped off the day before Citigroup's $100 billion bailout. What did John do? He bought Citi and doubled his money within a few days after the announcement! He did the same thing with Bank of America as well.

Senator Dick Durbin and Senator Claire McCaskill also had certain knowledge to buy Berkshire-Hathaway one day before that company bought millions of shares of Goldman Sachs at a greatly discounted price while offering a nice 10% return, thus boosting Goldman's shares immensely. Only these and perhaps a few others knew of the deal coming down due to their inside positions.

Peter Swiezer's book shows studies that on average, senators beat the market by an average of 12%. Likewise, the average corporate insider beats it by 5%, and hedge funds beat it by 7-8%. Should we assume that the senators are just a lot smarter than the Wall Street pros? Why wouldn't these politicians covet their positions of power and play by the rules? Add in corporate cronyisms and even though you were poor when you came in, you are a multi-millionaire when you leave Congress.

# Planned Collapse of Americanism

In 2012 Congress quietly passed the "Stock Market Act". I never heard about it, did you? The Wall Street Journal and many others had put a lot of pressure on lawmakers to stop the Washington political insiders within the White House, and on Capitol Hill, from abusing their insider knowledge of coming changes out of Washington that could affect certain stock prices and select markets. Unbelievably, it was legal for them to practice this up to that point. Even though the bill passed, it reportedly had many loopholes. You don't say! Well, in April of 2013, changes to key parts of the bill were passed to the delight of certain lawmakers, essentially gutting out some of the best provisions of the bill. New provisions made it so that top Federal employees did <u>not</u> need to disclose their financial holdings anymore! This applies to the President, Vice President, members of Congress or candidates for Congress, or staffers on Capitol Hill as well as other top Federal posts. Basically, it gives them a green light to thievery, and as long as they don't disclose their financial records, they will be o.k. and legal! Huffpost Business, Mark Gongloff, 4/17/13 article "Stock Act Change made it easier for top Federal employees to inside Trade".

But you needn't have worried too much, for Obama, the Federal Reserve and his socialists wanted you to be protected from the economic ups and downs! Yes, even though they and their banking, corporate givers are largely responsible for the bank failures that brought America to its knees, they certainly do have plans to save all our butts by 'Nationalizing' your 401k plan, even a part of your savings as well. Doesn't it feel great that they all have your financial security at heart? This plan is very likely to be exercised after the next financial crash, when hard cold cash is in short supply. At such a time, the government needs cash like we all need water! I am 100% serious

Obama had previously talked of the plans for a nationalized pension system. What better time than when the next really bad market crash comes along if he is still in power or if Hillary winds up in the oval office? The U.S. government may nationalize most or all of the pension system, 'safely' holding most or all your money, paying a small interest on it, perhaps 1-2%. They just want to make your money more 'secure' and put it to better use, you see, like paying on the national debt interest! I wouldn't describe loaning your hard-earned money to a bankrupt government a safe investment, but that's just me. That's socialism for sure.

Verifiably, the world is realizing that the King Dollars days are limited. Our foreign creditors will demand far more than the measly 1% that our own government will pay you for the money, so the un-federal reserve will be happy. Such will make our foreign creditors happy indeed, since their debts owed by the U.S. will be insured inside of state sponsored "Publicly Held Pension Holding Vehicles." Too cheer you up though, don't worry, but it's just that most countries throughout history who take this severe action, initiate it just before a collapse of their economy to rob the people and payoff the bankers, again. They then move on to another money system. For them, it works well to use YOUR money trying to prop up a failed system. Don't worry, just like Obama promised when he was in office eventually the government will be forced to insure your nationalized money with "the full faith of the U.S. government."

If you haven't noticed, my predictions aren't being swayed too much by the election of Pres. Donald Trump to any large degree. Although there will be upward hiccups in the Trump presidency, the long-range facts don't change a thing the fact that to be successful, Trump knows he must start the renaissance to a new American century!

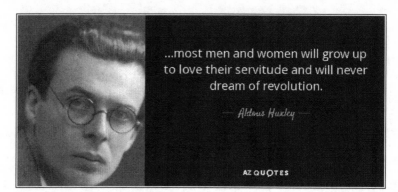

*Let's not allow the above to take place!*

# .13

# WALL STREET'S VAMPIRE SQUID

## ( Or How Goldman Sachs Robs America )

Many don't really understand the reality that Wall Street, government regulators, politicians still haven't fixed the reasons for the out of control markets of 2008 that caused the great recession/depression, and yes, that may even be a purposeful ploy. Taking the public's money and running up the debt, the un-federal reserve had managed to at least juice up the big banks and Wall Street though.  Yes, similar to the way they juiced up the credit markets that created the government insured housing bust of 2007. Yet, Joe Six Pack hadn't seen hardly any difference in his own private economy called financial hell.  America's rust belt is faring the worst which is why 80% of them voted Trump and rejected the establishment politicians.

Even though the regulators instilled around 100 new financial regulations after the 2008 crash,  many of the new regulations did not stop the banks from being far riskier by 2017.  But the new rules did limit the financial activities of regular retail mom and pop investors and small businesses according to many.  It choked off much of the free market mechanisms that business needs to prosper. The need of and the distinctions between big and small were not addressed.  This is big government in action.  Thankfully, President Trump has made major changes to the 2010 Dodd-Frank banking bill which had many flaws.  Now mid sized and small banks are less bound to unreasonable rules put in place originally.  Small businesses also are feeling some relief.

One thing that the biggest six banks have always fought against has been the resurrection of the 1933 Glass Steagall Act which Pres. Clinton had foolishly gotten rid of in 1996 at the behest of the big six banks.  Most economists blame the loss of the GSA as the reason for the 2008 crash.

Most assumed that after the 2008 market crash, and the ensuing unofficial economic depression that had crippled the American economy, perhaps our leaders would have acted more responsibly to make things right when it came to the use of bailout money. Using mostly the current or past 'uppities' of the "Goldman Sachs Dream Team", these guys were largely calling the shots as to how the bailout money was divvied up.  Is it no longer a question that the newly positioned Treasury Secretary / Goldman Sachs front man Treasury Henry Paulson was pulling off the old "create a problem-offer a solution-fix problem" technique when he cried to the world out loud that the bankers needed $800 billion dollars within 24 hours or the whole economy was going to crash into Armageddon!  The result was a fastly initiated, no terms, bailout that sent money out to the banks, with nearly zero restrictions on how they used it!  A huge chunk of the bailout money primarily went to Goldman and to other the big banks that contributed to the crash in the first place with few if any requirements as to how to how the money was to be spent.  If you hire snakes to run such a big money program it is your own fault. Yes, the wizards of Wall Street.

At the height of the panic, Goldmanite Hank Paulson, the captain of the economic sinking ship of America, and his insiders, made it look like it was all just "too complicated" for anybody but their own wizards to figure out how to fix the mess in the markets. Well, these same types of guys who put their "Plunge Protection Team" into action when the market was sinking, couldn't manipulate the market enough to stop the bleeding. The PPT is capable of manipulating the markets to large degrees by bidding markets up or down to stabilize them, holding huge government reserves to do the job when needed. Even though that didn't work so well, it was left to them to figure the rest out. What they did indeed figure out was how to fleece the public again, just like in 1929!

Perhaps the largest and most crooked of the mega banks on Wall Street is Goldman Sachs, a de-facto criminal organization.

In 2009, Rolling Stone Magazine's Matt Taibbi wrote a long and infamous article entitled "**The Great American Bubble Machine**" which was pointed largely against Goldman Sachs lifetime of thievery at every turn. While Goldman Sachs is arguably the world's most powerful investment firm, Matt calls the firm: *'A great vampire squid' wrapped around the face of humanity, relentlessly jamming its blood funnel into anything that smells like money."*

Matt really has a way with words for sure. The article goes on extensively to show how the firm has been behind every financial crash. There is so much more on dubious Goldman's past, it's a great read. Incredulously, this financial octopus on Wall Street rewarded their employees an AVERAGE of $662,000.00 in 2009 during the great recession and market crash! Should we think this was all earned perfectly legally and ethically? The firm's profits went through the roof at the same time regular people were being devastated. Perhaps not so surprisingly, in April of 2016, the octopus was fined $5.1 billion dollars by the Federal government for its huge role in packaging and selling billions of dollars of fraudulent mortgages that were a large part of the reason for the 2008 financial crash.

Goldman Sachs 2014 yearly statement admitted it made $8.48 billion in profits for itself, yet only paid 18.6% taxes. Forgive me, I must be wrong, right? After all, the big corporations swear they are taxed too much with a top tax of 35 percent! They only claimed half of their profits as U.S. profits, the rest being shifted into dozens of offshore tax havens, skipping half their tax liability! Other tricks are to pay upper salaries in part by issuing stock that is actually let's say $200 dollars a share yet valuing it at only $100.00 per share as far as for compensation purposes. The list goes on.

In 2017 Goldman made $12 billion dollars. I guess that beats 2014 by a whole lot. American tax laws allow large U.S. corporations to spread their riches amongst many differing tax havens, even allowing them to set up foreign entities that aren't more than just a P.O. Box somewhere far off like Belize. This is called a tax inversion. It is legal, another favor that our U.S. Congress afforded the big corps years ago. Did you ever hear anything when this law was passed? Shhh! You weren't supposed to! With such capabilities, many pay zero taxes!

For instance, Apple and G.E. pays nearly zero taxes on worldwide corporate profits. Such abuses are widespread. Why are the elites always getting politicians to pitch for lowering corporate taxes? It's because they would rather pay zero, nothing to do with being fair.

In another RSM article, Matt Taibbi shows an example of Wall Street crookedness that was written on 11/16/14, entitled 'The $9 billion witness; Meet J.P. Morgan Chase's Worst Nightmare.' A former JPM deal manager named Alayne Fleischmann was witness to, and according to her words, *"Tried to stop massive criminal securities fraud."* In short, JPM was forced to pay a $9 million dollar "shut up fee" to not disclose to the public the issue. This was just part of a larger SEC investigation involving Bank of America and others for wrongdoings.

In April 2015 there was a filmed sit-down interview between Ex-Goldman heads Hank Paulson, Robert Rubin and Tim Geithner that was moderated by Sheryl Sandberg at the Milken Institute, discussing the 2008 crash. When the subject of the growing income inequalities experienced since the 2008 crash was brought up, Paulson responded as follows; *"O.K., well...income inequality. I think this is something we've all thought about. You know I was working on that topic when I was at Goldman Sachs"* at which point Robert Rubin broke in and laughingly exclaimed *"In what direction?* *"You were working on increasing it!"* Immediately, Paulson fastly and boldly laughed out loud, **"Yea, we were making it wider!"**

Paulson and Geithner were the two of the most important people directing the 2008 bailout plan and its terms, and both were from Goldman Sachs! As hard as it may be to believe when the messiah Hank Paulson was asked; "how and where" the $350-billion-dollars part of the bailout money was spent or allocated by the banks. He was quoted as saying **"I don't know, I didn't ask".** Yeah, how convenient! They're all in on the gravy train. Today, Goldman Sachs is estimated to be worth over $2.1 Trillion dollars. This is much more than most countries around the world are worth! Yet, in 2015 Goldman Sachs announced they were firing over 1,000 employees and moving them to the Orient for far less money. This, even though they have enjoyed record profits since the 2008 crash.

PhD. economist Dean Banker says that the true purpose of the insane bank rescues was *"a massive redistribution of wealth to the bank shareholders and their top executives."*

# Nobel Prize winning economist, writer Joseph Stiglitz and many others have called today's American system as **"socialism for the rich."** I couldn't agree more.

PhD. economist Michael Hudson says; **"the financial parasites (banks) are "sucking as much money out as they can before jumping ship."**

We all naively expected our government to safeguard and sparingly use the U.S. taxpayer's money (err, obligations) that are being handed out. Yes, like making extra sure the banks who took the money agreed to certain conditions, like promising to use and lend a prescribed and agreed percentage of the money to small and medium size businesses to boost the economy. Or, requiring government oversight of how the huge funds were managed in the interest of all involved, especially the taxpayer.

What American citizens got was a crooked un-Federal Reserve handing out hundreds of billions of dollars with unlimited freedom to their banking buddies. These crooks injected and guaranteed loans to their crony banks around the world over a trillion dollars of taxpayer money, without hardly a single string attached. Most smaller and better capitalized banks didn't need the money or want it but were forced to accept it! No requirements for a portion of the loot to go towards small business loans, nada! Very little money went to the small guy, again.

Thank you, Hank Paulson, Timothy Geithner, Larry Summers, Loydd Blankfein and all those within the Goldman Sachs Dream Team who were picked to essentially run the bailout, run its terms, nearly the entire bailouts terms. These Goldman guys and their replacements are always the grim reapers for the public's interest, yet the White House is overwhelmingly filled with them, past and present, especially as to the highest economic positions, simply because they have garnered so very much power across the entire banking world due to their longstanding dealings with foreign banking. Paulson alone had made over a thousand trips to China over the span he was Treasury Secretary. And yet, Timothy Geithner (by his own admission) failed to pay the U.S. Treasury the taxes he owed because he couldn't follow the yes/no prompts of the elementary Turbo Tax software. During the fallout these boys were managing more money than nearly anybody, anywhere on the planet earth had ever tried before.

## THE BLACK SWAN NAMED 'NET CAPITAL RULE'

Nearly all economists agreed that the 2004 revisions of the 1975 Net Capital Rule regulating banking risk takings, as well as the failure to renew the Glass-Steagall Act in 1996 by President Bill Clinton were the two primary causes for the collapse of the markets. Both reversed decades old SEC rules that kept the big banks in check, protecting the public from the chances of reckless and risky bank gambling's, especially as to loan to reserve ratios. But in 2004 under Pres. Bush's watch, the SEC amended the Net Capital Rule, allowing the top 5 banks (those with at least $ 5 billion dollars of reserves) to engage in very high-risk loan to value ratios in relation to the home loans they were making. High risk takings were now codified into law!

The revision of the Net Capital Rule made it possible for the biggest banks to make an incredibly larger number of home loans. Exactly three times as many, and more importantly the risk was on the backs of taxpayers in fact if they failed. Instead of the longstanding loan ratio of 10 to 1 loan against reserves, it was increased to 30 to 1. And once these loans were packaged into bundles of 30 and sold off, the leverage ballooned to 90 to 1! Without the loan ratio safeguards inside the old Net Capital Rule, it was no wonder that the crisis happened. The banks got bailed out and life goes on. Today the banks are richer than ever. This was a staged event by the banking elites, the Bush crime syndicate and the Rothschilds aka Federal Reserve. Everyone made out but the taxpayers.

Today, the Net Capital Rule still has not been changed back to the old rules and the risk remains. The Glass-Steagall Act also remains impotent of safeguards. New safeguards are often dismissed as too little, too late by providing only miniscule and overbearing safeguards in other areas of finances. Assuredly the bankers, hedge funds and Wall Street love it how it is. And the crony politicians don't dare try to fight them! There's a saying about modern banking: *"All profits to the bankers, all risks to the taxpayers."*

Perhaps left with no other choice, fans of big government falsely believed that these Goldmanites, politicians, kleptocrats, and Barackocrats could manage trillions of dollars, the healthcare system, complex economic policies, war policies, and control the climate of the planet. Yes, even though most have next to zero hands-on experience with actually creating money, running a business nor anything else of substance outside of the Washington beltway. The statists are always fast to be on the scene when the takings are the greatest. While the manipulations are aplenty, just like in 1929 and leading into and during every downturn or moment of opportunity. It's no incident that virtually every year the SEC, the FBI, and such government enforcement agencies engage in huge lawsuits against Goldman, J.P. Morgan, Bank of America and all of the top banks for illegal and dubious money dealings, even upon their own customers. These corruptions and stealing's include riggings of the Libor's interest rates, rigging foreign exchange rates, evil dealings related to the subprime real estate debacle and nearly every financial instrument that can be abused. This is their history. But these lawsuits aren't limited to just Goldman.

Even though Goldman is normally at the top of the banking crime chain, nearly all of the top banks have similar lawsuits and fines that are usually just a very small fraction of what they absconded with. As a matter of fact, since the 2008 crisis there had verifiably been at least $140 billion dollars in fines given to just the top six American banks for their corruptions! Yep, the big six aka the trojan horse. Goldman Sachs paid a $550 million dollar fine in 2010 for misleading their investors and betting against them in the 2008 crash. That is just two weeks profits from the firm, big deal many say. And after they paid the fine their stock got a pop of $800 million immediately! CNBC Article, Financial Section 07/15/10 entitled: "Goldman Sachs Will Settle Fraud Case For $550 million". Crime really does pay.

Even when these robber barons are caught, nobody ever goes to jail! It has been estimated that the typical fines they incur typically comprise less than 5% of the money they made off the scams, so they figure it's a small price to pay. It's "pay to play" for the U.S. government who is so hungry for cash. Honestly, could a small business get away with such behavior? Of course, they could not, but small fries are easy targets. In the 1700's anyone caught speculating was hung!

D.C. politicians, especially democrats, were told by the Federal Reserve that if the bailout was approved, a handshake agreement took place the they would promise that a good percentage of the bailout funds would be used for business loans in order to spur the economy. The two-page document spelling out the terms of the $700 billion in bailout money didn't include any safeguards for the retail consumers! The entire first page was filled with exclusions of liability to the banks in fact. It was drawn up literally overnight in the wake of the 08' crash at the urgent behest of Paulson. That too was a false flag event calling for the Hegelian Dialectic *"Create a problem, offer the solution, fix the problem."* It never happened, and as a matter of fact, a year later new small business loans were being made at half the rate of before of the pre-crash levels. Big banks rarely have real concern for ever day people. Such was amplified after the 08' crash.

## WHAT THE HECK IS SHADOW BANKING?

Well, that's what I said when I learned of this not talked of anomaly of much importance! Much lesser known of the 2008 crash was a boom and collapse of the huge, largely hidden and unregulated "shadow banking system", that the elites and many large traders use for trading largely outside the jurisdiction of the authorities. Because of how it is set up, this fairly secret night time operation escapes oversight or supervision by the S.E.C. Today, it is estimated that this banking system is in danger of collapsing again, but this time it is bigger than ever, estimated to have grown to control an astounding 75 trillion dollars of trades under its roof. To keep this in perspective, please remember that the U.S. official debt is "only" 20 trillion dollars! The shadow banking sector is actually bigger than Wall Street, with assets larger than all the traditional banks together, and lacks most of the transparency of its workings. Such numbers are not meant to be conceived by human beings.

Over the past decade, the shadow banking system has become a truly worldwide phenomenon and is a major threat to the entire global financial system. In China, shadow banking has been growing by leaps and bounds, perhaps worse than the one on Wall Street, causing extreme concern amongst the Chinese.

In fact, according to Bloomberg, one top Chinese regulator has referred to shadow banking as a "Ponzi scheme". Their growth has caused the man who is now China's top securities regulator to label the off-balance-sheet products a "Ponzi scheme," because banks have to sell more each month to pay off those that are maturing.

And what happens to all Ponzi schemes eventually? In the end, they always collapse. And when this 75 trillion-dollar Ponzi scheme collapses, the global devastation that it will cause will be absolutely unprecedented.

Bond King Bill Gross, who is intimately familiar with the shadow banking system, came out in 2016 with a major warning about the lack of liquidity in the shadow banking system… Gross says that *"Mutual funds, hedge funds, and ETFs, are part of the "shadow banking system" where upon these modern "banks" are not required to maintain reserves or even emergency levels of cash. Since they in effect now are the market, a rush for liquidity on the part of the investing public whether they be individuals in 401Ks or institutional pension funds and insurance companies, would find the "market" selling to itself with the Federal Reserve severely limited in its ability to provide assistance."*

Bill Gross expects a *"run on the banks"* before too long. The way this is set up, it too is a Ponzi scheme. Combine this situation with a larger upcoming crash in the stock markets and we will likely see an avalanche of collateral hell coming out of the derivatives markets, credit markets, debt markets and perhaps a dollar collapse. America and the world might be looking at a monumental collapse that we haven't seen since the 1929 Great Depression, arriving in 2018 to 2020 likely! As far as shadow banking is concerned, everything is just fine as long as markets just keep going up and up and up.

During the rushed 2015 Federal Budget negotiations, high pressure was put on Congress to actually reinstate the Glass-Steagall Act, including the Volker Rule. Sen. Elizabeth Warren, a populist liberal, took the lead. Citibank, the biggest funder and manipulator of rigging banking laws, threatened to cut off democratic election money if Congress bucked. As usual, big money won out and Glass- Steagall was never reinstated. As a result, in the coming crash, the losses from derivatives is expected to be double or triple what was experienced in the 2008 crash. Experts expect the coming derivative time bomb to run into the many trillions of dollars, possibly taking down the entire system! Just as bad is that most all other markets and corporations are more leveraged and more heavily bet on than 2008 also. The FDIC, the Federal Reserve will be on the hook, and asked to guarantee losses, but this time everyone knows they will be unable to pull it off. Besides, a new Federal Reserve rule/law came out in 2016 that dictates to the markets that NO normal bailout will be forthcoming in the next financial crash! All the tricks in the box have been used. There is nothing left except to go out and ask for help from others of which the IMF is on ready alert and ready to implement a single global money soon. This will be the final gig! New World Order, check!

This next time, it won't really matter all that much that citizens worry about the debt problem anymore, as it might not matter anymore. It seems apropos to repeat the story of writer Ernest Hemingway after he went bankrupt. When asked how he became bankrupt, the reply was: *"Two ways. Gradually, then suddenly"*. As in 2008, the coming crash will come about when the markets just seem fine, even booming. The pigs will be "fattened up for the slaughter." The fact that the un-Federal Reserve (think Rothschild's) will no longer guarantee Wall Street failures is a monumental move that would only be made because of the knowledge that there will be no more king dollar. It appears to look like some elites know that this is the last dance for the American economy as we know it. What comes next? I am 100% sure that the big players are preparing accordingly, using their inside information. What we will likely see come down will be monumental and life changing, something that nobody alive has lived through in America! This won't be a picnic folks. This needs attention to protect the financial system from another meltdown as well.

# .14
# INVERTED FASCISM?

For those who don't know, fascism IS socialism, and socialism is in most respects part and parcel to communism in the end analysis. There is much confusion as to what fascism really, actually stands for. Understand that the primary components of fascism is authoritarian, nationalist political ideology that exalts nation (and often race) above the individual. It always includes a centralized autocratic government headed by a dictatorial leader, severe economic and social regimentation, and forcible suppression of opposition. It often claims to be concerned with notions of cultural decline or decadence and seeks to achieve a national rebirth by suppressing the interests of the individual, and instead promoting cults of unity, energy and purity. For the leftists who protest against Trump often call President Trump a "nazi" using as many ad homenem objections about him as they can muster. These types, and the media both use slander and identity politics to destroy their oppositions are using Marxism 101. Do many of these know that nazi is actually what their own party has stood for and helped greatly to benefit for the last 50+ years? Don't get me wrong reader! BOTH political isles are responsible to differing extent for leading us into this inverted fascism that has put the big corporate owners and deep state in charge of our lives.

In economics, fascism sees itself as a third way between laissez-faire capitalism on the one hand and Communism or Socialism on the other. It acknowledges the roles of private property and the profit motive as legitimate incentives for productivity, but only insofar as they do not conflict with the interests of the state. Fascist governments tend to nationalize key industries, closely manage their currencies and make massive state investments. They also tend to introduce price controls, wage controls and other types of economic planning measures (such as state-regulated allocation of resources, especially in the financial and raw materials sectors). We can see that in America, our government doesn't control industry. No, the corporations control Washington using "inverted fascism" of the American sort.

The term "fascismo" was coined by the Italian Fascist dictator Benito Mussolini (1883 - 1945) and the self-described "philosopher of Fascism" Giovanni Gentile (1875 - 1944). It is derived from the Latin word "fasces", an ancient Roman symbol consisting of a bundle of rods tied around an axe, used to suggest "strength through unity". It was originally used to refer specifically to Mussolini's political movement that ruled Italy from 1922 to 1943 but has subsequently also been used to describe other regimes.

**Fascism usually involves some "some or all" of the following elements:**

* Nationalism (based on the cultural, racial and/or religious attributes of a region).

*Totalitarianism (state regulation of nearly every aspect of public and private sectors).

# Planned Collapse of Americanism

*Statism (state intervention in personal, social or economic matters).

*Patriotism (positive and supportive attitudes to a "fatherland" (America), often mixed with a spirit of individualism to the extent that the leader allows.

*Autocracy (political power in the hands of a single self-appointed ruler).

*Militarism (maintaining of a strong military capability and being prepared to use it aggressively to defend or promote national interests).

*Corporatism (encouragement of unelected bodies which exert control over the social and economic life of their respective areas).

*Populism (direct appeals to the masses, usually by a charismatic leader).

*Collectivism (stress on human interdependence rather than on the importance of separate individuals).

It usually also expresses **opposition to the following:**

*Traditional Liberalism (policies of minimal interference by government, both politically and economically)

*Communism (specifically Marxism, but generally any communal social organization).

*Democracy (majority rule and competitive elections with freedom of speech, freedom of the press and some degree of rule of law).

We must ask, why is the fasci symbol being used inside the White House behind both sides of the podium in the House of Representatives as well as nearly every Washington monument? The axe within the fasci symbol was used for the term "Axis Powers" for the fascist countries in the Second World War. Symbolisms live all around us, but are we aware of what they mean? Todays fasci symbol, used all throughout American government, is just another hidden symbol of the elites. When it is used today, it represents people and countries bound together under a common centralized dictatorship of which the axe represents. Not only was this used by Ancient Rome back in the day as a symbol of "Supreme Authority" but was also used by the original "Axis Powers" of Europe in the first half of the 20th century, prior and during WWII to create unity amongst the socialist countries of Europe. Numerous governments have used the image of the fasces as a symbol of a powerful state since at least the end of the Roman Empire.

In Rome, In the eighteenth century, the fasces received a second life, when the young United States and republican France started to use ancient Roman symbols. Both were progressive revolutionary nations that imitated the Roman republican Constitution. Source:Fasci/Livius.org/ 2005.

Note below all the differing places around Washington D.C. that display the fasce symbolisms so readily noticed by the knowing.

- A fasces ring the base of the Statue of Freedom atop the United States Capitol building
- A frieze on the facade of the United States Supreme Court building depicts the figure of a Roman centurion holding a fasces, to represent "order"
- The National Guard uses the fasces on the seal of the National Guard Bureau, and it appears in the insignia of Regular Army officers assigned to National Guard liaison and in the insignia and unit symbols of National Guard units themselves; for instance, the regimental crest of the 71st Infantry Regiment (New York) of the New York National Guard consisted of a gold fasces set on a blue background
- At the Lincoln Memorial, Lincoln's seat of state bears the fasces—without axes—on the fronts of its arms; fasces also appear on the pylons flanking the main staircase leading into the memorial
- The official seal of the United States Tax Court bears the fasces at its center
- Four fasces flank the two bronze plaques on either side of the bust of Lincoln memorializing his Gettysburg Address at Gettysburg, Pennsylvania
- The seal of the United States Courts Administrative Office includes a fasces behind crossed quill and scroll
- In the Washington Monument, there is a statue of George Washington leaning on a fasces
- A fasces is a common element in U.S. Army Military Police heraldry, most visibly on the shoulder sleeve insignia of the 18th Military Police Brigade and the 42nd Military Police Brigade
- A fasces also appears shoulder sleeve insignia of the U.S. Army Reserve Legal Command
- Seated beside George Washington, a figure holds a fasces as part of *The Apotheosis of Washington*, a fresco mural suspended above the rotunda of the United States Capitol Building.

The most interesting to me is the State of Colorado emblem (not shown.). Not only does it display the fasci, but it presents the illuminati famed "seeing eye" sitting within the illuminati triangle. This classic illuminati symbolism is not to be mistaken for anything else! Is this all by chance? The gold fasci is the Roman. The rear of the Liberty dime has the fasces symbol boldy stamped on! Coincidence?

## IS AMERICA A QUASI FASCIST COUNTRY?

For those stuck in their normalcy mode, the above question would seem preposterous! The purpose of this subchapter is to exemplify how America's ideologies actually link up closely with the very definition of fascism, although let's easily come to such conclusions too quick! A close look above does buck the conventional thinking about what America really consists of, regardless of what the U.S. Constitution calls out for! Looking at how much fasci connections there exists all across Washington governmental structures, America certainly is a mix of ideologies, but I contend that fascism is a much bigger part of America than most are willing to accept! If we look at the policies of the neo-set that have run American war policies for the last 75 years, we can easily see how fascism is a major part of our foreign policy, flowing over into the war economy. It started at least going back to WWII. Democracy in America is a very watered down one, for corporate money and self promotion are the true goals of most of the lawmakers, politicians in America. Don't forget too that democracy is the kindred soul of socialism. It plays the enabler.

Perhaps the main difference between Hitler's fascism and America's style is that we have an 'inverted style' of fascism, a term made by a celebrated professor noted below. It cannot be ignored that Hitler's form of fascism <u>controlled the corporates</u> in nearly every way, allowing them to operate so long as they acted as a government arm of the military and every single fiat he gave them to follow! Since at least the 1930's America has increasingly run a system of government quite the opposite of how our country was meant to operate.

Famed Princeton Professor Sheldon Wolin within his book entitled "Democracy Incorporated / Managed Democracy" nailed the crux of what has transpired in the last 50 years or so in America…

According to Sheldon Wolin and writer Chris Hedges, *"we have an inverted fascism/socialism where corporate power portends to honor electoral politics, freedoms, while at the same time pillaging and destroying whatever representative democracy we started off with. In the end, the corporate forces have become so corrupted and manipulative that their powers upon our so-called democratic government so as to make representative democracy impossible."* Who could say it better than Wolin!

*"We go through periods of sleep-walking. We have to relearn of lessons known since the birth of the nation. Capitalism has its virtues, but it has to be carefully watched, observed and sometimes controlled".*

Wolin refers to democracy as "episodic, not continuous". Furthermore, he has coined the term and called today's American system as "inverted totalitarianism" which represents the "political age of corporate power and the political demobilization of the citizenry." The importance of the statement below cannot be overstated!

The passing of Wolin in 2016 was a sad day, for he was brilliant to say the least. He pinned down the truth, even putting a name on it like that nobody else I knew.

This marriage of corporate and government cronyisms have put a spear into the heart of our republican form of democracy. Going further, it should be said that America could hardly be defined truthfully as a "republic" anymore. America has become the American Empire just like Rome, Hitler's Third Reich, Mussolini and several other fascist governments.

Mussolini (a fascist trailblazer) famously said *"fascism should more appropriately called a corporation."* Wow, that is such a profound, true statement. He knew that the fascism operates much like a corporation under sheets. Further along I give you the readers a chance to chew on the idea that the United States is its own corporation!

America has tons of real history proving that even before WWI and moving forward, the biggest and most powerful men in power and business helped in huge ways to bring about fascist tenets to America. They helped Hitler in many ways toward his ascent to power. The biggest American and European bankers loaned Hitler billions of dollars, including Preston Bush, grandfather of the Presidents Bush family. The Bush family has been a proponent for Fascism since Prescott Bush. The Bush family are the ultimate insiders. They are aligned with the new world order creating a globalist corporate fascism across the world. Of the handful of top wealthy families, nearly all favor fascism for it benefits them the most! Their descendents and families are still pulling the strings as well as billionaires such as George Soros whom push the same agenda. These are nearly all on board with this agenda. They are using the fascist global architecture we see playing out today. We can see the tenets of fascism within much of American operations.

Below, notice the reverse side of the U.S. dime and an older one-dollar coin. Notice the fasci symbolism. You see a bundle of fasci rods, an axe and fasci wreaths wrapping the rods. Romans used the fasci and were Fascists, under a totalitarian governement and with the Caesar as it's dictator. Why is it still inside your congress, on either side of the flag in congress they are advertsing a new world fascist order. This axe is the origin of the term Axis Powers for the fascist countries in the Second World War. The symbolism is of people and countries bound together under a common centralised dictatorship, the axe. Not only was this used by Ancient Rome back in the day as one of its Symbols of "Supreme Authority", but also by the Original "Axis Powers" of Europe in the first half of the 20th century prior too, and during WWII. Worldwide, governments and other authorities have used the image of the fasces as a symbol of power since at least the end of the Roman Empire. It has also been used to hearken back to the Roman republic, particularly by those who see themselves as modern-day successors to the old republic.

Below. see the Nazi symbol once used on most of their uniforms (depicted in generic yellow). Does the one-dollar coin as well as the dime with the fasci symbolism stir up ideas to ponder? The universally recognizable fasci symbolisms are shown within the black outlined box. Next, two fasci symbols as the backdrop to the Congressional House Chambers, one on each side, gold colored.

The Washington monument and Lincoln's memorial chair also displays fasci columns under his hands at rest. It could take pages to show the many fasci symbolisms made part of many notable Washington D.C. monuments all around the capital areas. This clear connection shows the founding fathers admiration for the ideology of nationalism, a strong leader, strong military and some (not all) of the fascist dogma. To be remembered, behind all of the hoopla of what we are told about how our government works, well, little of it actually works according to the way it is supposed to work! The power brokers, elitists families and elitist non-governmental organizations (NGOS) that make much of our official policies are examples of elites working from behind the scenes, often in coordination with other to bring about favorable outcomes for themselves as individuals foremost, then as a group. Groups such as the Bilderberg Group, Trilaterals, Council on Foreign Relations explained elsewhere herein are used as prime examples. The fasci and its historic meanings have much to do with their true agenda.

**Fasci symbols such as those used behind the podium of the House of Representatives and the armchair of the Lincoln Memorial for instance exude the sense of powerful government and much more.**

# THE BIG FLIES SHOULD BE IN JAIL!

*"Laws are spider webs through which the big flies pass through and the little ones get caught"* Honore de Balzac

Actor Matt Damon made a short, insightful yet scathing attack on Americas present directions and those in control presently. This is not an endorsement of Mr. Damon's politics in general, but in short format Mr. Damon rightly expressed the following thoughts which I wholeheartedly agree with...

*"We have the wrong people in jail, and the wrong people out of jail. The wrong people in politics and the wrong people out of politics". "Many people associate civil disobedience as a bad thing, when civil obedience is the problem". "Western civilization has regularized and maximized the injustices we had before the laws". "Much of the rise of Hitler and Stalin were that the peoples fell in line and displayed obedience!" "Nixon and Brezhnev had more in common than we had in Nixon! These types shake hands and have cigars together. They agree on international laws and the goals of world integration, order. They are globalists at heart, not sovereign citizens of any particular country in their heart. They really like each other." Matt Damon*

Quite true, right? These internationalists have little if anything in common with the needs of you and me! They are fronts for the power grabbers no matter what it entails. Perhaps if we got back to the spirit, principles and aims of the Declaration of Independence, we could take back our nation! As I say many times herein, "Get rid of the bums" before they get us!

The huge growth of the U.S. laws as well as the social and military state, has squandered trillions by the neo liberals and neo conservatives who promote unjustified wars, unnecessary and expensive bureaucracies, waste on all levels, and a Wall Street extraction machine that has looted tens of trillions of inflated taxpayer's dollars over the years. Both neo sets are in favor of techno-fascism. Both favor large government that micro manages and claims to offer all things to all people. The public has naturally resorted to the socialist mindset of "gimmie-mine" at the very same time that it has nothing else to give but bankruptcy. The hardest hit has been at the expense of the downtrodden and homeless. Our great country has thus devolved into a depraved state of economic and moral brokenness for large sections of society, so much so that far too many earnest people have just given up looking for work, accepting public welfare and numerous other benefits that equal or beat the benefits of a part time job. This is an example of a socialist state that has been robbed of its life and that can't create jobs anymore unless it abandons its failed economic policies described throughout this book.

Naturally, these rather large sections of American society have turned to lives they never imagined when they were young. Millions have fallen into a spell of lost confidence as to ever regaining the past or moving ahead in the future. The horizon they see looks dim. These are the American's that only but a handful in Washington can relate to as they gorge on fine wine and 5 star eating establishments. Such discouragement drives people to do things they would never have thought of. Drug, alcohol, spousal and child abuse, violent crimes, divorce and depression, even homelessness. These are the un-talked of, the "off-the-record, longly un-accountables" who don't even show up as unemployed any more. At the same time, the justice system has unfairly pointed its finger and all its resources *disproportionately* towards blacks and the poor whose lives are too often destroyed by an unfair court system. Especially for relatively minor offenses, misdemeanors.

**The U.S. has the highest rate of incarceration rate in the world,** sporting an incarceration rate of approx. 1000 people per 100,000 of population. The next highest rate is for either New Zealand or Spain, both only at around 154 per 100,000! There are currently at least 6.6 million people in the United States either in jail, on probation, or on parole. Of those, 2.4 million are incarcerated, and sixty percent are there for non-violent drug offenders. That number has quadrupled since 1980! Unfortunately for many reasons, blacks in particular are largely targeted and the stats show it. Blacks comprise 12.6 percent of the U.S. population but are incarcerated for drug offenses at a rate 10 times higher than that of whites-resulting in 35% of the overall prison population. Another 30% are illegal aliens. The rest of the world's laughs in disbelief that America shells out around sixty thousand dollars a year to house illegal immigrants! I say that if a candidate doesn't push hard to eliminate "Sanctuary Cities" they should be expelled from their job! What if we sent most of the illegals back home and spent the many billions of dollars towards the downtrodden Americans in order to bring jobs and hope to them? No, there is no money to be made or kudos from the globalists state under that solution.

Meanwhile, corporate corruptions, government cover ups, misdeeds, swindling, as well as banking industry fraud in the trillions of dollars goes unabated. These well connected, and financially able types often have corporate or government immunity for their actions. These always move on to their next fraud, without fearing any personal liability and culpability for their egregious actions. As such, it is truly a government run only for the elite and well connected, can anyone disagree? The largest banks in particular are consistently fined by the SEC for fraud, misrepresentations, false reporting and such. Little do they care! The fines typically are only for about 1/10$^{th}$ of the profits they already made off the misdeed.

*"The more corrupt the state is, the more laws it has to pass",* Roman senator, historian, Tacitus, 56 AD-120 AD

Every sane person wants fair justice, fair fines and/or jail times. With many thousands of added laws being enacted every year onto private citizens, even minor infractions can bring on out of control fines, fees, attorney costs, bail costs, loss of your job, and even jail time for what used to be considered very minor infractions with small fines attached. A simple argument between spouses can erupt into jail time due to politically correct judges. Simple cases of recreational pot smoking, unpaid fines, driving without insurance, missing a court date and dozens more of such are enough to wind up in jail! Good people who went just a little off the track can have their lives almost ruined, at least for a time. These are often incarcerated, sometimes losing their job and/or housing because of lost income or lost job. This is where many a broken soul has found his or her new drug dealer that promises a new outlook.

Many a parent(s) can lose their kids for an extended time once a neighbor calls the authorities with an unsubstantiated or overblown claim of one type or another. Once the state gets their hands on the kids, it can be a nightmare for poor people that cannot afford to hire good representation. All for being less than perfect, in a world that has failed to offer proper education, good jobs or much other hope to bring them out of their situation.

For somewhat larger offenses, today's justice system can seem Orwellian at times! Because of huge, immense profits to be made by the state, and the corporations who service them and their broken cities (of which many are broke), these look at the court system as a money machine to continue paying for their expanding state. Yes, a state that is filled with often unneeded or overpaid jobs that guarantee retirement benefits that nobody else can hardly afford in the private sector. The politically correct enforcers, judges and bureaucrats have succeeded in jamming up the court system and jails by aiming at an unprecedentedly large percentage of people with fairly petty offenses, creating the largest jail system in the world with the highest per capita incarceration rate in the world also. Today there are 2.4 million people incarcerated in American jails, and even though America holds only 5% of the world's peoples, it holds 25% of the world's prisoners! It has grown 500% in the last 30 years. Private prisons generate $70 billion dollars a year for this industry! Correction Corporation of America, the GEO Group, Wackenhut are main private prison providers, and they have immense sway in lobbying congress every year to invent new laws that put even more people in jail for extended times. The company Global Tel-Link is a telephone provider to 57% of the prison system. They often charge up to $17 dollars for a 15-minute call, even though stats show that a prisoner that is able to connect with his family is far less likely to commit crimes while in jail and once let out.

The war on drugs has proved a complete failure when considering those people in jail on first drug charges. The only reason drug statistics have fallen slightly is because those in jail are not counted anymore. The more they throw in jail, the more it skews the stats. The war on drugs has provided ballooning prison populations, by increasing arrests for petty offenses such as marijuana possession. America has the longest first-time drug offense sentences (5-10 years), of developed nations. Studies have shown that the possibility of prison time does not deter crime before it happens, and it may actually encourage prisoners to engage in. Recidivism rates are sky high. In actuality, prison time prison creates a cycle of crime and imprisonment in impoverished neighborhoods. Information provided in part by Attn.com article: "Here are 6 companies that get rich off prisoners." by Ashley Nicole Black.

For the poor, paying the bail bondsman is impossible. So, one may sit in jail for weeks or months before being able to settle his/her case. Affording a competent, concerned attorney on the outside is an impossibility, so one is often left with a shitty plea bargain, even if innocent. If bail is put up, the suspected is left in debt to family, and possibly left without a job to return to, regardless whether innocent of the crime or not! Many return to the streets and double down on drug sales in order to pay for their court costs and bail bondsmen, increasing their chances of being re-arrested. The court system today is perhaps the largest money generator in government services. It is a boon to counties, attorney's, bondsmen, jails, public jobs sectors, builders of new facilities, and the list goes on. This is what happens when the state is more concerned about building an ever-bigger bureaucracy than helping the accused to get real help. This is also the time when the state is fastly preparing and approaching conversion into a fascist or dictatorial state.

On the bright side, with the advent of DNA evidence, less crime suspects are being falsely imprisoned or at least being released. For those who already served many years, it is very unfortunate they lost years of their lives while innocent. Often it has been found that the prosecutors pushed so hard for a guilty verdict, only to boost their career. It is verifiable that prior to DNA technology, one out of three suspects involving serious crimes were falsely jailed, often for many years or even life. At this point, perhaps it is time to throw in a bit of truthful humor about the court system.

The great, late George Carlin had a funny, somewhat true quote. I love this one!

*"The real reason we can't have the Ten Commandments in a courthouse? You cannot post Thou Shalt Not Kill, Thou Shalt Not Steal, Thou Shalt Not Commit Adultery, and Thou Shalt Not Lie within a building full of lawyers, judges and politicians. It creates a hostile workplace environment!"*

The statists and technocrats are gearing up for revolts against the coming upheavals we are beginning to witness. The coming socialist utopia will definitely need a profit generating, growing, ever larger court system, even larger than we witness today, and accordingly it will need added jails to carry out "justice" against the millions of dissidents, those who can't, or won't, deal well with the new, stricter and stronger state. Such a state often doubles up on any supposed infractions upon the new state, however minor or unfair.

We have two systems of justice, but they won't tell you that. Joe six-pack is thrown into jail for smoking a few joints or saying the wrong thing at a traffic stop when he is being shoved around by a cop with an attitude. Yet, Hillary Clinton never serves even 1 minute in prison for up the many felony counts of endangering America's security by having her own illegal, private and susceptible email server while she was Secretary of State of the United States. She disobeyed many, many top security rules, lied about her emails to the FBI and courts. After learning of a subpoena to confiscate around 30,000 of her emails, she proceeded to hire a firm to erase her emails from the government. Hillary employed a sophisticated tech firm to bleach the files, then smash the files into smithereens! All this, while continuously denying any wrongdoings!

In another instance, Hillary verifiably took a pay for play bribe when she accepted a $2.35 million-dollar donation to the Clinton foundation from Ian Teffler, CEO of Uranium One. Clinton made it possible for Tefler to sell 20 percent of Americas uranium reserves from his uranium mining company to Russia! All stamped and approved by Hillary. I thought that would be considered treason? The New York Times published an article revealing the 2005 trip's link to Mr. Giustra's Kazakhstan mining deal. It also reported that several months later, Mr. Giustra had donated $31.3 million to Mr. Clinton's foundation with a promise for $100 million more! Around that time, Bill

Clinton also received $500,000 dollars for a speech he gave in Moscow from a company promoting Uranium One Hillary has had at least 5 obvious Federal Offenses and misdeeds, all requiring around 10 years in prison. Yet she will never see a jail cell! Her Deep State operatives have done all that is humanly possible to shield her from harm.

Meanwhile, Joe six pack is still waiting in jail and lost his job because of some small mistake! It has oft been claimed that the criminals and the elites are in the wrong places and their place in society would be better reversed. Perhaps most of the real, truly most damaging crooks are the ones who are our rulers.

*"We hang the petty thieves and appoint the great ones to public office"* Aesop

## IT'S A TAXING SITUATION (or is it?)

Just one small example of how Washington skews the tax rates in favor of big corporations is to consider this corporate paid tax scheme that was put up for consideration by the neo-con political hack named Sen. Eric Cantor elected House Speaker. in 2015. In 2014 as the upcoming 2015 Federal Budget was being worked on by the Republicans, Sen Eric Cantor presented a Republican budget for the new year, and it was immediately criticized for being just what it was, another scheme to shift more tax liabilities onto the backs of middle class Americans His plan just showed how, by supposedly giving a few miniscule breaks to the small guy, the corporate interests were scheming to change the corporate tax rates into only two rates. Namely, 10% for most smaller corporations, and 25% for the well off. Most corps are small, these small firms typically pay a lower rate in reality anyways, nearly always paying at least the 10% range regardless. The problem with this proposed plan was that the current rate for corporations with incomes above $335,000 is officially set at 35%. Yet it is extremely hard to find a corporation that pays anywhere near a 35% tax! After all the allowed deductions and tax schemes, the average large corporation in reality pays from zero to 16% as I show in the chart below.

Big business can yell all it wants about the US having the highest tax in the world, but the 35% number is hardly ever paid! It isn't hard to see that the large majority of big corporations only pay an average of 16% and are not paying anywhere near the supposed 35 percent rate! This is a fairy-tale, untrue statement focused on the dumbed down, unsophisticated public in order to garner support for what might amount to a zero effective tax rate if they could have their way! Effective is the key word my friends. Many already pay zero, such as Apple and General Electric. The effective rate has been falling since 1950 as the chart below shows. Don't we all wish we could only pay a 10% tax? Many call this "socialism for the rich".

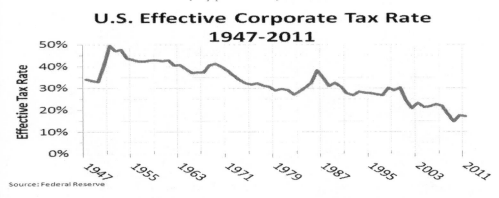

## U.S. Effective Corporate Tax Rate 1947-2011

Effective Tax Rate — 50%, 40%, 30%, 20%, 10%, 0%

1947, 1955, 1963, 1971, 1979, 1987, 1995, 2003, 2011

Source: Federal Reserve

As we can see, actual (effectual) corporate taxes have been tanking since 1950 when it was 50%. Today the actual rate being paid is averaging around 16% for all corporations. Not to go on too much, but if the top 1% already have captured nearly all income increases in the last 20+ years, and the 400 richest Americans have more wealth than the bottom 150 million Americans all put together (over half of all Americans), should we really be talking about an even larger tax break for the very wealthy, when they largely pay a far less percentage in taxes than Warren Buffets secretary does. A wage earner making $26,000 per year now pays an average income/ payroll taxes of $6,084, which breaks down to 23.4%. By the time his/her state income taxes, gas taxes, sales taxes and various other typical taxes are paid, he is paying closer to 50%. And that doesn't count the big one, property taxes! Yet the rich have over 3000 I.R.S loopholes.

The GAO (General Accounting Office) of the U.S. government reports that between 1998-2005, clearly 2/3 of all corporations operating in the U.S. paid zero taxes! So why do the politicians unanimously cry out that if we don't lower corporate tax rates, it will stifle our economy? It's a bald-faced lie by politicians in order to keep the corporatist gravy train coming in. The system can no longer stay afloat with such top-heavy favoritisms toward the large corporations who play tax games and escape nearly all taxes while shifting the debt onto the back of American citizens! Make it fair and let Americans spend it in the economy!

## THE TAX REPRIATION LIE!

Perhaps the biggest lie handed out by President Trump and Republicans is that if we offer the corporations holding trillions of dollars of profits inside of offshore accounts a one-time real great tax break, they will bring it back into the United States and spend it on creating new jobs and new factories! Gee, doesn't that sound swell guys? Want the truth? Some history behind this scheme follows.

**The following is from an article in the Sentinel on 4/27/17 by columnist Zaid Jelani:**

"From 2004 to 2005, the Bush administration and Congress tried a one-time tax repatriation holiday, cutting the rate to 5.25 percent. It was named the American Jobs Creation Act. Yet a Senate study in 2011 found these corporations brought $312 billion they had stashed overseas back to the United States, avoiding $3.3 billion in taxes as a result of the repatriation rate.

The top 15 companies that took advantage of the holiday **actually reduced** their total U.S. employment by 20,931 jobs the top five executives at the top 15 repatriating corporations saw their annual compensation increase by 27 percent from 2004 to 2005 while increasing their spending on stock buybacks to 16% from 2004 to 2005 period, thereafter upping it to 38% from 2005 to 2006! the report surveyed studies of all 840 corporations that took advantage of repatriation and *concluded that there was "no evidence that repatriated funds increased overall U.S. employment."* So, what did the companies use the money for? The report found that two things increased dramatically after repatriation: executive compensatin stock buybacks, bonuses, retirement plans, etc. etc.                                                        Supporting        articles: https://www.gpo.gov/fdsys/pkg/CPRT112SPRT70710/pdf/CPRT-www.brookings.edu/.../**dont**-fall-for-corporate-repatriation Repatriation Tax Holiday A Failed Policy.

William Lazonick, an economist at the University of Massachusetts Lowell, has long studied the issue of stock buybacks. He noted in a Brookings paper published in 2015 that corporations have essentially established a "buyback economy": Between 2004 and 2013, 454 companies in the S&P 500 Index did $3.4 trillion in stock buybacks, "representing 51 percent of net income. These companies expended an additional 35 percent of net income on dividends." "Why are you giving these companies any tax breaks when the vast majority of the **profits are just being used to boost stock prices?**" he asked in an interview with The Intercept, further saying "Corporations are hardly concealing the fact that they'd like to repeat the 2004 tax repatriation experiment." Look, American companies are sitting on more cash than they have in their lifetimes and they still aren't investing in new factories or new jobs! What makes it believable that this time will be different.

# .15

# THE ROTHSCHILD SYNDICATE

## MANIPULATORS OF ECONOMIES, WARS & THE WORLD

### Lessons on Modern Banking

*"The first truth is that the liberty of a democracy is not safe if the people tolerate the growth of private power to a point where it becomes stronger than their democratic State itself."* Franklin D. Roosevelt, 1942

Central banks are all quasi-legal private banks. Irregardless the official statements, America's twelve central banks are largely owned by the Rothschild banking family, their inner circle of the wealthiest corporations in America, often acting as fronts for its hidden owners. Eustace Mullins was the top Federal Reserve researcher of all time perhaps. In his book 'The Federal Reserve' Mullins reported that the top 8 stockholders of the New York Fed in 1983 were:

- Citibank
- Chase Manhatten Bank
- Morgan Guaranty Trust
- Chemical Bank
- Manufacturers Hanover Trust
- Bankers Trust Company
- National Bank of North America, and
- Bank of New York.

According to Mullins these institutions in 1983 owned a combined 63% of the New York Fed's stock. These American banks, in turn, were owned by European financial institutions. Since the commercial banks in the New York Fed's district elect its board of directors, the London Connection is able to use their American agents to pick the Bank's directors and ultimately control the whole Federal Reserve System. Mullins explained it all this way:

*... The most powerful men in the United States were themselves answerable to another power, a foreign power, and a power which had been steadfastly seeking to extend its control over the young republic since its very inception. The power was the financial power of England, centered in the London Branch of the House of Rothschild. The fact was that in 1910, the United States was for all practical purposes being ruled from England, and so it is today* (Mullins, p. 47-48).

He remarked further that the day the Federal Reserve Act was passed in 1913, *"the Constitution ceased to be the governing covenant of the American people, and our liberties were handed over to a small group of international bankers"* (p. 29).

Hidden behind these front corporations and large banks, the ownership of and profits derived from this money machine are not who you think they are. Chase Bank was Rothschilds American front man during the creation of the Federal Reserve, so it is no shock at all that Chase is a major owner as even the Federal Reserve itself admits. The un-Federal Reserve has so very many ways to manipulate money without oversight, well, it is stupendous! This type of gargantuan money machine could never be contained. In 1910 this entire scheme was set up amongst the wealthiest of the world at the Jeckyll Island Hotel in Georgia as I cover.

The Rothschild family has been around for more than 230 years and has slithered its way into each country on this planet, threatened every world leader and their governments and cabinets with physical and economic death and destruction, and then replaced their own people in these central banks to control and manage each country's pocketbook. Worse, the Rothschilds also control the machinations of each government at the macro level, not concerning themselves with the daily vicissitudes of our individual personal lives. Except when we get too far out of line.

F.D.R. warned of the banking elites during his time in politics. Here is one of his quotes: *"Fascism is the ownership of the government by an individual, by a group or any other controlling private power."*

F.D.R was specifically talking about the infamous "money trust" of the time whom, together, had basically taken control of the country and ransacked it to feed their riches. F.D.R knew exactly who caused the Great Depression that America was reeling from for he was a Fabian as well. The largest culprit by far were the Rothschild's and their banking implants from England. And nothing has changed.

If one is to understand the American and world economics at all, it is imperative to realize just how the world's private central banks actually operate, how they engineer depressions and recessions for the benefit of themselves and the big spenders in Congress.

We have just passed up the 100th anniversary of the un-Federal Reserve, and most Americans still don't know what it actually is or how it functions. But understanding the Federal Reserve is absolutely critical because the Fed is at the very heart of our economic problems. The agency was sold to the public that it would "end financial panics". Yet since the Federal Reserve was created, there have been 18 recessions or depressions, the value of the U.S. dollar has declined by 98 percent. Without a private/un-Federal Reserve bank who illegally runs our central banking system, it would have been much harder for our leaders to justify the costs connected with many of the unwarranted, expensive, deadly invasions across the globe. Since its inception our debt has grown over 5000 times over. I didn't make that up! This insidious debt-based financial system has literally made debt slaves out of all of us, and it is systematically destroying the bright financial future that most our children & grandchildren were supposed to have.

At this point the world is inevitably and irreversibly on course for the most unbelievable economic crash-ageddon that the world has ever witnessed, but the longest and most painful part of the whole process will be a very, very long period of total government control over nearly everything, especially that thing called MONEY.

With a little patience, the following read will reap a wealth of understanding as to exactly how the Rothschild's brought their rapacious, tricky central banking scheme from England to AmericaTheir somewhat proprietary "system", is hard for most people understand their ploy.  This is why their scheme has been so easy to hide its working from the public.  Only one person in a thousand truly understands the scheme. This rapacious system has become a permanent American fixture since passing the Federal Reserve Act of 1913.

In their beginnings in the 1700's, the Rothschild bankers made all types of loans, but soon learned that they could make far more money by lending money to countries rather than individuals. Rothschilds learned that they could finance otherwise unaffordable wars and social programs for countries willing to pay the price. They do not discriminate whom they lend to in such cases, for they often fund both sides of a war.  If you think about it, they and their central banking creations have been able to fund US warring's for a long time.  Don't forget, our wars create big deficits and debts as well as huge profits. We don't have the money, so we borrow the money from these private bankers, the un-federal reserve.

The Rothschilds would fund both sides of the same war most times.  For instance, the War of 1812 was one case.  That was the war that Rothschild cleverly made tens of millions of dollars simply by betting on the winner. The five brothers ran banks in five major European cities, making it possible to loan all of Europe.  The loans were very safe since the return of their money was guaranteed as the borrowing country put up hard state assets and the payments would be made through taxations. The Rothschild's devised and capitalized on the system of creating money out of nothing in actuality!  If that wasn't enough, they also created systems of making far more money out of that "nothing" than anyone could fathom. Fractional reserve bank lending and the monetizing of debt. They created our debt-based economies out of nothing more valuable than your newspaper. And of course, you know from the 2nd chapter that the Rothschild's and the British Monarchy had long ago taken actual control of America under a separate corporation and Admiralty Law.  After you read the following quote, think for a minute.

**"I care not what puppet is placed on the throne of England to rule the Empire, ... The man that controls Britain's money supply controls the British Empire.  And I control the money supply."**                    **Baron Nathan Mayer Rothschilds**

Mullins, Eustace (1983), Secrets *of the Federal Reserve*.  Staunton, Va.: Bankers Research Institute.

# THE GREATEST SCAM IN HISTORY

Pardon me if I go on a lot about the Rothschilds and the Federal Reserve but I feel so strongly about the subject and its destructiveness upon America that well, I just can't help but want to expose the Ponzi scheme. share the immensity and details of it since so few are clueless about the subject. Yes, clueless. And oh, what a mistake! So here we go. If more people knew just how flawed the whole concept and workings of our country handing over its money functions to a private bank, we could replace this agency with a U.S. Government run central bank and skip the middle man Ponzi scheme.

How did the Federal Reserve come to be? After the Panic of 1907 roiled the American economy, Americans wanted banking reform. The next year Congress passed the Aldrich-Vreeland Act, which was officially said to be needed simply to "make the money supply more elastic", meant to temporarily alleviate the stresses during emergency currency shortages. Nelson Aldrich established the National Monetary Commission, which recommended the Federal Reserve Act. In 1910, Aldrich and executives representing the banks of J.P. Morgan, Rockefeller, and Kuhn, Loeb, & Co., secretly secluded themselves for 10 days at Jekyll Island resort, Georgia under the guise of a duck hunting trip. The executives included Frank Vanderlip, president of the National City Bank of New York, associated with the Rockefellers; Henry Davison, senior partner of J.P. *Morgan* Company; Charles D. Norton, president of the First National Bank of New York; and Col. Edward House, who would later become President Woodrow Wilson's closest adviser and founder of the Council on Foreign Relations. There, Paul Warburg of Kuhn, Loeb, & Co. directed the proceedings and wrote the primary features of the Federal Reserve Act. By no accident, Henry Davison of J.P. Morgan acted in capacity as the silent partner of Rothschilds, the real power behind the new private bank. This bill allowed a group of elitist bankers to create the Federal Reserve System in 1913. Morgan's own bank, The Morgan Guaranty Trust, was allowed to be among the inner circle of primary owners of the Federal Reserve. Does not the name MORGAN come up a lot? Although all involved were amongst the most powerful men in the world at that time, the new bank was definitely engineered with Morgan (Rothschild) being the primary powers behind it all.

The bankers knew that the public would reject any new bank that gave the impression that it was government bank, for the public were weary of another such bank. The public had been sadly disappointed in the first two government banks. If the name of this new entity sounded like the priors, (the First and Second Banks of America) it would surely never pass. So they cleverly named it the "Federal Reserve". So official sounding, its "Federal" after all, and it's got reserves, and it's a bank for us! Wrong on all counts. While debating the issue of this new entity within Congress, it was becoming apparent that getting a majority might be impossible. But nothing is impossible when the biggest money men of the world want something big.

Late at night, during the 1913 Christmas vacation, a very small assemblage of bought off Congressmen who supported the new Federal Reserve legislation (many buddies of the banking cartel), gathered in the capital to secretly vote for its passage without the opposition being around. These had had previously promised the opposition that they would wait until Congress reconvened <u>after</u> the Christmas holidays. Well, they lied!

On Dec. 22, 1913 in the dead of night, the legislation was secretly passed, and the rapacious un-Federal Reserve became law. A naïve President Woodrow Wilson had been convinced by the bankers to favor the idea also but lived to regret it. He was after all a university man and knew little of finance. He left it to the banksters to advise him on the matter, predictably being convinced to sign on if it would end all financial panics in the future. Ha! The banker's scheme to print free money, charge the government (the people) interest on fictitious money was basically complete. Source in part: Mullins, Eustice. The World Order as well as dozens of other books, publications on the federal reserve.

**Six years later, President Woodrow Wilson had regrets about the passage of this act when he admitted:** *"I am a most unhappy man. I have unwittingly ruined my country. A great industrial nation is now controlled by its system of credit. We are no longer a government by free opinion, no longer a government by majority, but a government by the opinion and duress of a small group of dominant men".*

Just prior to passing the Federal Reserve Act early in 1913, Congress passed a hotly debated 16th Amendment to institute an income tax. Many scholars and judges agree that the 16th Amendment was never passed and approved properly, but it still flies. The income tax was first called a "war tax" to help pay for WWI but was never cancelled, eventually becoming our Federal Income tax. Happy were the socialists who wanted to expand the state. That took money. With WWI beginning in Europe, America would also need the added funds to pay for America's part in the war. The Rothschild's and bankers already had a big contract to fill... funding a planned world war! It also cemented a permanent, unconstitutional tax in reality.

Never talked of is the fact that in 1914, at the beginning of WWI, the brand new Federal Reserve loaned $25 billion dollars to American allies! This was just one of many such examples of the "Reserve" funding the war. The war we couldn't afford otherwise. Federal Reserve phony baloney debt that the taxpayers would have to pay back from the sweats of their labors. Again, money out of nothing, only backed by a small amount of gold and the sweat off our brows.

The part most people miss in this whole scheme of creating both a private Federal Reserve and an income tax at virtually the same moment in time is the following: The Rothschild's and some politicians knew upfront that this combination would allow America to borrow for nearly anything it desired and worry about it way down the line! Costly wars that could never have been afforded before, could now be fought. Europe could not have afforded WWI but now they could, with a loan from the U.S. whom now had the ability to just print money! Favors could be bought around the world. Big social programs could begin, etc. Most importantly, the Rothschild's and their fellow bankers could make billions upon billions of dollars in interest, fractional reserve lending and a dozen other ways that hardly anyone else could dream up. These were a den of thieves (and still are). The Rothschilds profits said to be sent back to England, usually converted to gold (a real form of money). And the new income tax would of course help pay for the interest owed to the un-federal reserve (for a while at least). Parts from Eustice Mullins book - Secrets of the Federal Reserve as well as extensive reads in bibliography section 'Federal Reserve'.

*"Gold is money. Everything else is Credit" J.P. Morgan*

Authors note: Well, some things don't change, do they?

## CREATING MONEY OUT OF DEBT!

Ask yourself this question, if you were given a money printing press and a legal contract to print and issue all the money you wanted, infinitum, wouldn't you? What if you could charge interest on that paper you printed at full face value for whatever amount you wanted. The government has done exactly that. The most awesome power the un-federal reserve has is in the power to CREATE out of nothing. In return, the future productivity of America's citizens is partly confiscated in order to pay back the money forgers. This is what the Federal Reserve is REALLY ABOUT! America has legislated away their countries future growth and handed it over to the English Monarchy and the U.S. Corporation. Yet, according to the Supreme Court, this transfer of power is in direct violation of the law. "Congress may not abdicate or transfer to others its legitimate functions" Schechter Pultry v U.S. 29 U.S. 495, 55 U.S. 837.842 (1935)

The whole scheme is predicated on new money being increasingly printed, more new debt while constantly expanding it faster and faster to keep the Ponzi scheme from collapsing. It is only when they keep this inflationary / money destruction thing going that the huge scam can possibly continue on! The jig is up any day.

*"By a continuing process of inflation, governments can secretly confiscate an important part of the wealth of their citizens."* John Maynard Keynes.

So you see, we really are a debt-based economy!" As crazy as that might sound, it is absolutely true. The problem is this: if we ever were to try and appreciably pay down all the Federal debt, it would cause another Great Depression worse than in 1929! The attempt would pull so much money out of the economy to pay the debt that it would cause money to dry up in the economy nearly immediately. This is already a problem.

Following is a simplified explanation of the inane method in which currency and credit is currently created in the United States. This system benefits a few elitists at an exorbitant cost to We the People! The average American contributes his hard work earned from January until at least May in large part to support this corrupt money extraction machine. Once this new un-Federal Reserve central bank was established in 1913, all bills in circulation were gold certificates, backed by the Treasury with pure gold. Sounds good, right? But within one year, the gold standard was relaxed, and within just a more few years, the Fed began replacing gold certificate bills with "Federal Reserve certificates". No guarantee of gold backing anymore. The money was now unofficially backed by only 40% gold. That meant that 60% was not backed by gold. Do we smell a scam starting already? Of course, this new policy of money debasement is always what allows governments the power to steal without nearly anyone realizing it is going on. Debasing the value of America's money our money had begun, always a bad sign. The Rothschild's scam in reality had just debased our currency by 60% with nobody realizing it! Now, the Federal Reserve was able to print just about as much 'money' as the government asked the central bank for. All the government had to do was write an IOU, leave it to the Treasury to sell government bonds, (pieces of paper backed by promises). This is the Rothschild's trademark.

Another ploy to increase the banking industry's ability to increase its ability to take more risks with public's money was to change the safety ratio of our money under their management (aka a reserve requirement) from 21.1% down to only 11.6%. Soon after that, they lowered that requirement dropped to only 9.8 percent! Today it is often far less.

Nearly immediately after taking the helm of being the caretaker of America's money, the new un-Federal reserve had already taken three huge steps to not only debase the US money, but also lowered the safety margin of money held in their banks! Today's reserve requirements have been watered down to only average around five percent! This means the bank only holds about five dollars for every one hundred dollars in the case of a run. The FDIC insurance fund is supposed to cover the rest, but in the case of a "run on the bank", it only has enough cash to cover about 1% of the nation's cash needs. For every $100 dollars held in the bank, only $5.00 is held in the bank to cover it. Imagine, between the 60% haircut of gold backing, plus the reduction of reserve requirements by over 50% by 1917, the newly hired un federal reserve was able to print and expand their Ponzi scheme tenfold. The US government was able to borrow and fund a world war and spend nearly endless money by mortgaging the nations hard working peoples. The modern un federal reserve uses clever types of Ponzi styled money management that includes creative types of debt, complicated financial swaps, derivatives, and dozens of other exotic methods to create money out of nothing more valuable than plain old paper and printing costs. And yet it is all guaranteed by the future labor to be produced by the entire nations working forces! The early, oftenly naive FR supporters including politicians, could not have even conceived just how far the FR would decimate the earning capacity of the United States peoples.

Just one example of how the top banking interests make out big during wars of which they play a part in engineering, we can see how J.P. Morgan (the Rothschild's American agent) soon began a near monopoly on underwriting war bonds for the U.K. and France, through the Rothschild's Bank of England. With this near monopoly, J.P. and the Rothschild's profited tremendously as they just printed more money whenever the need arose. Was it just a coincidence that JP and the Rothschild's bank got involved in this setup? History shows the close relationship between JP Morgan and the Rothschild's. Morgan was in fact Rothschild's American connection, business partner. This partnership was instrumental in bring the Federal Reserve to life without the name Rothschild hardly ever mentioned! This partnership, as well as some others within the elite "money trust", made huge Federal Reserve loans to suppliers of armament factories in Britain, France, Russia, England, as well as financing both sides of the war. We must again realize that these bankers have used their monetary and political clout to encourage or create wars throughout their entire history for their financial gains! They care less if their actions maim and kill millions.

The Rothschild's were so powerful, the brothers own mother had once said: *"If my sons wanted to end wars, there would be none."*

Historians often cite that the particular timing of the Federal Reserve's beginnings was tied closely to the profitable prospects of W.W.I soon to come.

In 1933, just prior to WWII, the Rothschild's also created the largest private central bank of the world, known as the Bank of International Settlements aka the B.I.S. It is located in Basil, Switzerland. The BIS is the most powerful banking entity in the world, controlling from behind the scenes the entire world's central banking system. It was originally set up to manage the settlement payments agreed upon inside the Treaty of Versailles at the end of WWI. It is called the "Central Bank for the central banks". It is that powerful.

Interestingly, from the very beginning of WWI the Rothschild's Hitler practically ran the BIS in order to assist himself in the numerous secret money transfers to and from America, Germany and the European investors whom were quietly funding his side of the war. This entity allowed Hitler and his financial backers to escape any world scrutiny of "trading with the enemy". Hitler laundered billions of dollars of money, products, gold, art and other valuables back and forth through the BIS in order be able to go around all the trade embargoes and such that were imposed upon Hitler during the war. This arrangement allowed Hitler to do an end-run around all the various economic trade boycotts that had been placed upon Germany during the war. Reportedly, Hitler absconded with at least a billion dollars out of Germany toward his own stash.

As we can see, the Rothschild's looked upon this WWII as just another extremely profitable business to support! They didn't take sides, just the money. They also created extreme Rothschild debts for their own benefit. Not such a sterling first few years for the primary central banking institution of the world to reminisce about!

Of course, between 1913 and today a lot has happened involving the same big players of money as well as their successors as I covered elsewhere. Today, it is surmised quite intelligently by many astute historians that the Rothschild's, operating through hundreds of differing banks, corporations and a multitude of various surnames, still harness a majority of ownership and control over the Federal Reserve, the BIS, the European Central Bank, the IMF, World Bank and perhaps half of the world's total wealth. It is widely accepted that the Rothschild's (Jewish), own 80-90% of the state of Israel, and control much of Israel's policy makings through AIPAC as well. For those whom cling to the left's mantra that America's Founders ideas are all pass`e and irrelevant, I suggest you read the following quote from good old honest Abe Lincoln.

*"The central bank is an institution of the most deadly hostility existing against the Principles and form of our Constitution. I am an Enemy to all banks discounting bills or notes for anything but Coin. If the American People allow private banks to control the issuance of their currency, first by inflation and then by deflation, the banks and corporations that will grow up around them will deprive the People of all their Property until their Children will wake up homeless on the continent their Fathers conquered."*

*Signed; President Abe Lincoln*

# .16

# OUR <u>UN</u>-FEDERAL EXPRESS

As we all know by now, our Federal Reserve System is about as "Federal" as Federal Express! It's perhaps the biggest Ponzi type scheme ever invented and threatens the existence of our nation by bankrupting us with insidious banking methods that wind up created money out of debt! This system was contrived to benefit the Rothschild / J.P. Morgan partnership, the U.S. "money trust" as it was called, the English Monarchy, European banks and other epic money men of the time. As covered in more detail, this entity called a Federal Reserve was no more Federal than Federal Express and actually has no real reserves! This <u>non</u>-federal reserve (of which I usually omit capital letters on purpose), was passed as law by a late night, minimalist Congressional vote on Christmas eve of 1913 when most of Congress was on vacation for the holiday. The dirty bankers told congressmen not to worry, they would wait until they got back from Christmas vacation. Sabotaged!

After passage in 1913, the rapacious style of the Rothschild's monopolized / British centralized private banking was now finally established in the U.S.A. These were all part of the infamous, despised "Money Trust" of the times.

And they didn't have your best interest at heart. And if you don't know, the FR entity is a private corporation, is not a branch of the Federal Government, or under its control, and it has no "reserve" either. Surprised? It has no real budget, has no audits by our government, is not accountable to anyone, not even Congress or the President, and no one can supervise its running's, so it has almost no restraints! It gives us vague statistics ever so often, but many complain it's not enough and not often enough. Yet this agency has more control over the country than the President in many ways. Why should they care what our government says of this?

It was former Chairman of the Federal Reserve, Alan Greenspan who was quoted;

*No other action of any other agency can overrule any actions we take."* It is truly a monopolistic organization that can manipulate, steal, cook the books and pretty much do whatever it wants with the money it prints up!

On November 27, 2011, a frustrated Bloomberg News sued the Federal Reserve under the Freedom of Information Act, in order to force them into revealing exactly who all the firms were who received the $2+ trillion dollars in bailout money and government guaranteed loan funds, and what exactly was used as collateral in exchange for the cash within the 11 different programs employed by the FR. Judge Loretta Prisca of the U.S. District Court ordered the FR to hand over the information, but the FR shot back to say that they are an independent agency, not part of the Federal Government. Bloomberg reported that "the Fed performed trillions of dollars of off-balance sheet transactions as of 09/2012". They shouldn't have been surprised! Where did this money go? Who knows!!

This agency has a license to do whatever it wants with our money with no repercussions! Source; Columbia Journalism Review, Ryan Chittum, story 8/25/09. This is how the FR can do literally anything it want to with U.S. taxpayer's money and they can't do one thing to stop them. Did you ever hear a peep out of the Main Street media about this?

In 2013 the Federal Reserve just "lost" $9 trillion dollars, with no accounting for it. That's $9 trillion dollars that they expect you, me, even our kids and grandkids to pay! Under sworn testimony to our U.S. Congress, Elizabeth Coleman, the Inspector General to the Federal Reserve couldn't account for it! She kept saying "I don't know". It appears that the money likely went into the big banks and investors pockets. Very likely the same crooks that "own" the private stock in the Federal Reserve. No accountability, nada! It seems inconceivable that our government or military needed such a gargantuan amount of funds for a secret black budget project or such. Even the black budget has numbers that are transparent, just not where it went. So where did it go? This was an amount equal to half of our official debt of $29 trillion dollars. Fmr. Housing Secretary of HUD under Reagan, Catherine Austin Fitts has been a leader in researching just where much of this money likely was funneled to. SolariReport.com

Many have complained that the Federal Reserve's highest positions are inordinately and heavily weighted with Jewish representation. Who would've thought? Past and current FR presidents, board members and such are primarily Jewish and well connected to the cabal who really run the Federal Reserve. Obviously, this is no mistake. These are concerned that this private corporation called a private federal reserve, is overly represented and heavily influenced by the really big Jewish banking, investment, and Wall Street heavy hitters as well as largely owned by the Rothschild's under sheets. In recent times, these critics are complaining more and more that the Jewish elements are conspiring with, and often sharing secret information, preferential treatments and favors to their fellows on Wall Street.

The Rothschild's, the Goldman Sachs types, have all been accused many times of trying to control the financial world for themselves. As an example of their control, the Rothschild's descendants meet twice daily in London, under the Bank of England, to dictate to the world what the world price of gold will be. They also dictate what the "Federal Reserve System" will do with America's finances Of the 12 Federal Reserve Board members, nine are Jewish. Since 1979, past Fed Chairman's were Bernanke, Greenspan, Volcker, and the current Janet Yellen. In 2015, all 5 five board members within the FR Board of Governors are Jewish as well, even though only 2% of the population is Jewish. The five names in 2009 were, Ben Bernanke, Donald Kohn, Kevin Warsh, Randall Krosner and Frederic Mishkin. That being said, this Jewish cabal is without a doubt operating at the helm of the "good ship lollipop" called central banking. These are controlling monetary policies affecting not only Americas economy, but the worlds too in many ways to a tune never before experienced, without constraints. They believe that this power has allowed hugely special favors and treatments in the billions and trillions of dollars between the private Federal Reserve and the central banks, the world's top banks and Wall Street firms for instance. They also assert that the Jewish firms get the best treatments and favors. Just one example follows: Virtually all those in charge of the 2008 Wall Street "Bailout Team" were current or former top executives at Goldman Sachs and Jewish. Hank Paulson was S.E.C. head! These were the guys that were almost exclusively put in charge of the bailout amounts, to whom largely decided the terms and distributions of cash, and the mindboggling loan guarantees in the trillions of dollars, etc.

Timothy Geithner, (a Trilateral and CFR member), Larry Summers, (CFR) Hank Paulson (Secretary of Treasury during the 2008 crash), Robert Rubin were, or had been all Goldman Sachs guys of the highest posts. Goldman's new C.E.O. was also involved in the transactions and how money would be distributed to favor G.S. and friends. Paulson tapped former G.S. banker Neel Kashkari to take charge of the distribution of the $700 billion injection of cash, thereby guaranteeing G.S. a nice share of it. Kashkari currently serves as the Minneapolis Federal Reserve as a president. Crime pays off I suppose.

Needless to say, Goldman Sachs wound up getting $10 billion dollars plus another $24 billion of guarantees, etc. according to news sources. If one dares to look, a very, very large percentage of Washington D.C.'s selections as to whom shall serve in the capacity of anything to do with finance or money have been past employees of Goldman Sachs! Citibank (remember they are the ones who are always fighting against any talk of reinstituting Glass-Steagall) took the most money, namely, $2.5 Trillion, Morgan Stanley took $2.04 Trillion, Merrill Lynch $1.9 Trillion, et al. Amazingly, in August of 2009, Sen. Ron Paul and Alan Grayson did actually accomplish (with the General Accounting Office) a partial audit of the Federal Reserve as an amendment to the Dodd-Frank bill upon its passing. Sen. Barry Sanders and Jim DeMint tried to get a total audit but were unsuccessful. Nevertheless, one of the largest discoveries was that the un-Federal Reserve had passed out $16 Trillion dollars to banks and corporations all around the world, some not even asking for it! This scandal largely went behind the doors of the unfederal reserve system without any public oversight! Nearly as much money as our official debt! How much do we know about the details? Nearly zip.

Why hasn't there been any type of government investigation into this seemingly criminal act? Oh, that's right**, the private unfederal Reserve cannot be audited**! Sorry for my French, but what a bunch of bullshit! Sorry for my temper, but this is your money and my money (aka sweat and toil) that they have license to play with! Too keep it in perspective, the amount exceeds the entire Gross Domestic Product (GDP) of the United States of $18 Trillion dollars for 2017! This was an unprecedented showering of cash upon many, many of the worlds big players, especially banks. For the Rothschilds, the shareholders and their shadow corporations, THIS is where real the money is at!

Although the proof is there that huge amounts of the public's money got absconded, well, you must realize that at such high levels, nobody ever caught or gets put away. Instead, the government is happy just handing out huge fines to feed a starving Washington. Billionaires nearly never go to jail, have you ever noticed that? For those who know the dubious history of the FR, and their cohorts in financial crimes, this should be no surprise.

*"People who will not turn a shovel of dirt on the project nor contribute a pound of material will collect more money from the United States than will the People who supply all the material and do all the work."* Henry Ford

## ROTHSCHILDS LITTLE HELPER

"By this method, government may secretly and unobserved, confiscate the wealth of the people. And not one man in one million will detect the theft".

Quote of John Maynard Keynes, architect of today's monetary policies. He is the most famous, influential and followed economist in America from 1933 until today. He was also a Fabian socialist.

With the above quote, how could anyone, anywhere, not interpret this as a criminal admission that our Federal Reserving Banking system is in reality an illegal banking scam? The same economist that America's elites have put so much confidence in since 1930, leading into today is still John Maynard Keynes. Keynes is the architect of America's official economic model, used right up till today. Hence, there is the problem. Finally, the establishment economists are beginning to admit that Keynesian economics has failed. Well, it failed for the everyman anyways. The wealthy thrive on the system. He was an ardent Fabian socialist, one-worlder, as well as a eugenics leader, serving on the Governing Council of the Eugenics Society from 1937-1944! This was/is social Darwinism, part and parcel to the Fabian belief system, as well as most all one world globalists as well. These types are nearly always of an atheistic bent, as well as having socialist underpinnings.

Keynes believed in spend and spend "monetary" policies, and of course, abhorred the gold standard that just might force him and his one world socialist elites to restrain from spending beyond the nations means! Most Presidents and Federal Reserve Board Chairman's have been using and following his economic policies since 1930. Keynesian policy fits perfectly into the globalist's goal of quietly bankrupting America in order to slowly take control in Fabian fashion. As you will see with much more proof herein, large amounts of what we see developing today in America and the world can be traced to the Rothschild Banking model to control all the world's money. Rothschild tactics have bankrupted many nations before in their history, but America will be their Grand Slam if they pull it off! Why would they want that? Monopolized global corporate ownership.

Whether one believes it or not, every single president, their running mates, and nearly everyone in the White House administrations have been Keynesians, going back since at least the Great Depression! Without it, Washington D.C. politicians would be held to be far more disciplined. So here we are today, after 80 years of Keynesian policies, BROKE! The rich are far richer though.

As soon as the un-Federal Reserve was established in 1913, it was the Rothschild's bought economist Keynes himself whom adopted the concept of eliminating gold as a standard of the monetary system of the nations of the world. His notion of a managed currency (that he sold F.D. Roosevelt on twenty years later) was an old socialist catch-all, espoused by the Fabians since the turn of the century. It is a fundamental concept of State-Socialism. It was during this period (1913) that Keynes adopted the concept of eliminating gold as a standard of the monetary system of the nations of the world. His notion of a managed currency (that he sold F.D. Roosevelt on twenty years later) was an old socialist catch-all, espoused by the Fabians since the turn of the century. It is a fundamental concept of State-Socialism.

## HOW ABOUT A GOLD STANDARD?

Some critics of the gold standard claim that it doesn't work and didn't prevent the busts from occurring throughout our countries history. I contend that although it is not perfect, their thesis is wrong and here is why: Our government's lack of spending disciplines, lack of a gold standard to peg the dollar at a fixed value, fueled by an un-Federal Reserve system that allows a lack of spending discipline, has taken us down the road we are in. These private bankers have abused both the fractional reserve system and the gold standard, thus giving license to create far, far more currency than the amount of gold held in reserves. Without gold backing (like we see today), we see what an extended period of a non-gold, abused monetary policy has gotten us! Inflation has decimated our dollar.

Many, not all, of our Founding Fathers had seen this evil system working in England under the Rothschild's and knew how usurious and destructive it would become if it was allowed to operate in the United States! In case you didn't know, only about 2 percent of all money accounted for in the U.S. economy is actual hold in your hand cash, the rest is on computer screens. Don't you feel better?

As you now know, Congress wrote within the U.S. Constitution Article 1, Section 8 requiring that the U.S. government would assume the sole responsibility to "PRINT, COIN ITS OWN MONEY, regulate the value thereof, and of foreign coin!" So here we are today contracting the job out to a private central bank, but let's go back a little in time… It all goes back to the Revolutionary War.

You won't find it in history books, but the primary reason for the Revolutionary War was a fight not just over the Souths banking and slave businesses, but a plan by the British and Rothschilds to control our entire banking system. Not usually known is that the Rothschild's paid for the war on England's side at no interest, in order to get their private banking system implanted into the new America! The Brit's wanted to take control of America as I explained in the chapter Schools of New World Order. But when the Brits lost the Revolutionary War, the US Government went ahead regardless and included the Rothschilds in establishing and participating in the funding's of what would become known as The First Bank of the United States, which ultimately was abolished. Years later, a Second Bank of the United States was tried, again partnered with the Rothschild's. Ever since they have been at the helm of our banking's in order to manipulate and control America's banking system.

# Planned Collapse of Americanism

The Rothschild's have tried very hard to hide their involvement in our money system but is there for all to see. It took them over a hundred years to really pull it off, but they did and still do. They own America! The whole $20 trillion in fact! Oh, that's right, they own most of the world as well. The Civil War between the South and the North was also largely for the same reason, using slavery as the ruse. The Rothschild's wanted desperately to monopolize on the souths new banking business.

After many economic booms and busts that were the fault of the state and national banks, banks rightfully got a bad rap, prompting the public to not trust banks nearly at all by 1907. Many of these banks practiced abusive forms of fractional reserve theft, as well as making far too many loans, had printed and lent out far too much money compared to the small gold reserves they had on hand. Obviously, the money lost much, or all, of its worth eventually through either rampant inflation and devaluation, robbing the bill holders of the full value of the money in their wallets!

These same banks who made loans when times were good would call in these same loans when people were struggling due to engineered crashes. Personal and business failures usually skyrocketed, bankruptcies went through the roof, causing farms and businesses to go bust. Even then, many of these predatory banks were Rothschild's connected banks in America and played a large part of the boom and bust economies of the US. Yes, the same homegrown scheme they mastered at their own Bank of England. It is widely acknowledged that the big banks lent far too money towards far too many railroad wildcat firms in the 1800's towards the building of new railroad lines that weren't really feasible in the first place, often running out of money, thereafter going broke. The banks often knew these risky bets by their customers were probably doomed for failure. This tactic is no accident, it has been done time and time again throughout history.

Going back to the beginnings of America, when wars need to be funded, the same techniques were used by the bankers, in particular by the Rothschild's and their American counterparts such as J.P. Morgan, teamed up with our own government. Often, they sold far more war bonds than there were funds to pay them back, as well as printing insane amounts of paper money which became nearly worthless. Some examples of this were the Continental bills which financed the American Revolution, and secondly, Lincolns Greenbacks to finance the Civil War. In both cases, the banks kept supplying far more notes, bonds and dollars than there was in gold available to back them up. This secret, yet purposeful plan by the government and banks was a hidden war tax. Those who bought the bonds and held Greenbacks or Continentals eventually realized that they couldn't buy near as much with those same bills. This was thievery in disguise in order to fund a war.

The Federal Reserve has now bankrupted the nation and the world in reality. Don't worry though, the FR's real owners and their banking crony's will be fine. You see, they already have made their money, so even if the news reports claim that the banks lost billions of dollars in the next crash, to them it won't really matter. The depositors and the government will again be on the hook, not them. They will have already taken their winnings for the last many years and are going to saddle Americans with the debt,

AGAIN. But due to friendly corporate laws, no one is ever prosecuted. It is evident that the Rothschild's cartel and power elites of the world aren't ready to let go of their crooked scheme of an un-Federal Reserve System. The big money crowd loves intentional inflation, market bubbles, the leveraging of it, the ability to harness it for their own gains. These elite bankers and Wall Streeter's are pawns upon society, just as a large number of the uber-rich are as well. It truly is a system for the elites that keeps on giving.

## THE EASIEST MONEY SCHEME EVER INVENTED

It was Robert B. Anderson, Treasury Secretary under Eisenhower, who truthfully admitted in 1959: *"When a bank makes a loan, it simply adds to the borrower's deposit account in the bank by the amount of the loan. The money is not taken from anyone else's deposits; it was not previously paid in to the bank by anyone. It's new money, created by the bank for the use of the borrower."*

Fractional reserve lending is another quick sleight of hand that nearly no one is aware of, or if they do, they really don't understand it. Here is an explanation of fractional reserve banking directly from the website of the Federal Reserve of New York. This tactic is used every day by the Federal Reserve as well as your bank. It gives you a good idea of how this crooked, yet legal scheme works. First off, this method is and inflationary, counterfeiting scheme to make the bankers richer.

Here's the actual wording in the Federal Reserve Newsletter to describe it: *"If the bank's reserve requirement is 10%, for example, a bank that receives a $100-dollar deposit, may lend out 90 dollars of that deposit. If the borrower then writes a check to someone who deposits the $90 dollars, the bank receiving that deposit can lend out $81 dollars. As this process continues, the banking system can expand the initial deposit of 100 dollars into a maximum of $1,000 dollars of money."* If that seems unbelievable, it's right on their website! It is not uncommon that the reserve requirement is only 5%, so in that case, the ability to multiply money in the economy is twice the 10% rate used above, allowing up to $20,000 of loans.

Going beyond the illegitimacy of this scheme, the government loves this process because it allows more and more unbacked money to float around and be used in the marketplace than what would normally be expected. Once these expanded amounts of loans are taken out to the marketplace by its borrowers, the money is usually spent to buy items like homes, cars, businesses and whatever. So here comes the part the government loves! The entire $20,000 (that grew from the original $1,000) of loaned money is just fiat money, backed and secured by guess what? No, not gold, but more debt! But you and I are on the hook for the debt. As insane as that sounds, it will only work for a finite time, until the Federal Reserve runs out of its options and creative abilities to fleece us. Money out of nothing! Henry Ford knew the dangers of the Federal Reserve...

*"People who will not turn a shovel of dirt on the project nor contribute a pound of material will collect more money from the United States than will the People who supply all the material and do all the work."* Henry Ford

Here's the other part that state governments just love. Example: At a 10% state tax rate, much or most of the $20,000 above is given over to the state tax authorities automatically upon the first go around of buying goods with the loaned money, often equaling $2,000.00! (except for real estate), which is twice the amount of the initial deposit!) Farther down the line, this money is multiplied many times by the innumerable amount of ensuing transactions out in the marketplace. Now get ready for this: 92%-96% of "money" in the system is not created by the government or the Federal Reserve, but in the banking system itself as a result of this system of ever growing transactions from just one original deposit of money. Every time the same money changes hands, the same money is taxed again and again, flowing into the Federal and State Governments coffers. They pay interest to the Federal Reserve for borrowing money they shouldn't have borrowed.

Imagine, using the above example, all this activity and taxing began from just a one-time $1,000 deposit! This is just one example why the average worker is suffering, drowning in debt with little buying power left. It is of course a little more complicated than this simple example, but the point of this book was to make it fairly easy to get the idea across. You may ask "why don't we print and regulate our own money and ditch the Federal Reserve. Well, for many years before 1913, when we ditched the Rothschild's, we had the longest run of economic growth ever! America printed its own money, we had independent state banks to regulate separately, we often didn't abuse fractional lending and we respected the gold standard. We really excelled. When the banks behaved, so did the economy. Unfortunately, most of our countries banking history shows an abuse of the banking system by those able to unjustly profit from it using deceitful tactics that often took the banks out, lost the customers deposits in the process.

The big bubble ready to explode upon this pumped up stock market in 2017 seems likely to a commercial credit bust. You see, the big banks such as J.P. Morgan are borrowing billions of dollars of bonds (government debt) at a rate never witnessed before from the unfederal reserve, then turn around and loan it out ten over! This has many technical implications that could turn dire with the slightest downturn.

As explained further in the Rothschild's section, once they brought their own Ponzi scheme banking of (the FR) to America, they created one boom and bust period after another, allowing them to extract large sums of assets (often gold) from the banking system just before it was purposely crashed. This is a technique that makes them abundantly wealthier every time they abuse the banking system and steal wealth through various slick techniques that the average citizen has no knowledge or understanding of.

**Quote; "Neither paper currency nor deposits have value as commodities, intrinsically a 'dollar' bill is just a piece of paper. Deposits are merely book entries." Modern Money Mechanics Workbook" Federal Reserve of Chicago, 1975**

One of the best full explanations on the whole issue of what money really is, how it is manipulated, its history and its fraudulence is explained in free videos created by Mike Maloney within his series entitled Hidden Secrets of Money on YouTube.

# ENDING THE FEDERAL RESERVE!

The following are facts to consider when it comes to ending the un-Federal Reserve.

1. Congress has the power to shut down the Federal Reserve any time that they would like. But right now, most of our politicians fully endorse the current system because of how they can use it to benefit the most powerfuls within the establishment, the corporations and so forth. Nothing is ever going to happen until the American people start demanding change.

2. The Federal Reserve has become so powerful that it is now known as "the fourth branch of government".

3. The greatest period of economic growth in U.S. history was in the late 1800's and other periods when there was no central bank.

4. The Federal Reserve was designed to be a perpetual debt machine. Under Admiralty Law, the British Royalty and Rothschild's sent us into a system that was intentionally designed to trap the U.S. citizens and government into a perpetual debt spiral from which it could never possibly escape. Since the Federal Reserve was established 100 years ago, the U.S. national debt has gotten more than 5000 times larger.

5. A permanent federal income tax was established the exact same year that the Federal Reserve was created. This was not a coincidence. In order to pay for WWI, as well as fund the coming socialist state as well as the huge government debt that the Federal Reserve would create, a federal income tax would be necessary. Here's the catch: From that point on American workers would be obligated to give up much of their sweat and toil in order to continue paying for the unaffordable, unrequired debts that the government and the elites would continue running up.

Even though at least for a few years America's gold reserves were held as collateral to the Rothschild's under this shady and misunderstood structuring of money policies, even those reserves could not even cover the debt being run up. So much money was printed that the gold was confiscated by FDR in order to pay the Rothschild's and central banking apparatus for the default on the debt that had been run up. This was the first bankruptcy the U.S. went through! Since that time, the gold standard has never been completely reinstated technically. The whole idea was to transfer labor and wealth from our pockets to the federal government, and from the federal government to the bankers.

6. The period of 1870 until 1913 (when there was no income tax and no Federal Reserve neither) was the greatest period of economic growth in U.S. history.

7. Today, the U.S. tax code is about 13 miles long.

8. From the time that the Federal Reserve was created until now, the U.S. dollar has lost 98 percent of its value.

9. From the time that President Nixon took us off the gold standard until now, the U.S. dollar has lost 83 percent of its value.

10. During the 100 years before the Federal Reserve was created, the U.S. economy rarely had any problems with inflation. But since the Federal Reserve was established, the U.S. economy has experienced constant and never-ending inflation.

11. In the century before the Federal Reserve was created, the average annual rate of inflation was about half a percent. In the century since the Federal Reserve was created, the average annual rate of inflation has been about 3.5 percent, often times far more and it eats away at your wages.

12. The Federal Reserve has stripped the middle class of trillions of dollars of wealth through the hidden tax of inflation.

13. The size of MI has nearly doubled since 2008 thanks to the reckless money printing of the Federal Reserve.

14. The Federal Reserve now knows that all their normal tricks aren't working anymore on the economy, and that real economic growth is now impossible to create.

15. The Federal Reserve has been consistently lying to us about the level of inflation in our economy. If the inflation rate was still calculated the same way that it was back when Jimmy Carter was president, the official rate of inflation would be somewhere between 8 and 10 percent today.

16. Since the Federal Reserve was created, there have been 18 distinct recessions or depressions: 1918, 1920, 1923, 1926, 1929, 1937, 1945, 1949, 1953, 1958, 1960, 1969, 1973, 1980, 1981, 1990, 2001, 2008.

17. Within 20 years of the creation of the Federal Reserve, the U.S. economy was plunged into the Great Depression.

18. The Federal Reserve created the conditions that caused the stock market crash of 1929. Past F.R. Chairman's now admit that the response by the Fed to that crisis made the Great Depression far worse than it should have been. Ben Bernanke, Alan Greenspan are two examples. The infamous and highly criticized past "easy money" policies of former Fed Chairman Alan Greenspan set the stage for the great financial crisis of 2008.

20. Without the Federal Reserve, the "subprime mortgage meltdown" would probably never have happened.

21. If you can believe it, there have been 10 different economic recessions since 1950. The Federal Reserve created the "dot-com bubble", the Federal Reserve created the "housing bubble" and now it has created the largest bond bubble in the history of the planet. Yet, the FR was sold as the answer to end recessions, depressions, promising a forever stable market!

Quote: Congressman Charles Lindbergh, 1921 "Under this Federal Reserve Act, panics are scientifically created." From his own book Economic Pinch, published 1923.

**The Federal Reserve is "the gift to the elites that keeps on giving"!**

**Deficits = intergenerational theft!**

# 17.

# The 1933 Bankruptcy of The United States

It's unusual when one comes across a statement such as above. It is something that most people would never think seriously about, for obvious reasons. But what if it was true? Your lifestyle would probably be much improved from what it is now! What I have reprinted below is a speech before Congress by Rep. James Traficant Jr. on the Floor on March 17/1993. Traficant was a character, and perhaps it could only be him that would be so boldly truthful in front of Congress. HERE IS HIS SPEECH!

**Representative James A. Traficant Jr. (D-OH)**

Congressional Record, March 17, 1993

Vol. 33. page H-1303

Introduction and text from James Traficant's book, *America's Last Minuteman*:

This speech has been written in several books. Many people still write to me asking for information and details about the speech.

Some are confused because the speech was actually inserted into the record with only the first part delivered on The House Floor.

Floor debate is usually limited. I had only one-half minute, thus, I made the first remarks, then asked unanimous consent to have my total, prepared speech inserted into the Record and it was.

I never read or gave a "prepared" speech on the Floor but did on occasion use the segment of Record known as "Extension of Remarks" when I needed more time to make my point.

The following is the complete text of my speech.

---

"Mr. Speaker, we are here now in chapter 11. Members of Congress are official trustees presiding over the greatest reorganization of any Bankrupt entity in world history, the U.S. Government. We are setting forth hopefully, a blueprint for our future. There are some who say it is a coroner's report that will lead to our demise.

It is an established fact that the United States Federal Government has been dissolved by the Emergency Banking Act, March 9, 1933, 48 Stat. 1, Public Law 89-719; declared by

President Roosevelt, being bankrupt and insolvent. H.J.R. 192, 73rd Congress session June 5, 1933 - Joint Resolution to Suspend the Gold Standard and Abrogate the Gold Clause dissolved the Sovereign Authority of the United States and the official capacities of all United States Governmental Offices, Officers, and Departments and is further evidence that the United States Federal Government exists today in name only.

The receivers of the United States Bankruptcy are the International Bankers, via the United Nations, the World Bank and the International Monetary Fund. All United States Offices, Officials, and Departments are now operating within a de facto status in name only under Emergency War Powers.

**The federal Government exist in name only.**

With the Constitutional Republican form of Government now dissolved, the receivers of the Bankruptcy have adopted a new form of government for the United States. This new form of government is known as a Democracy, being an established Socialist/Communist order under a new governor for America. This act was instituted and established by transferring and/or placing the Office of the Secretary of Treasury to that of the Governor of the International Monetary Fund. Public Law 94-564, page 8, Section H.R. 13955 reads in part: "The U.S. Secretary of Treasury receives no compensation for representing the United States?'

Gold and silver were such a powerful money during the founding of the United States of America, that the founding fathers declared that only gold or silver coins can be "money" in America.

**Only gold or silver!**

Since gold and silver coinage were heavy and inconvenient for a lot of transactions, they were stored in banks and a claim check was issued as a money substitute. People traded their coupons as money, or "currency."

Currency is not money, but a money substitute. Redeemable currency must promise to pay a dollar equivalent in gold or silver money. Federal Reserve Notes (FRNs) make no such promises and are not "money."

A Federal Reserve Note is a **debt obligation** of the federal United States government, not "money."

The federal United States government and the U.S. Congress were not and have never been authorized by the Constitution for the United States of America to issue currency of any kind, but only lawful money, gold and silver coin.

It is essential that we comprehend the distinction between real money and paper money substitute. One cannot get rich by accumulating money substitutes, one can only get deeper into debt.

**A Federal Reserve Note is not money!**

We the People no longer have any "money." Most Americans have not been paid any "money" for a very long time, perhaps not in their entire life.

Now do you comprehend why you feel broke? Now, do you understand why you are "bankrupt," along with the rest of the country?

Federal Reserve Notes (FRNs) are unsigned checks written on a closed account. FRNs are an inflatable paper system designed to create debt through inflation (devaluation of currency).

Whenever there is an increase of the supply of a money substitute in the economy without a corresponding increase in the gold and silver backing, inflation occurs.

Inflation is an invisible form of taxation that irresponsible governments inflict on their citizens. The Federal Reserve Bank who controls the supply and movement of FRNs has everybody fooled.

**Inflation is simply, just another tax!**

They have access to an unlimited supply of FRNs, paying only for the printing costs of what they need. FRNs are nothing more than promissory notes for U.S. Treasury securities (T-Bills) - a promise to pay the debt to the Federal Reserve Bank.

There is a fundamental difference between "paying" and "discharging" a debt. To pay a debt, you must pay with value or substance (i.e. gold, silver, barter or a commodity).

**They pay only the printing costs!**

With FRNs, you can only discharge a debt. You cannot pay a debt with a debt currency system. You cannot service a debt with a currency that has no backing in value or substance. No contract in Common law is valid unless it involves an exchange of "good & valuable consideration.

Unpayable debt transfers power and control to the sovereign power structure that has no interest in money, law, equity or justice because they have so much wealth already.

Their lust is for power and control. Since the inception of central banking, they have controlled the fates of nations.

The Federal Reserve System is based on the Canon law and the principles of sovereignty protected in the Constitution and the Bill of Rights.

In fact, the international bankers used a "Canon Law Trust" as their model, adding stock and naming it a "Joint Stock Trust." The U.S. Congress had passed a law making it illegal for any legal "person" to duplicate a "Joint Stock Trust" in 1873. The Federal Reserve Act was legislated post-facto (to 1870), although post-facto laws are strictly forbidden by the Constitution. [1:9:3]

The Federal Reserve System is a sovereign power structure separate and distinct from the federal United States government. The Federal Reserve is a maritime lender, and/or maritime insurance underwriter to the federal United States operating exclusively under Admiralty/Maritime law.

The lender or underwriter bears the risks, and the Maritime law compelling specific performance in paying the interest, or premiums are the same. Assets of the debtor can also be hypothecated (to pledge something as a security without taking possession of it.) as security by the lender or underwriter.

The Federal Reserve Act stipulated that the interest on the debt was to be paid in gold. There was no stipulation in the Federal Reserve Act for ever paying the principle.

**"No stipulation to pay principle."**

Prior to 1913, most Americans owned clear, allodial title to property, free and clear of any liens or mortgages until the Federal Reserve Act (1913) "Hypothecated" all property within the federal United States to the Board of Governors of the Federal Reserve, -in which the Trustees (stockholders) held legal title. The U.S. citizen (tenant, franchisee) was registered as a "beneficiary" of the trust via his/her birth certificate.

In 1933, the federal United States hypothecated all of the present and future properties, assets and labor of their "subjects," the 14th Amendment U.S. citizen, to the Federal Reserve System.

In return, the Federal Reserve System agreed to extend the federal United States corporation all the credit "money substitute" it needed.

**Our private property is now collateral.**

Like any other debtor, the federal United States government had to assign collateral and security to their creditors as a condition of the loan. Since the federal United States didn't have any assets, they assigned the private property of their" economic slaves", the U.S. citizens as collateral against the unpayable federal debt.

They also pledged the unincorporated federal territories, national parks forests, birth certificates, and nonprofit organizations, as collateral against the federal debt. All has already been transferred as payment to the international bankers.

Unwittingly, America has returned to its pre-American Revolution, feudal roots whereby all land is held by a sovereign and the common people had no rights to hold allodial title to property.

Once again, We the People are the tenants and sharecroppers renting our own property from a Sovereign in the guise of the Federal Reserve Bank. We the people have exchanged one master for another.

**Tenants and share croppers!**

This has been going on for over eighty years without the "informed knowledge" of the American people, without a voice protesting loud enough. Now it's easy to grasp why America is fundamentally bankrupt.

**Why don't more people own their properties outright?**

Why are 90% of Americans mortgaged to the hilt and have little or no assets after all debts and liabilities have been paid? Why does it feel like you are working harder and harder and getting less and less?

We are reaping what has been sown, and the results of our harvest is a painful bankruptcy, and a foreclosure on American property, precious liberties, and a way of life.

Few of our elected representatives in Washington, D.C. have dared to tell the truth.

**"We are reaping what has been sown."**

The federal United States is bankrupt. Our children will inherit this unpayable debt, and the tyranny to enforce paying it. America has become completely bankrupt in world leadership, financial credit and its reputation for courage, vision and human rights. This is an undeclared economic war, bankruptcy, and economic slavery of the most corrupt order!

**"Wake up America! Take back your Country."**

THE ABOVE SPEECH MADE QUITE A STIR INSIDE CONGRESS THAT DAY! IF TRAFICANT HAD AN HOUR OF ALLOTED TIME, HE COULD HAVE LAID OUT ALL THE SPECIFIC FEDERAL HISTORICAL LAWS AND ORDERS THAT SUBSTANTIATE HIS CASE EVEN MORE FULLY. IT IS LIKELY THAT THE FULL TRUTH WOULD LIKELY HAVE CAUSED HIM EJECTED FROM THE ROOM! YOU, THE READER MAY NOT UNDERSTAND HIS CLAIMS, AND THAT IS UNDERSTANDABLE. THIS IS THE KIND OF STUFF THAT IS DANGEROUS TO PRINT!

TRAFICANT'S SHOCKING CLAIMS SEEM PREPOSTEROUS. HOW COULD HE ACTUALLY GET UP THERE AND SPOUT THIS SILLINESS? JAMES TRAFICANT WASN'T, AND STILL ISNT, THE ONLY ONE WHO CAN CITE THE DOZENS OF ACTUAL LEGAL PRECEDENTS THAT BACK UP THIS THEORY! PERHAPS IF IT WASN'T SO PROVABLE IT WOULD HAVE DIED LONG AGO, YET THERE ARE STILL MILLIONS WHO BELIEVE THE THEORY TO NOT BE JUST THEORY.

THERE IS A LOT THERE TO CONSIDER SERIOUSLY. THE FEDERAL RESERVE DOES OWN EVERY ONE OF US AS CHATTEL TO THE INTERNATIONAL BANKERS. THE BANK OF INTERNATIONAL SETTLEMENTS CONTROLS THE ENTIRE BANKING SYSTEM LIKE A GODFATHER. THE BIS IS OWNED BY THE ROTHSCHILD'S. NEED MORE PROOF? IT ALL STARTED THERE.

JAMES TRAFICANT WAS FAMOUS FOR NOT PLAYING GAMES IN CONGRESS. HE MADE QUITE A REPUTATION OF SPEAKING THE UNABATED TRUTHS DURING HIS ENTIRE POLITICAL CAREER. TO EXPLAIN AND PROVE EACH POINT AND THIS ENTIRE CHAPTER WOULD TAKE ANOTHER BOOK, SERIOUSLY.

Believe it or not, I try not to be a conspiracy buff. Only after countless hours of slow (some would call "boring") study did I come to the conclusion that Traficant's claim is valid enough to seriously be considered, because if one goes deep into America's deep history, there are tons more facts to back up this fact! America IS a corporation. I can hear many of you laughing out loud about now. I agree that most of these types of claims are bogus. But this is one that been around for some time and has a serious following for good reasons I believe. Since it seems so unlikely to be true, nobody wants to believe it!

Governments are notorious for not telling the public what they need to hear for chance of discovery of how they have been robbed or lied! So many times, the truth is right in front of you to view but you never saw it. My forthcoming follow-up book will delve into this fascinating story to much greater degree!

The big state must protect its secrets and it abilities to fabricate lies about how our government really operates. Hitler knew this fact. When Hitler told a lie, it was usually a huge one. Hitler repeatedly said the following:

*"Make the lie big, make it simple, keep saying it, and eventually they will believe it."*
Once learning how the Un-Federal Reserve works, this quote of Hitler's really proves just

how gullible the voters were in 1913 when the Federal Reserve Act was allowed to become law. After that, America did not really own its money anymore!

*"Nothing in this world, nothing, works the way you think it does. There's always more to the story." – Jordan Maxwell*

Should we give our leaders the benefit of the doubt? Should we believe the political leaders who disparaged Traficant and his assertions? Have their disparagement of Traficant validated them one little bit since the day of the above indictments made by Traficant in front of congress?

They had so much to lose if the big lie came out! And today the situation is perhaps too far along to fix without economic mayhem for all Americans!!

A few years later Traficant was expelled from Congress on made up bribery charges and sent to prison. Traficant was just too honest, and his congressional district loved him! They always get rid of the exposers for they are dangerous to the deep state, international bankers, and those who don't play ball with the statists in Congress! I suggest readers watch the film below, Congressman of Crimetown.

Van Susteren, Greta (2009-09-10). *"Exclusive: Traficant – 'I Was a Target. ... I Must Have Been Doing Something Right'"*. Fox News. *Retrieved 2009-11-13.*

*Buy American: The Untold Story of Economic Nationalism – Dana Frank – Google Books*. Books.google.ca. *Retrieved 2013-03-27.***Jump up** ^ Milan Simonich, Pittsburgh Post-Gazette, Rep. James Traficant: 'He's perceived ... to have almost magical powers', April 12, 2002

*Traficant: The Congressman of Crimetown, 2015, Documentary film*

# 18

# HOW TREATIES TRUMP THE CONSTITUTION

*"Illegal we do immediately. The unconstitutional takes a little longer."*
*Henry Kissinger.*

Kissinger was at least honest. One of the main weapons the world globalist/corporate bodies have used to accomplish their goals of world domination has been to disguise trade and environmental treaties as just a way to improve trade, create more jobs at home, and maybe even help to protect the environment. Since the international corporations are onboard with the U.N. goals of a one world corporate government, they also know full well that provisions in such lengthy bills contain thousands of pages of legalese that easily escape close inspections. There is always a plethora of exceptions, vague wordings ripe for interpretation and loopholes galore. That being said, not one person in a million would have the time, aptitude, or even care to read it! As the old saying goes, "The devil is in the details."

President Trump knows this is all true. He is fighting hard to reverse and at least renegotiate the terrible treaties that were assembled using a thought process called "globalism" and putting America secondly! Joe citizen has been told little if anything about these immensely important treaties that have been drawn up and foisted upon unsuspecting hard-working Americans. Americans just know something has been wrong with the job situation for many years, and realizes it is getting worse year after year. This silence on the airwaves has been perpetrated on purpose because if Americans really understood these treaties, and how their lives are actually being sold down the river of globalism, these unconstitutional treaties could never have passed!

Today, the top 200 corporations are bigger than the combined economies of 182 countries and have twice the economic influence than 80 per cent of all humanity. It is this unbelievable power that makes it possible them to virtually dictate to the world's leaders how markets are going to be built or changed with their interest's paramount, and all these so called "free trade treaties" are a big part of their end game towards total control.

Going back to the real beginnings of these free treaties was NAFTA in 1992. And it was Henry Kissinger who was the primary defender and force behind the treaty that was to begin the corporatist takeover of the American and world economies. Make no mistake, Kissinger knew that this was the impetus for a one world order. Kissinger was trained by Mr. One Worlder... Zbigniew Brzezinski, on the "tricks and trades" of the new order way back around 1970. Brzezinski was the water boy for Rockefeller. Prior to NAFTA passage, it was Mr. Kissinger, then a prominent leader of the CFR/Trilateral, Illuminati's, and nearly every other major one world organization whom wrote an out of character yet truthful quote in the L.A. Times, prior to the passage of NAFTA. Quote: *"What Congress will have before it is not a conventional trade agreement, but the architecture of a new international system...a first step toward a New World Order."* Henry Kissinger

This was 1970, not 2017 yet no one really listened or understood what he meant by that statement. For once, Kissinger was telling the truth. Something he rarely does.

American's have short memories and attention spans. NAFTA immediately stole millions of American jobs and was set up by the global elites. We were supposed to compete with Mexicans who work for Mexico's .89 cents an hour minimum wage! How could we compete with a country that doesn't offer unemployment insurance, health insurance, labor laws, child labor rules, unions, nor have environmental laws? And permits? Fuhgeddaboudit! Presidential candidate Ross Perot ran on a platform to stop NAFTA, but the elites stopped him dead in his tracks twice. This was the beginnings of the end for American wage equality.

NAFTA has failed miserably as far as American jobs go, creating a huge outflux of jobs to Mexico that never have come back home. According to prior AFL-CIO Pres. John Sweeney, *"The trade deficit with Canada and Mexico ballooned to twelve times what it was pre-NAFTA, reaching $111 billion dollar in 2004 alone!* Obviously, jobs went elsewhere. This is free-trade? Companies such as Carrier, Black & Decker, Chrysler, Stanley and Callaway Golf have all left America in large part. Can we blame these companies this late in the game? They can hire Mexican workers for $6.00 per day and leave behind the $25 to 34.00 per hour American worker.

The TPP will only amplify these problems tenfold. NAFTA is a lesson of history that proves the lie of globalism and "free trade." Trade deficits spiraled out of control within one year after NAFTA'S implementation. We can remember Pres. Candidate Ross Perot warning of a giant "sucking sound" that sent millions of American jobs to Mexico during that time. These deals are always bad for America! Currently we have the TPP, TISA GATT, NAFTA, SPP, CATFA, PNTR, TAFTA as well as several more un-free trade treaties working against the autonomy of the world's countries, their sovereignties, and decimating the wages of the developed world's citizens for the benefit of the supranational corporations. Luckily, President Trump will renegotiate NAFTA.

## THE TRANS PACIFIC PARTNERSHIP

The TPP agreement would create an economic union of 11 countries from the Pacific Rim; Singapore, Brunei, New Zealand, Chile, Australia, Peru, Vietnam, Malaysia, Mexico, Canada and Japan. Below, please see just how, if ever passed, this could be the lynchpin to the new world order and their dream creating a worldwide trade system wherein anything goes, especially screwing over the consumers across the globe.

Bill Moyers says the new TPP is an *"Investors Rights Agreement, not a free trade agreement."* I wholeheartedly agree!

I might add to that: The TPP is not a traditional "Trade Agreement". It is a Bill of Rights for the Corporations! Hillary calls this the "gold standard."

According to President Obama, the TPP is *"The most progressive trade deal in history."* Well, I suppose President Obama was telling the truth, but like so much coming out of Washington D.C. today, it wasn't conveyed in an honest way that most of us could understand its implications. Remember, it's all about words and symbols! When the President or any progressive uses the world 'progressive', most don't comprehend the actual meaning of that word, but if you've been reading this book, you know that word is code for "socialist/communism". He didn't mean good for historic America at all!

The TPP will be good for the .001%, aka the global corporatists, the hugely wealthy one worlder's whom want to limit competition, get away with anything they deem necessary to maximize profits, that is for sure. President Obama pushed through a "Fast Track" trick to get TPP into the pipeline early in the game, bypassing Congress. What else is new? The deal is a stealthy delivery mechanism that could not survive public scrutiny, and the pact aims to severely curtail government authority at all levels.

Many criticize that the document is 5,544 pages long, and so full of technical fine print legalese, so hard to understand, full of confusing open-ended rhetoric, that eyes tend to just glaze over. It is a great read before you go to bed I suppose. And it great statist fashion, it was purposely constructed to peruse in that fashion. And besides, the politicians responsible for signing really important bills like this don't really have much say on the matter, which I explained. Pres. Obama signed the pre-agreement with the other nations and indicated that only a straight up vote on the final draft would suffice its passage. No changes whatsoever, all or nothing. Isn't that nice he did that for us? It made the process so much more "streamlined", just as we could imagine him saying in his slick political talk!

According to one U.S. News and World Report, Economic Intelligence section:

*"The TPP is written by lobbyists, for the legacy industries, and they are using it to limit their exposure to competition in the marketplace. This sure sounds like global monopoly. There is a broad range of special interest giveaways. It contains:*

*Provisions that would extend patent protections while restricting governments from negotiating lower prices on pharmaceuticals.*

*Provisions that would privilege major banks and financial institutions over credit unions and the emerging sector of public banks.*

*Provisions that would disadvantage organic farmers and others who adopt safer and more environmentally-sound agricultural practices. No longer would it be required to label dangerous genetically modified foods. We would lose all regulations and labeling. No longer subject to state or federal legislation or FDA or USDA oversight. Say goodbye to having a choice in the choice of what food qualities to choose from*

*Provisions that would ban local and state governments from extending preferences to locally produced goods such as foods and other services. No longer would "Buy America" be allowed. Local employers could no longer be supported this way. Neither could local farmers.*

*Provisions that would extend the dominance of coal and oil, as well as hinder alternative energy producers by blocking regulations and deployments of smart grids and other infrastructure."*

Governments could be sued for not conforming to the new rules within the TPP! From article "Obama's Pacific Trade Deal is No Deal at All." David Broadwin, Co-founder and board member of American Sustainable Business Council.

A joint analysis by Sierra Club, World Wildlife Fund and the National Resources Council came to a conclusion that the TPP does away with a robust system for addressing environmental rules, fearing that it will only offer up watered-down versions.

*"The TPP raises significant concerns about citizen's freedoms of expression, due process, innovation, the future of the internet's global infrastructure, patents, and the right of sovereign nations to develop policies and laws that best meet their domestic priorities. In sum, the TPP puts at risk some of the most fundamental rights that enable access to knowledge for the world's citizens. It's a powerful trade deal that locks out all public input of the drafting process."* Source: The Electric Frontier Foundation.

Elizabeth Warren (D-Mass) proclaims: ***"The TPP nearly makes it impossible to enforce rules that protect hardworking families, but very easy to enforce rules that favor multinational corporations"***

WikiLeaks founder, Julian Assange says that the TPP's companion treaty called TISA, if implemented as well, would essentially set up open borders!

Yet, it was the UN's top trade official, Alfred D. Zayas made an out of character comment about the TPP and TIP agreements and the effects that their implementations will have on the populations of the world.

***"It will bring a dystopian future wherein which the corporations and non-democratically elected governments call the shots." Alfred D. Zayas***

Luckily again, President Trump has vowed to cancel TPP, or just go the way of separate agreements for each country involved. This sounds like just too much common sense for many in Washington politics! Especially for those and their big corporations who have much to lose if the President is successful!

# 19

# ILLEGALS & THE NORTH AMERICAN UNION

*"Get all the debt up, move jobs abroad. Instead of re-engineering your skills, we're going to dumb down America so that the middle class will disappear".*

An early warning about these free-trade agreements voiced by Katherine Austin Fitts, Fmr. Asst. Secretary of HUD for Bush I, 1995. She knows the real globalist plans.

Within the next few years, the long awaited, largely hidden, upcoming North American Union was expected to be approved, but it seems that newly elected President Trump will likely reverse it as he had promised. But it tells a whole story. The open border policies we have noticed in recent years along the Mexican border have verifiably been purposely perpetuated by the globalist inclined Presidents Carter, Bush and Obama administrations in order to push forward the idea of the North American Union, connecting both nations with seamless borders.

The Center for Immigration Studies reported that *"government data shows that since 2000, all of the net gain in number of workers (ages 16-65) holding a job has to gone to immigrants (legal and illegal)."*

Yet the far left makes the communist argument that if we don't continue this trend of welcoming anybody and everybody, we are racist! One thing becomes clear...The Democrats want illegal immigrants to vote while the Republicans want illegal immigrants for cheap labor. Neither side of the political isle REALLY want the illegals gone unless it begins to hurt their votes or profits depending on the party! In order to restore Americanism, American jobs, balance America's budgets and keep the American dreams alive, we must change the argument that claims we must take in and pay for the 12 million illegals already here, for they don't pay into the system anywhere near what they cost taxpayers (covered much more inside the chapter 'Neediest Suffer the Most".

Meanwhile we still have a V.A. scandal wherein the VA cancelled some forty thousand tests and required treatments to veterans with cancer and other diseases. A second set of appointment books was devised, thereby missing scrutiny. One VA Hospital in Arizona alone was found to have lost perhaps hundreds of veterans who were put on a phony "wait list" that never really existed in reality. Yet at the same time, in 2014 Arizona alone spent $700 million on illegal aliens. Who comes first we should ask our government servants? Billions of dollars are spent on illegals while full citizens die for lack of care. In the meantime, hundreds of billions of healthcare dollars have been spent on illegal immigrants whom because of the very nature of how they came here, have no business being here. The libtards justify the inconsistency out of compassion? It is refreshing to have a President who has made this a top priority and done something about it finally! Just like so many other issues brought to the table by the party that has had 8 years to fix any one of them, they lay it on Trump as though the many ignored problems have been his doing. Such hypocracy! Did you know that the big issue of separating illegal immigrant children from their parents when caught was created 30 years ago? Yet the Main Street news sources made it sound like this was a new problem created by this new Republican President! This is why we must pay attention to the truth and history.

All this talk of racism this, racism that is largely promoted by far-leftist socialists who want to increase the divisions in America. These know that many of their offensive and slanderous threats are very difficult if not impossible for the average debate opponent to deal with. After all, once you are accused of something, it is YOU that must prove you are not guilty of the accusation. Most will avoid such confrontation completely, even allowing the other side to win the argument! Politicians shake in their boots if anyone decries them as being racist. This is Marxism 101, and Americans are good people who don't know how to deal with this type of clever and unfair debate tactic that is so effective. Infamous Marxist agitators such as Saul Alinsky, Bill Ayres and near all far left activists know this smear tactic and it is standard practice in their playbook. Yet so many viewers of news fall for these clever deceivers who use the tactic. And yet all through President Obama's 8 years we witnessed racism rising to levels not seen the 1960's, while divisions across America hasn't been bad since the Civil War!

Border agents have had their hands tied behind their backs, releasing 90% of detainees and wishing them well. Tens of thousands of illegals are now being housed in hide-away modern temporary facilities with air conditioning in border cities along Texas, Colorado and California borders before being processed for near guaranteed entry into the U.S. You won't know this listening to the Mainstreet news sources though. This has been a hush-hush project but is a red flag as to how serious the elites are in taking forth the agenda of mass assimilation of cultures. Standard practice for the border agents is to feed, clothe, shower and offer directions as to where to go for welfare and other generous government programs that are availed. President Trump has doubled down on border security by allowing border agents to do their job better without their hands being tied up behind their backs as they were during Pres. Obama's reign.

Most now know that our border states in particular have experienced record numbers of drug cartel killings, American citizens killings, billions of dollars of illegal dangerous drugs, the importation of MS-13 hard core gangs, rapes and other societal plagues coming across our border for the last many years. Little covered is the situation of cartels training and cooperating with ISIS members 4 miles from American border near El Paso, TX. Yet border patrol agents are often outnumbered, outgunned by the cartels, often causing the agents to just pull back and let it them go along their way. Unfortunately, this policy of easy release followed President Obama's orders given to Jeh Johnson shortly after the president assuming office in 2013. DHS docs. released in 2013 made a majority of illegals immune to arrest and relegates border agents to the role of social workers. They cannot even deport or detain without approval from top officials in Washington as reported by Breitbart on 6/30/12, editor Brandon Darly. The docs. do not specifically order agents to allow illegals to freely pass into the U.S., but rules clearly say, "don't waste your time" because the illegal assuredly won't be put into detention, sent back, or deported. With these policies in effect, why wouldn't the official rates on apprehensions be low? While glowing stats show a decrease along heavily guarded sections, there are not stats for where fencing just stops with nothing beyond but grass!

Even Border Agents such as Mike Scioli are quoted "Border fences are like speed bumps in the desert". Del Rio, Texas Border Patrol Chief Randy Hill admitted that even the new fencing will slow illegals crossers only by minutes". He didn't say stop them, just slow them a bit. Even the triple fencings along the most heavily travelled sections don't. The Migrant Policy Institute found that 97% of the persistent immigrants do succeed after several tries. According to Breitbart, TX. 1/15/15. Farmers and homeowners along the border have had to deal with new illegals crossing their private lands. There have been dozens of verified killings of landowners by illegals and drug runners as well as thousands of others along the border in general.

Tim Foley of Border Recon leads a group of patriots whom privately monitor the Mexican border. He admitted that once these illegals cross our southern border, they have more rights than American citizens. In order to avoid false persecution, his types of independent patriot American citizen groups must film every move, lest be falsely incriminated by illegals who would love to claim they were mistreated or falsely apprehended and rewarded with financial rewards for the claim (and have been successful in some cases).

Unfortunately, under Obama, those caught crossing the border had a high probability of staying in the U.S. indefinitely if they played the game right. Only those with bad rap sheets are likely to be sent back in short measure. The others, if they get to know how to work the current system are likely to eventually receive welfare, free schooling, lunches, food stamps, medical care, home care, college, child care, private English lessons and the list goes on. These even are likely to receive a free plane ticket or bus ride to the city of their choice. I already hear cries from liberals that "Illegals cannot get welfare". But as I said there are ways if you know how to work the system. We have millions who have shown they know how.

It is reported that because of our open border policies, drug trades account for at least $60 billion dollars a year moving across the border for profit. There are many drug cartel who make billions for themselves from this trade. Even quite a few cops and politicians on both sides make out. It is a well-known and verified fact that our own CIA plays a part in the illegal drugs business in Mexico and around the world, but that's for another book. And our top leaders of Washington and law enforcement are all too aware of the documented long running plan to merge the U.S., Mexico and Canada into the North American Union within a few years. Some surmise at this point that America's immigration heads figure *"what difference will all this worry about the border thing mean in the long run? Besides, we have the North American Union coming soon!"* We must remember, this dismantling of borders is the long-term plan by the progressives in both political parties in order to get their new one world order into reality. Hopefully, the new President Trump White House administration won't be complicit in their borderless plans

Unless President Trump overturns the North American Union pre-agreement for a borderless length of Mexico/American stretch, we are in deep trouble soon. Even if Trump does in fact turn back the clock on this terrible agreement does not mean that the following administration doesn't reimplement it at a later date! This is what I talk about

# Planned Collapse of Americanism

when I talk of how the Fabian plan works slow, even allowing setbacks at times. They use patience. This plan has quietly been in the works since at least 2005 when President Bush, Mexican President Vicente Fox and Canada's P.M. Paul Martin met in Waco Texas with the Council on Foreign Relations (no surprise), the Mexican Council on Foreign Relations, and the Canadian Council of Chief Executives, and there have been subsequent meetings in order to coordinate their plans. The plan, once finally implemented, is intended firstly to circumvent the three countries legislatures, their Constitutions and end sovereignty. Secondly, once accomplished, it would create a borderless North America, including Canada as well. All would essentially become a global corporate controlled continent without barriers to trade or capital inflows for business giants. The America we remember would be no more than a shadow of the past. Avoiding this outcome is likely only secure until the end of President Trumps reign as President of The United States though.

Disturbingly, America's access to vital resources, especially to water and Canada's oil, will also be endangered. Secretly, over 300 initiatives have been crafted in order to create the impossible job of coordinating the continents policies on energy, food, drugs, security, immigration, manufacturing, the environment and public health, as well as militarizing the 3 nations for enforcement, aka the world army! Part of the agreements is a provisions for a possible false flag event that crosses all 3 borders, calling for emergency assimilation aka a North American Union. This would follow the modus operandi of the elites. By the way, under this agreement, if you support your local businesses you could face a fine.

As a final note, if you aren't convinced of the immense dangers that these treaties engender, and the end game, please read the following proof of their long overdue plans within a 1996 United Nations report entitled "Our Global Neighborhood publication (420 pgs.), it outlines a plan for "global governance." It was called during the **1998 Conference on World Governance** for the purpose of submitting to the world the necessary treaties & agreements by the year 2000. You can check it out. Yes, they're a little late with the end game, but please notice that the report stresses heavily on "treaties and agreements" that tear down sovereignties of nations or their ability to create or write their own individual laws that protect their own people's interests! One source: Chronological View of the New World Order by D.L. Cuddy, PhD.

# AGENDA 21 & POPULATION CONTROL LIES

The global warming scare is nothing less than a scheme by the wealth-transfer specialists to move money from the middle and upper classes to the uber-elites of a new world order, aka a global domination of the world's economy, the demotion of the earths citizenry to become nothing more than the welfare clients of the international oligarchy.

In order to believe or not believe in the theory of man-made global warming or other claims of man being the primary causes of anything related to the health of the planet and peoples, one must dig a bit further than the main street media's 30 second blips warning of global catastrophe. One must go beyond the praising's of Al Gores Inconvenient Truths propaganda or the rantings of other leftist political figures screaming "the sky is falling" for there is much proof that going far back, global warming was fake.

In 1969, the UN introduced the beginnings of what become began Agenda 21. Unbelievably, a large portion of the world are still unaware of this global plan. At first glance, it sounds so innocuous, calling out for better living conditions, health conditions, education and so forth around the earth within a coordinated effort of all nations under the umbrella of a kind and caring 'United Nations". Oh, isn't that wonderful! Truth be known, the U.N. is a world body of socialist one worlders whom want to actually run the entire planet! If that didn't sound scary enough, it is now realized that our very way of life would be turned upside down and thrown into a Marxist society with complete government control over every aspect of human life. Agenda 21's main claim is that the peoples of the earth are ruining its ecosystem, creating too much Co2 gases and making it unfit for human survival, and survival of earth as well, unless we completely change our way of life and habits, according to the U.N. plan and directives. Plans are to destroy the industrial complex.

In 1972 (when global cooling was their mantra) there was the Earth Summit, which was the launch pad for what would become "Sustainable Development." Since then, there have been many follow up Agenda 21 summits, highlighted by the Rio Earth Summit in 1992, being the largest and most telling of their plans. What came out of that summit was an innocuously named 40-part, 27 principle document. The tenor of which these are summed up as a call for international government, which defers to poorer states at the cost of richer ones. Accordingly, Agenda 21 writings show it to be against private property ownership, (a hallmark of communism) single family homes, fireplaces, air conditioners, private insurance, car ownership, appliances, individual travel choices, privately owned farms, and much more. Reading the agreement(s) clearly state that nearly all human movements are to be monitored, forcing us all to live according to the U.N.s new world utopia. We could likely live in a world of community rituals instead of churches, riding bicycles instead of cars, human rights instead of religion?

Human populations are to be severely reduced to save the environment, while private property rights are cancelled, individual rights giving way to the needs of communities, needs of the community determined by the governing body, people are to be packed into human settlements, islands of human habitation situated close to employment centers and transportation. The main blame is put upon the capitalist system, the more developed countries and peoples who just consume too much of everything. Furthermore, is to pit the poor against the better off, disparage the "rising consumption of the rich" as well as forcing PPP's (Private Public Partnerships partnerships), where the government decides which companies and corporations are allowed to stay in business and receive special tax breaks, grants, and the governments powers of Eminent Domain and Government monopolies. These are all the tenets of Marxism. Source: Canada Free Press: Sustainability: The new Code-Word for Stealth Marxism/ Kelly O'Connell, 7/1/12.

By 1976, the United Nations was ready to articulate a general policy on land use. This policy is stated in the final report of the first U.N. Conference on Human Settlements (HABITAT I), held in Vancouver, British Columbia in 1976.

According to the new policy within the document, the <u>U.N. asserts in loud Marxist terms that land is not to be held privately</u> before long. **This objective has now been codified into international law in the form of the Convention on Biological Diversity, its actual wordings as seen below:**

*"Land...cannot be treated as an ordinary asset, controlled by individuals and subject to the inefficiencies and pressures of the free market. Private land ownership is also a principal instrument of accumulation and concentration of wealth and therefore to social injustice; if unchecked, it may become a major obstacle in the planning and implementation of development schemes. The provision of decent dwellings and healthy conditions for the people can only be achieved if land is used in the interest of society as a whole."* Source; U.N. Conf. on Human Settlements (Habitat 1), Vancouver B.C. May 31 to June 11, 1976. Preamble to Agenda 21, item 10 of the Conference Report.

The U.S. has signed onto these principles and has enlisted over 700 U.S. cities to go along, folks! This type of global plan could not be implemented without a large and well-funded group pushing through its priorities. For that, Agenda 21 has the International Councils of Local Environmental Initiatives (ICLEI), already deeply ingrained in America today, and part of the United Nations. The organization claims it is the "domestic leader in on climate adaptation, sustainable development on the local level."

The environmental cry is a ruse to create such a big problem, that no less than a world effort is required to fix it. Ah yes, a world government is needed to handle it! ANY QUESTIONS?

Since its inception, nearly all recent Presidents have signed on. All of the environmental laws, protocols, green planning and such is largely pushed by Agenda 21. That all sounds like good stuff, so why fight that you might say? It is a large part of a long-term plan by the one world globalists to use 'environmentalism" as a ruse to place more and more power onto the states of the world. These impositions of thousands of new environment laws came out of the Rio Summit of 2013. In 2015, Agenda 21 has become Agenda 2030, which is the prior on steroids and fast track

Pres. Teddy Roosevelt's initiation of National Parks was a great idea since we all want to protect our nations beautiful and critical lands. But the left has used a good idea as the springboard into world governance. UNESCO has already designated 47 U.N. Biosphere projects locations around the world, covering 70 million acres. This designation allows the U.N. to bypass U.S. Congressional authority to manage the Federal Reserves in the United States! The Wildlands Project tells how most of the land is to be set aside for non-humans. This is already law. Irregardless of protocol or the Constitutional requirement, At the direction of President Carter, the U.S. State Department entered into an agreement with UNESCO (M) in 1979 to launch a U.S. Man and the Biosphere Program. Congress was not consulted, nor was any state legislature consulted, as 47 U.N. Biosphere reserves were quietly designated in the United States!!

The land use philosophy of the non-American world was fully incorporated into international law and norms, with the support of the United States government. These sites are already designated as World Heritage sites, and as such are off bounds unless allowed by government. Upon their decision, all of it could be closed off at the drop of a dime by the United Nations. Approval of the U.S. Congress is not required for the U.N. or any one of its programs to take control of these lands! This includes our National Parks and Forests, wetlands. Think…Yellowstone Park, Statue of Liberty, Independence Hall, Monticello, Great Smokey Mountains, Grand Canyon and all unique American Landmarks! All under ultimate control by the U.N. Yes, you read that right. (Infowars, Spy Witness News, 2009.) With these tactics, the U.S. Constitution is not a problem for the globalist inspired, democrat and republican politicians and presidents to deal with! This is INTERNATIONAL LAW (with big important letters) we're talking about! Treaties override the U.S. Constitution after all. Today, the world even has an International Court of Justice through the U.N. (a precursor to world law).

According to Agenda 21, it only allows for small apartments (high density housing) where 100-200 sq. ft. is predicted to be an average apartment size. People valuable to the state will of course receive better treatment. The plan requires a reduction from 7 billion peoples down to around 2 billion, as has been openly confirmed by many of the U.N.'s members and one world devotees. I guess we are going to overrun our resources according to their reports. Those U.N. people and all of the "caring" one worlders are really just looking out for you, so relax! Does it ever seem that those who call themselves "progressives" are actively wage war on progress? In the environmental globalist's terms… "Sustainability" is un-talk for central planning, global government and un-growth.

All of these measures work together to achieve the original goal of the Man and the Biosphere Program: to conserve most of the planet for wildlife, forcing people into "sustainable communities." This objective has now been codified into international law in the form of the Convention on Biological Diversity.

So-called "progressives" actively war on progress. For example, Deanna Archuleta, Obama's Deputy Assistant Secretary of the Interior told an audience in Nevada: "You will never see another federal dam." But wait, isn't hydropower renewable energy? It doesn't used oil or coal. It generates energy from naturally flowing water! What could be more renewable than that? Progressives are at war against mass prosperity.

Multiplied, such insane policies adds costs for nearly everything you must purchase, including water in this case. There are now thousands of insane and costly edicts contained within nearly all products produced across the plant. Some justified, but most not. We all want to do the right thing for the environment, and we can always find some reasonable and actual improvements to products to improve their safety, reduce highly dirty emissions, but we had most of those handled as far back as the 1990's.

These, the unleashed governmental, environmental powers behind the New World Order, the maniacal and high profiteering 'green' scam artists, these know of "no limits" to the unreasonableness of these edicts placed upon you and I, nor do they care! Just another HUGE reason to reject the large statist state we have been entering into.

Freedom requires responsibilities and accountability. Unfortunately, throughout history there are examples aplenty of nations that have been forced to choose between a heavy-handed government or freedom and responsibility. Unfortunately, it is human nature for people to choose the first.

The natural urge for people to "belong" to a collective is still so very strong, that it matters little of what the collective represents. People easily fall into the fantasy land belief that a big controlling government can accomplish what they promise. Today, the young in particular have been faced with a long, suffering economy and the responsibility of providing for themselves and/or their families. These millions are overwhelmed at making enough income to pay for private health insurance and other government provided services available for their benefit. Many can easily succumb to the states purse strings and powers, even if it means giving up liberties, freedoms and rights. Tens of millions of Americans have given up their freedoms for goodies and so-called "security" offered by an insincere new state of America. Thus, the elites pounce on this vulnerability. This, and the threat of a crumbling environment is at the very essence of a new world order, using global warming and other created hysterias to whip up compliance.

Realize that after the accomplishment of their plans for a one world government and Agenda 21, property rights will become a thing of the past. This is the hallmark and endgame of the global elites behind the new world order. This places citizens into "subjects" to be used as lowly paid serfs for the globalists, perhaps 10-15 years away if not stopped in their tracks.

Is it any wonder why today's communist party members (as in the last 100+ years) across the globe are told to rally at global warming parades, rallies, anti-establishment policies, action committees and such? But you won't dear hear the mainstreet news report their easy to spot attendance! This too is no mistake. Below is just one example of thousands of which I speak. Below is from an article printed April 30, 2017 by S. Noble, Independent Sentinel Politics.

*"While thousands marched past the White House with hundreds waving communist flags, the media ignored it. The Hill and other media outlets praised the march but didn't bother to mention the red flags. They had an entire story around "nine clever signs from the climate march" but never noticed the communist."* Just an oversight I ask, or is the media complicit in the far, far leftist agenda?

# .21
# GREEN FALSE FLAGS

*"The urge to save humanity is almost always a false front for the urge to rule".*     Henry L. Mencken, Famous American editor, critic (1880-1956).

Isn't it amazing that so many people of the past were so much more insightful and longer term thinking than today's mob mentality? Will we still take heed of such wisdoms, or throw them out with the garbage? There is no way to cover all of the possible evidences and facts on this subject within the room allowed in a single section book, or many book together. But this subject does require a significant part of this book for the global warming or global cooling theories need to be shown for what they are.

In 1970 on the official "Earth Day" the environmentalists, scientists warned us we faced a "New Ice Age". In 1974, David Rockefeller in his annual Rockefeller Report (page 22) called for a global cooling conference and said in it, "the future indications of the global cooling trend are now underway." Time passed, and that theory went the way of the horse-buggy. Since around 1985 they claimed we have a problem of global warming. This 1970 theory was first claimed by President Obamas then chief scientific climatologist. The same guy now says that we have a warming problem. Will they make up their mind?

Nearly all these insiders and their allied scientists who are proponents of this new theory are either receiving a government grant in exchange for favorable reports to help make the government's case, work for the gov't directly, or have been fooled by bad science. The proponents of the green movement have long said that anyone who fights and disputes their lies is receiving money from big energy companies, but the truth comes out. CFACT, a free market think tank that has teamed up affiliates Ron Arnold and Paul Driessen and wrote an eye-opening book called 'Cracking Big Green.' Some of the highlights of the book are as follows: The Big Green was formerly known as the Iron Triangle, known as *"A mutually supportive relationship between power elites",* as told by Mark Tapscott, the Washington Examiners executive director. Accordingly, Big Green consists of "government agencies, special interest lobbying organizations, and legislature over their interests". Today, it includes well financed, major environmental groups such as the Sierra Club and the Natural Resources Defense Council. To these, add wealthy foundations and corporations that fund them.

It will no doubt astound many readers to learn that there are more than 30,500 American environmental groups. And as just an example, they collected more than $81 billion from just 2000-2012, according Giving USA Institute! According to IRS Form 990 reports of non-profit organization, it was discovered that just among the 2012 incomes of the better-known environmental groups, the Sierra Club took in $97,757.678 dollars and its Foundation took in $47,163.599. The Environmental Defense Fund listed

$111,915,138 in earnings, the Natural Resources Defense Council took in $98,701,707, National Audubon Society $96,206,883. These four groups alone took in more than $353 million in one year. The list goes on and on but suffice to say that many of the environmental groups get nearly half their revenue from private foundations like the Pew Charitable Trusts, the Rockefellers Brothers Fund, Walmart's very own Walton Family Foundation. Starting with 81,777 foundation donors, the top 50 donors out gave these green groups $812,639.999 dollars (2010 figures) according to the Foundation Center's vast database. By 2016 the number had grown to over $2 billion dollars! This doesn't include at all the governmental donations. Just astounding! Like the rest of nearly every other venture, follow the money trail. With just a little research one will find that all of these foundations are on board with the one world agenda.

If you wonder why you have been hearing and reading endless doomsday scenarios about global warming, the lowering or rising of sea levels, the disappearances of species and forests for decades, the reason is that a huge propaganda machine is financed at levels that are mind boggling and very profitable. In the 1970's the Rockefeller led scientists claimed that the earth was going into a new ice age. When that didn't pan out, they came out with global warming in the 1980's. Now, the doomsday campaign has been changed to "Climate Change." I guess that covers them either way the pendulum swings! The reality is that the climate is always in a state of change and is largely determined by the Sun and other factors such as the oceans and volcanic activity.

Most scientists have determined that humans play virtually no role whatever in climate change. Many say perhaps .01 degrees at most! Big Greens claims that carbon emissions have influenced the weather enough to cause whatever climate change we are witnessing. This claim has long been disproven and debunked by most scientists who are not on a government grant or somehow collecting from the green lie. Co2 gases have a positive effect on our plants and trees as anyone knows, as without it trees and humans would die. It is a naturally occurring byproduct of photosynthesis, and it never has been considered seriously as a pollutant. It is a net positive by far!

In 1984 Al Gore had warned that *"By 2013, the ice caps will be nearly gone"*. Not surprisingly he was wrong as he always is. Today the ice caps have increased by over 60% over much of the earth. The problem is, the corporate owned news and other media continue to tell the Big Lie of global warming. Oh sorry, they renamed it global 'change' now that they aren't so sure, and they see it starting to cool. The effects on our lives is higher costs on nearly every front and much more that most don't see.

Without this scam, billions of wasted dollars could be utilized to actually improve earths living conditions and economies for the entire planet if we could put many of the lying financial globalists in jail, getting them out of our way towards real progress. But that isn't their agenda. It's about milking the world's economies and incomes as much as they can, lining their own pockets and controlling billions of people. Trillions of dollars are being made. Al Gore is just one of thousands who are profiting handsomely. Good old Al has gone from a worth of just a couple of million dollars while Vice President for Clinton, into being worth many hundreds of millions, near all derived from the green movement. Al made millions from his largely discredited "Inconvenient Truth" movies that have been discredited, his speaking engagements, plus a Wall Street business partnership with his partner David Blood with a corporate name of "Blood & Gore Corp". That's not a misprint! Capitalizing on pending cap & trade legislation, they attempted to enact a Chicago brokerage house that would buy, sell or trade carbon credits to companies that had a surplus or lack of credits. Fortunately, his hoped-for cap and trade legislations never got approved by the new Republican Congress, and the whole scheme collapsed. Not to worry though. Between 2008 and 2011 their company, named Gore and Blood (I'm serious), made over $200 million dollars from suckers like Ford, Am-Track, DuPont, Dow Chemical, International Paper and many more including several states, cities and universities who all bought in on the scam and became losers. Parts of above taken from article in Forbes/Opinion section, 11/3/13, entitled 'Blood & Gore: Making a Killing on Anti-Carbon Investment Hype', L. Bell Contributor.

Favored government contractors benefit greatly as well, obtaining swell green contracts worth millions, even into the billions. These enjoy the many millions of dollars in profits from government mandated 'green' equipment and upgrades towards military, local and state government applications. For the banks, add in lucrative bond sales, and financings for business and consumer solar and green upgrades projects.

Peak oil is a term that for 45 years been used to describe that premise that the world is running out of oil. Around 1975 they claimed we would run out of oil in 8 years. That was nearly 45 years ago! Everyone now knows that America has hit upon more oil than in Saudi Arabia right here in North Dakota! In November of 2016 another oil gusher of epic proportions was discovered in Texas. Today we one of the largest exporters of oil to the world! Again, this has all been hoopla to scare the world into submission of Agenda 21. One reason the global warming scare is on the back burners in most peoples minds today has to do with this fact that has turned out to upset the global power grabbers.

If you simply look at these top leaders of the green movement, they typically have multiple homes, yachts, personal jets, leaving a gigantic "footprint" on the earth's environment, as they would say! Al Gore, Bill Gates, George Soros, Pres. Bill Clinton, Hillary, Pres. Obama and nearly every single one of the very wealthy green supporters are huge polluting pigs who squander huge, obscene amounts of energy, pollute the air, create smog, etc. So, can you believe them by watching their examples? I suppose it makes them popular with any one of the 6 major media mega corps they surely work for (also one worlders.)

Facebook owner Mark Zuckerberg is the latest young Jewish billionaire to push the entire globalist agenda. These, who push for restrictions on nearly everything we do, always seem to require at least 3 or 4 mansions, at least one private jet plane & helicopter, their own limousines, a dozen cars, swimming pools, spas, and far more, all leaving an immense carbon footprint wherever they move around. Several 20,000+ sq. ft. residences seem to be the norm. They fly to and fro around the world on their toxic fuel spilling, behemoth jets designed just for them. Their palatial residences need constant heat or air conditioning, upkeep and watering of their big lawns, plantings, etc. Unsurprisingly, Hollywood types such as George Clooney, Angelina Jolie, Brad Pitt, Matt Damon, U-2 and nearly ALL of the megastars are always ranting about global warming, only to step outside their pollution spilling mansions and into one of their own gas guzzling limousines or Hummers, board upon one of their private jets, and trail off to one of their mansions in France or to some foreign destination! Another one hell of an example was when some truther's did a little research on Al Gore's personal life. He was caught being a big global warming 'hypocrite'. In truth, he leaves obscene "global footprints" everywhere he travels and sleeps! Besides having at least 6 residences, his primary one is estimated to be worth $10 million dollars in 1990 dollars.

As an example of just how overboard and heavy handed environmental and local politics have gone amok, Gary Harrington, of Eagle Point, Oregon had fought for 10 long years to defend his rights to collect rainwater and snow runoff on his 170-acre small farm in order to have water available should a fire break out on his property that laid in a very dry forested area. He obtained permits from the state Water Resources Board and all local agencies to proceed, but after he dug three small ponds around the property, the board changed their minds, claiming that the water was to be treated as belonging to a nearby creek that the water had been flowing from for years. In 2013 he was ordered to serve 30 days in jail, five years of probation on 9 misdemeanor charges, as well as a $1,500 dollar fine! It seems that rainwater or snow falling on or across your own property is no longer yours! This is government run amok and citizens must resist and fight against it. This is an example of "freedoms" being available only at the express permission of government. Mr. Harrington was appealing the decision. RT News, 7/30/2012 but in the end I understand he won the case after spending hundreds of thousands of his own limited funds. He nearly went bankrupt! Are we really

Many of these liars are making much of their riches on the backs of you and me. What a cruel joke on society! The Clinton (mafia) Foundation has made hundreds of millions off of the green movement and similar schemes. I guess it's alright in their little narcissistic minds to ask you and I to drive a Prius and ride bicycles everywhere, urging us all to eventually live in a 100-200 sq. ft. stackem-packem crammed apartment. Yes, this is within the Agenda 21/2030 stated goals.

*Al Gore was quoted in 2015 by Business Insider Politics that at the World Economic Forum in Davos, Switzerland that "we need to spend $90 trillion dollars on our planet to rebuild all our cities into smaller, planned, densely packed neighborhoods where no one needs a car."* Ninety trillion? Where do you think that will come from? Long planned has been a 2% U.N. world tax for starters.

Of course, the Marxist types around the world are on board, and have been since the 1970's at least. They know that environmentalism is the road to a socialist order that hands all power over to the state. It is as impossible to attain as true socialism is. Environmentalism is an atheistic, man-less, cultish religion of its own. The lefties behind this movement are devotees of Jean Jacques Rousseau of the late 1700s who has often been referred to as the father of environmentalism, a worshipper of nature. Rousseau's paeans to states, egalitarianism, and totalitarian democracy have shaped the Left for 200 years. These holds the earth's value far above the individual.

William Jasper, a veteran on the study of world affairs and a journalist with the New American magazine for 30+ years shows the religious tenets of U.N.'s intended new religion of the world within his book entitled: A New World Religion". He describes the new religion as *"a weird and diabolical convergence of New Age Mysticism, pantheism, aboriginal animalism, atheism, communism, socialism, Luciferian occultism, apostate Christianity, Islam, Taoism, Buddhism and Hinduism"*. If that isn't enough to make your head spin! This would be a disaster. What you get out of all this is a disguised Satanic religion in reality.

## M. STRONG: THE FATHER OF U.N. CLIMATE-GATE

The father of modern U.N. environmentalism/Agenda 21 programs was Maurice Strong. He was oft called *"The creator, fabricator & head proponent of global warming and climatism."* Mr. Strong was extremely involved with the U.N. operations and designing its long-term goals going back to the agencies beginnings.

Prior to joining the U.N. Maurice, Strong became a multi-millionaire at the age of 27 thru his own Canadian oil company, selling it at great profit. But even before beginning his oil company as a very young man, he worked at the new U.N. offices in New York City, in small capacities. Once catching the eye of Nelson Rockefeller, he was under his own personal guidance and grooming. Rockefellers are, and were always, perhaps the largest funders and leaders behind the entire U.N. organization, as well as nearly every one of the similar organizations. One could call Rockefellers the "Kings of the One World Movement".

In 1992, while Mr. Strong was the Secretary-General of the "U.N. Conference on Environmentalism & Development", much hyped as the Rio Earth II Summit, his post enabled him to be instrumental in the "success" of getting 178 nations to sign onto Agenda 21.

It was at this summit that he told a crowd of thousands, *"Isn't it the hope for the planet that the industrialized civilization collapse?* Isn't it our responsibility to bring that about*"?* Another of Mr. Strong's quotes: *"We may get to the point where the only way of saving the world will be for industrial civilization to collapse".* Yes, they want to de-industrialize and de-populate the world to save it.

It had been thought for years by many that he would become the General of the United Nations! In 1996 all roads in the UN led to Maurice Strong. To show you how influential Mr. Strong had been in this whole movement, I give you his posts at various hugely influential environmental groups of deception. Earth Council Alliance, Founder, Club of Rome member, The Commission for World Governance, leader. He was also the Founder/leader of the U.N. Environment Program and the trustee for the Rockefeller Foundation (the longest and strongest supporter of this world order agenda). Furthermore, a Founder of the following green/communist groups: The Planetary Citizens Group, World Federation of U.N. Associations, World Future Society, Global Advisory Council, World Wildlife Fund, Order of the Polar Star.

This man has/had spearheaded nearly all of the organizations involved with the environmental and one world order movement. All of these organizations and associated organizations are publicly approved and endorsed by our friendly United Nations. Most of these groups share their lengthy reports with the U.N. on the status of their research results, and achievements, toward the accomplishments of the one world agenda. These offer advices to the U.N. on their findings, share thoughts or recommendations to accomplish their new world order.

The infamous Club of Rome (a major player of the scheme), came out with a quote years ago that tellingly 'let the cat out of the bag' as to their real agendas as follows...

*"In searching for a new enemy to unite us, we came up with the idea that the threat of global warming...could fit the bill. The real enemy, then, is humanity itself. We've got to ride this global warning issue even if the theory of global warming is wrong, we will be doing the right thing in terms economic & environmental policy"* quoted from Timothy Wirth, Past President of the United Nations, currently on the Foundations Board, former Colorado Senator. The Club of Rome, is an advisor to the U.N.s environmental boards. Getting back to Maurice Strong, let's go to a quote out of Mr. Strong's mouth at the 1992 Rio Summit for Environmentalism, an Agenda 21 mouthpiece primarily...

Strong went on to make clear his agenda: *"It is clear that current lifestyles and consumption patterns of the upper middle class involving high meat intake, consuming large amounts of frozen and convenience foods, use of fossil fuels (car, planes, etc.), appliances, home and workplace air conditioning and suburban housing are not sustainable."* This is verifiably what they have planned for you, your kids, grandkids, and entire family! He also worked to spearhead the movement to impose a world tax of 0.5%, a total of nearly 2 trillion dollars a year that would be funneled to support the U.N. operations to grow exponentially. This would be an amount surpassing the entire income of the U.S.A.! This world tax goal is still a primary goal of the U.N. agenda, and will eventually get approved quite surely.

Quote: *"It is not feasible for sovereignty to be exercised unilaterally by individual nations, no matter how powerful."* *Maurice Strong*

Of course, there are many hundreds or even into the thousands, of top elites that are on board with the United Nations devious plan. I have no doubt that many of the lower level fans of this scheme actually just think they are just good citizens and believe the global warming hoax and also believe that all this U.N. talk is surely just a sane, logical response to the world problems of hunger, injustices, discrimination, wage inequality, etc. etc. Think Hollywood types, popular rap stars, Beyoncé and so many more. And don't forget the tree-hugger liberals and all the low information followers who abide by the latest "feel good" fads that are tugging at the heartstring. Yet don't ask people to really think or research into any of it. Amazingly, if you were to bring up the name Maurice Strong or Henry Kissinger at a Washington or Hollywood cocktail party, you would likely only see blank looks amongst the leaders or stars at the parties. Most of these types are clearly clueless and have bought into the politically correct lie, helping to steer our country right into the N.W.O. plans.

Perhaps one of his most profitable, illegal deals at the U.N. was Mr. Strong's involvement with the Food for Oil program in Iraq during 1995. During a U.N. investigation of numerous other misdeeds and briberies of that program, they came upon proof that a check for $988,885,000 was endorsed by a Mr. M. Strong, issued by a

Jordanian Bank. After that incident he left and took to China and as of 2010 was still hiding out there. Subsequently he was stripped of his 53 international awards and all other "merits" of his work. The agent giving the check to him was eventually caught and the U.S. Federal Courts found him guilty of bribing U.N. officials. So, the noble Mr. Strong was finally caught at his real game, ripping off the public ala the U.N.

Come on folks, I can't make this stuff up! If you're a crook, I guess it really pays to be included within the "inside circle" of these types of so called humanitarian organizations, especially the U.N. obviously. Besides all the connections and influences with the world's elites and leaders, Mr. Strong clearly claimed he was a socialist, saying *"I am a socialist in ideology, a capitalist in methodology"*. You see, he knew that to achieve socialism you needed capitalism first, followed by huge, crushing debt. After collapse comes his own version of capitalism, a one world state largely controlled by the elitist capitalist, overseen by the U.N.

Maurice Strong, besides being the architect and original force behind the U.N. global policies, also had an "interesting" (to say the least) personal life that reflected his belief system I think. Consider this: His "ranch" reportedly consists of 200,000 acres in Colorado and called Baca Grande. It has a colorful history since his ownership. Trying to keep this short, he got the ranch into the UNEP (environmental program of the U.N.), so he'd never have to deal with the Forest Service or Army Corps of Engineers. He believed Baca Grande was his Mecca for "Gaia" (mother earth), worshippers and mystics. Apparently, it also was a Satanic Cult. So, he built a temple to a Babylonian Sun God, and believed that this will be the new "Vatican City" of the New World Order! It is said that when he bought the ranch, a mystic told him that "The Baca would become would become the center for a new planetary order which would evolve from the economic collapse and environmental catastrophe that would sweep the globe in the years to come". To me, that sounds like something he made up at the time as a sort of hidden prophecy (or desire) of his own, vis-à-vis through a supposed mystic. And it gets weirder. Remember, this man was the mover, shaker towards the U.N.s goals, so in many ways was the pre-eminent dignitary in charge of our future life on earth! And the Satanic Sun God appears again and again with and around these same murderous thugs!

Many Presidents, not the least of including Bill Clinton and V.P. Al Gore (of course) have spoken at the compound's Satanic temple at different times. Al Gore reportedly was invited, and delivered a "sermon" at the temple, where during the service, sacred elephants and sheep walked the isles. Devout worshippers marched to the altar with bowls of fresh compost and dung. The temple is a round nature worship center with pagan rituals, escorting goats and cattle to the altar during services for a blessing. Satanists, Freemasons, and Illuminati's often worship the grotesque, horned and Satanic goat-god, Baphomet. It is still believed that many Illuminists continue to sacrifice to the unspeakable deity to this very day. The Masons believe the letter "G"'" (goat, geometry) represents their supreme deity. The Masons had much in common with the Illuminati's in earlier years while many claim they still do.

Satanic devotees revere the goat, especially the exalted Baphomet Goat head with twin horns and the 5 pointed star. Is this why they call followers of the new world order leaders as "sheeplings?' I do believe there is a connection there!

Again, one such notorious Satanist follower is Anton LaVey, founder of the Church of Satan who exemplifies such practices. Many, many evil, inhuman practices often take place within the worship areas they use, including at times, tortures, animal sacrifices and worse. Many of these leaders of the green and new world order movement are confirmed as quietly being either Satanic, sexually perverted, believing in themselves as their own Gods and such. They absolutely abhor the chains of Christianity and other religions as well. For these, the real God is the anti-God! They honestly believe that once the New World Order is here, we will worship the leaders of this movement as our Gods! These call upon mortal beings to consider themselves as their own gods in fact. I am absolutely serious on this note. This is a war of good against evil whether ones likes it or not. You will come across a quote from Rockefeller himself within the following chapter wherein he says that his types will one day be revered as gods! George Soros and others such as these have mimicked the same words in public interviews. These sickos feel they are here to save humanity for their own selves and Satan.

One of Mr. Strong's most avid followers and primary advisors was Strobe Talbot. Talbot was the textbook globalist with all the pre-requisite qualifications for someone who was to lead the world agenda, knowing exactly how to achieve it. His globalist credentials included the he is a Rhodes scholar (of course), a Yale Grad, President of the liberal & Godless Brookings Institute, Deputy Secretary of State 1994, and headed the Center for Study of Globalization 2000. Not to miss anything, he has served as director of the Council on Foreign Relations, trustee of the Trilateral Commission and a member of the Aspen Strategy Group, another new world order think tank. He was quoted during a Book TV interview with Arthur Brooks, saying "on terminology & methods to counter the "Climate Gate" effect & how "Climate Change" (previously Global Warming) is a fundamental building block of future Globalization planning". That's code words for global taxation and Cap & Trade.

Many of the very top leaders deep inside themselves seems to hold no high humanist or moralistic values to speak of. Looking at the past despotic actions of the most heavily involved names of this movement, i.e. Maurice Strong, George Soros, Henry Kissinger, Brzezinski, the Rockefellers, Strobe Talbott, plus a long list of other worldly movers and shakers, one only need take the time to investigate the real, actual history of these elites. Please notice the names that keep popping up in most all of the globalist organizations I have spoken of. Does being that rich make you like this? The jest of all this is that the globalism/globalist/corporate pirates have been using the very successful communist game plans laid out by communist conspirators as named herein. Lies, tricks, mind manipulations, unjustified fears calling out for more government, corporate ownership of most assets, etc., etc. etc. ALL a fraud.

# ELIZABETH SANGER
## PLANNED PARENTHOODS DEVILISH PAST

The far left has perpetrated one of the ugliest lies upon the American people since the 1970's. First, they convinced the Supreme Court to pass Roe vs. Wade, which brought to the forefront Planned Parenthood. Elizabeth Sanger was the founder of Planned Parenthood. Elizabeth Sanger is often touted by American media and libertarian groups as some kind of humanitarian leader of the women's rights movement. But how much do most of us know of her entire background? Firstly, she was a failed nurse whom never completed her nursing education. Within Sanger's 1920 book entitled "The Pivot of Civilization, she espoused "The extermination of human weeds" and the sterilization of "genetically inferior races", as well as "The cessation of charity, segregation of morons, misfits and the maladjusted". She believed that the "unfit" should not be allowed to reproduce. Accordingly, in 1920 Sanger opened her first birth control clinic in the Brownsville section of New York, an area largely populated by newly immigrated Italians, Slavs, Latins and Jews. Targeting those who she felt were 'unfit' and not "desirable" for a well sustainable society was her mission. She carried out her clinics "mission" while also gathering followers, promoting abortion, even eugenics.

Nineteen years later, in 1939, she organized the Negro Project, which focused on eliminating black births in poor neighborhoods. As her movement expanded, it focused largely in the South, where the highest density of blacks occurred. She believed them to be the "inferior race". The masses of Negroes...particularly in the South still breed carelessly and disastrously, with the result that the increase, among Negroes, even more than whites, is from that portion of the population least intelligent and fit...

Sanger knew that white people approaching black women would not work, as they would not trust their intents. So, Sanger made it a policy to send three or four black ministers out in order to "*travel into the black enclaves.*" Using their papal cloak, these could convince black women to make a "health visit" and/or and be convinced to abort her baby. Sanger was quoted that "The most successful educational approach to the Negro is through religious appeal. We do not want the word to get out that we want to exterminate the Negro populations, and the minister is the one who can straighten out that idea if it occurs to any of their more rebellious leaders." It would seem obvious at this point that nearly all of today's black African Americans, if informed of these quotes, would not continue to sanctify Margaret Sanger, and possibly see a different side to abortions. An example:

*"The most merciful thing that a family does to one of its infants and members is to kill it."* M. Sanger

In the 1930's she published the "Birth Control Review", exposing that she gave enthusiastic support to Hitler's horrific infanticide program, as well as championed Hitler's goals of Aryan white supremacy. Prior to W.W.II, Sanger commissioned Nazi Ernst Rudin, director of the dreaded German medical experimentations programs, to serve as an advisor to her programs. In the 1930's she publicly championed Hitler's goal of Aryan white supremacy.' Perhaps not so surprising, Sanger embraced Communism with a distaste for America. As her movement grew in power, influence and acceptance, Sanger began to the targeting of religious groups, particularly Christians and fundamentalists, as well as Catholics for destruction. Blacks, Hispanics, American

Indians she considered "Dysgenic Races", wishing the same for elimination. Many excerpts are from the book 'Killer Angel' by George Grant: Reformer Press.

Even though Sanger did not accept God, she did make exceptions if it came to support any group who would help her crusade to wipe out blacks and those less than perfect. Sanger even sought out the KKK as part of her crusade to kill those who were less perfect in her eyes, especially blacks. Here is a picture of her at a KKK rally in Silverlake, New Jersey in 1926.

Even with all this evidence of her prejudice toward blacks and her own eugenics and abortion clinics programs dubbed Planned Parenthood, the leftists and the black communities in particular, unassumably bow down to the name Sanger as though she was a saintly messenger for "women's rights". This term was an appealing sounding, slick and enticing marketing term created by the communistic one world globalists to naively believe that the Democrats were looking out for them and would bring them out of poverty. Today, 51% of younger black women have had at least on abortion, the highest rate amongst all groups of woman in America.

Sanger was a devout Fabian/Communist, anti-freedom and anti-God, as well as a devotee of the occult became a devotee of the Theosophy religion founded by Madame Blavatsky, carried on by occultist Alice Bailey under the name of the Lucis Trust (Lucifer) which today serves as an NGO for the United Nations under the name World Goodwill. Very clever title, eh? The Lucis Trust is based on repudiation of traditional God and endorses the worship of Lucifer, believing he is the light of the world, etc. Sadly, speaking, the Theosophy cult today has become the religion of many of the most powerful. It has occult forces behind the scenes in New York City, Washington D.C. and large cities in particular.

The "success" of Sangers movement leading up to today has been a huge accomplishment for the progressives, socialists, communists and/or one worlder's. They have succeeded in large part at destroying the idea of sanctity of life in many women's minds. Once this quality of being fully human is slowly disrupted or destroyed over several generations of peoples, what's next? Likely euthanasia once the elderly reach 80 years when combined with an irreversible disease? With the high costs and high profits that the healthcare system demands, the bureaucracy may justify state justified eugenic procedure? Such a policy is certainly within the realm of possibility at some point. Such goes a long way in fulfilling the socialist's desires for a eugenics-based society.

The depopulation views of Marxwell Taylor, Henry Kissinger, and others are echoes of the words from a 1996 full-page ad by Negative Population Growth, Inc. (NPG), that was published in *Foreign Affairs,* the official publication of the Council on Foreign Relations! There are scores of quotes and writings by many of the admitted one world leaders, citing that they are planning for at least a 70%-80% reduction in peoples on earth. For more proof, check out the U.N. Depopulation Reference: GBA Section 9.2.3.2., a U.N. publication. Methods to accomplish this mission must include a mix warring, famines, pestilence, pharmacological, nuclear, and nutritional means at the very least in order to realistically accomplish such a monumental, evil task.

## 22.

# GOVERNMENT ENDORSED "SLOW KILL"

The Overpopulation problem, aka Agenda 21, is a myth propagated by the financial elite who have determined that a far, far lower world population would more be advantageous to their plan to dominate and control all currently available natural lands and resources, including people, thereby increasing their influence, power and wealth.

Yet we know that the newest technologies can make it possible for people to live in places that were previously not thought suitable for a good life. Our supposed "over-population problem" does not exist in smaller towns, but the agenda 21 devotees even want those to curtail their lifestyles in the name of the planet. Even if such actually was a problem, large populations within highly concentrated cities would be the only target possible. Yet, the elites don't want to stop there. You see, it's all about handing over control of nearly all land, people and resources to the elites while making the remaining people left to work as serfs to benefit them.

It is largely affirmed that with improved farming and sanitation practices, large portions of the undeveloped world can support far more human activity. New smart cities could be built just as we see popping up around America and China without the use of a heavy-handed government to manage every nail used. Properly managed, the world could support more than twice the population than presently exists with no big problems. I believe that advances in farming and other technologies will soon allow for billions of additional people on the planet earth if it is intelligently managed on the basic levels. Yes, birth control, planned families and a myriad of other responsible actions (often by citizens themselves) could easily make the differences needed to intelligently thrive on mother earth. We cannot be seduced by the same leech's, the elites, whose main objective is total control!

With that being said, consider this small sampling of eerie statements coming out of the United Nations:

*"A total population of 250-300 million people, a 95% decline would be desired."*
*Ted Turner, founder of CNN and major United Nations contributor".* *Now <u>read the U.N.'s radical anti-human agenda to this end</u>!!

*"The present vast overpopulation, now far beyond the world carrying capacity, cannot be answered by future reductions in the birth rate due to contraception, sterilization and abortion, but must be met in the present by the reduction of numbers presently existing. This must be done by whatever means necessary."* <u>This language is included and made a part of</u> the **UNITED NATIONS ECO-92 EARTH CHARTER!**

According to an article published the New York Times, some of America's leading globalist billionaires, including David Rockefeller Jr., Warren Buffett, George Soros, Michael Bloomberg, (mayor of New York City) and Bill Gates have formed a secretive club that meets regularly for the purpose of determining how they can use their wealth and power to systematically slow down, even reverse, the growth of the world's populations.(http://www.thesundaytimes.co.uk/sto/news/world_news/article169829.ece)

## ELITE ENGINEERED DEATH VIRUSES

Proof came out in early 2016 that the Rockefeller Foundation had discovered the terrible Zika Virus that is taking lives all over the world and supposedly has the state in a state of panic. How could this be? DID MAINSTREAM NEWS TELL YOU THIS? Well, take a look at the official document below, proving that they developed it back in 1947! Worse yet, their website claims they had nothing to do with it. State of The Nation article "How is the Rockefeller Foundation connected to the Zika virus?" 2/09/16

**ATCC** | IN PARTNERSHIP WITH LGC STANDARDS

| PRODUCTS | SERVICES | STANDARDS | DOCUMENTS AND LITERATURE | CUS |

Home ▸ Products ▸ All Products ▸ VR-84™

# Zika virus (ATCC® VR-84™)

Classification: **Flaviviridae, Flavivirus** / Product Format: freeze-dried

| GENERAL INFORMATION | CHARACTERISTICS | CULTURE METHOD | SPECIFICATIONS | HISTORY |

| | |
|---|---|
| **Name of Depositor** | J. Casals, Rockefeller Foundation |
| **Source** | Blood from experimental forest sentinel rhesus monkey, Uganda, 1947 |
| **Year of Origin** | 1947 |
| **References** | Dick GW. Trans. R. Soc. Trop. Med. Hyg. 46: 509, 1952. |

Gee, does not the above document list the Rockefeller Foundation name as the Depositor of the Zika virus? That it came from an experimental monkey from Uganda? The Rockefeller Foundation and other sources have been behind the research and harvesting of hundreds of varying and dangerous drugs, viruses and vaccines going back much longer than this 1947 patent!

# Planned Collapse of Americanism

As a matter of fact, the CDC now owns the patent on the Ebola strain! The patent number is CA2741523A1 in case you want to verify that. We must ask how if they own the patent, how could it have been used WITHOUT their permission? Zika and Ebola are just two of the most recent diseases that are extremely suspect of foul play by either governments, or globalists. And yes, the CDC is not the all caring, compassionate agency you think it is. Scandals have surfaced over the past several years that show CDC involvement in unscrupulous practices often involving corporate kickbacks.,

Often these types of dangerously developed strains are used by our government in developing biological weapons and/or other nefarious uses. It is confirmed by numerous respected reports that all presidents since at least Pres. Eisenhower have allowed this type of research, and the creations of, deadly cocktail viruses to be employed within warring's, humans as well as other horrific uses.

The real controllers, the global-crats, whom include the Rockefellers Foundations and their ilk, have for many years been active in procuring and developing dangerous viruses to test on the world's population as part of their agenda of having complete control of nearly everything at their whims. Many of these concoctions have been formulated to possibly be used on enemy nations or their fighting forces in the case of warring, aka "bioterrorism." Others suspect Zika virus to possibly be used as a governmental false flag operation after riots begin in the U.S. Likewise, this could be the answer to justify the imposition Marshall Law roundups in the U.S once the virus spreads onto the general populations. Already we see this virus spreading in Florida and other areas at an alarming rate. Could this be the beginnings, or just a test program? The timing couldn't be better.

These same culprits have repeatedly put these strains into the environment as well as our bodies and our air in one way or another in order to watch its effects. Many now claim that clandestine operations within our government distribute many of these exotic and obscured diseases to perform live outdoor studies to assess just how it affects humans. As part of government and CDC research, mass sprayings in the air have been implemented to calculate how the differing races and ethnic groups react to the chemical ingests. For instance, who are most resistant or least resistant, what types of ailments/deaths are eventually determined to spike upwards a result, and so forth.

As history marches forward, the deathly effects of new and stronger cocktails of immunization shots put out by the drug industry has been proven to cause hundreds of thousands if not millions of added illnesses and deaths upon the innocents and unsuspecting at the constant urgings of the health authorities and schools. Another stat that has been noticed in recent years is the spike in autism in children with no official explantation. Yet, in the last few years there have been an increasing number of studies showing a definite link between new has reached epidemic proportions in just the last few years, fastly increasing from one in one thousand around 15 years ago, rising to one in every 30 today! The links are proven. Yet our government does nothing.

Just as Hitler experimented much the same way, these testing's can be used in dangerous and nefarious ways, especially in the hands of nefarious and plotting of one worlders planners such as the Rockefellers. They can decide how people should die, even pinpointing whom should die within selected populations. Serious science has likely determined that the HIV virus came from a particular breed of monkey, likely purposely introduced by the Rockefellers or similarly inspired elites and primarily sent into the black and gay neighborhoods in order to reduce their numbers as well. I truly hope that today such targeting of blacks is not the case, but history sends the opposite message. The monkey connection begins to sound just too similar to the Rockefeller financed origins of the Zika virus described above and of which was also derived from a monkey. The AIDS epidemic as well as scores of other newer, never heard of strains of various diseases are very suspect of intentional creation by government, but space does not allow elaboration.

Huge lawsuits multiply every year upon drug companies that peddle drugs with side effects, even deaths, of which they already had been aware of, yet failed or were complicit in not reporting the problems. There are even documented proofs of that shady agency called the CIA as being involved in some of these cases. The FDA and the drugs peddlers, who finance politicians with millions of dollars, are raking in tens of billions in extra dollars from these explosive and dangerous drugs through their cronyisms with our own government. Ridiculous increases in chemical concentrations and added chemicals placed into today's vaccinations exist only because of the lobbying actions of the slick pharmaceutical makers who give huge political donations to politician's election coffers if they cooperate. Today, the F.D.A. is given many millions of tens of millions of dollars every years toward pharmaceutical companies in exchange for laxness and guaranteed approval of dangerous drugs and fast track treatment, thereby bypassing most scrutiny. This has verifiably caused a conflict of interests by the introduction of money between the parties aka a "Nod-Nod, Wink-Wink" policy. These peddlers of slow death are feverishly intent on selling whatever they can, much like drug dealers with no regard to the damage done upon the buyers of his drugs. Yet, these drug dealers are never convicted or sent to jail. This brief indictment of the drug industry should at least spur interest to you readers who just can't believe that our government could do such things while colluding with the drug companies.

Katherine Austin Fitts, whom served as Fmr. Assistant Secretary of Housing under George H.W. Bush had at one time expressed concerns as to how the globalists intend to dispose of masses of peoples as a form of depopulation. Fitt's was quoted: *My simple calculations guessed that we were going to achieve economic stability on Earth by depopulating down to a population of approximately 500 million people. I was used to looking at numbers from a high level. To me, we had to have radical change in how we governed resources or depopulate. It was a mathematical result."*

Fitts concluded that social safety nets such as Social Security and Medicare would become broke and unsustainable unless populations were reduced. She concluded that by changing the actuarial assumptions in the budget, such as life expectancy, would be the only answer to the problem of which she claimed would mean *"Lowering life expectancy"*, *"Lowering immune systems and increasing toxicity levels combined with poor food, water and terrorizing stress will help do the trick."* That isn't an answer as far as I am concerned! Unprecedented scares over Ebola, Zika virus, E. coli and other potentially deadly viruses makes one wonder if this rash of man-made viruses, combined with the toxic, dangerous vaccines we are now experiencing are purposeful experimentation on the public as beta-tests for future pandemics that will be used for population control, or rather, slow kill. It always come down to MONEY.

# .23
# GET READY FOR THE BIG BAIL-IN

An article in Forbes Opinion page, 3/25/13 said: "Why a Cyprus-Like Seizure of Your Money Could Happen Here."

Plans are already in place for the instant confiscation of the money accounts of not only American citizens but also most of the worlds industrialized nations when the next major economic crises hits. No politician will ever tell you this scary fact though. It will likely come in three very fast steps. First, the president will announce a new economic 'crisis' for our banking system. This could be a market crash, a cyber computer attack on the banking system, or any number of other reasons, real or false flag. Two, a stock market shutdown and "bank holiday" is declared. Bank doors are shut. ATM's are closed. Three, a big chunk of your money is confiscated in the name of "fairness, common good, saving the system, blah, blah. A few days or weeks later, the banks will re-open, but like the incident, you will only be allowed to receive very small amounts of your money daily unless you are already wealthy. In the Cyprus case, pension checks were more than halved for weeks! And the FDIC? It only has enough reserves to cover about 1% of all accounts during a run on the banks. There is around $70 trillion dollars of debt out there in the world. And only enough money, gold to pay a tiny fraction of it! In a panic, what can we do?

An article reported by the Guardian in 2014 was entitled: Money in The Bank No Longer Belongs to You. Besides explaining the obvious, pointed out was just how tight cash is today, even in the banks themselves. Here is an example of this problem in the article;

"Stephen Cotton attempted to withdraw £7,000, a little over $11,500, from his HSBC account in the United Kingdom. Speaking on the BBC Radio 4 program Money Box, he recounted how staff at the branch refused to allow him to withdraw the money without an explanation of why he needed it, in addition to proof. In this case, Mr. Cotton intended to repay a loan from his mother. The bank demanded he produce a letter from her, verifying this. Cotton then found himself in the position of haggling with staff over how much he could actually withdraw; finally, he was allowed to take out £3,000." Further along in the article writes this: "The real reason behind such policies is that banks – and the governments that control them through regulation – do not believe that private citizens actually have any right to claim that the money in question belongs to them. According to a BBC News report, Douglas Carswell, a British Conservative Member of Parliament, says that such regulation of banks basically infantilizes [sic] the customer. In a sense your money becomes pocket money and the bank becomes your parent."

For sure, President Trump has a monumental undertaking to save the American Dream! In 2013, the Congressional Budget Office claimed that under current conditions, by 2023 there will be no money in the budget to pay for a military, all "entitlement" programs, and much more. At the time of this update (October 2017), President Trump is near passing a huge package of tax reforms that he says will provide a real boon to the economy. Already he has accomplished in providing an economy that produces over 3% growth, something not seen for decades! Other such monumental efforts will be needed to climb our way out of the gigantic $20 trillion-dollar national debt! And if interest rates rise even a little, all bets are off.

Unless President Trump can perform a miracle upon the American economy before 2020, get ready to expect bank "bail-ins". Yes, a "Bail in", not "bail out"! In this scenario, if you have over a set amount of cash in your bank account, your account will essentially be tagged for automatic debit as your part of shoring up the broken economy, much like happened in Cyprus. Some experts guess-timate the beginning number used to set off a debit would likely begin at the $100,000.00 level, depending on how dire the situation is presented to the country or to the world. If experience shows us anything, is that in this type of situation aka a bail-in, the more affluent will suffer the largest percentage of takings in the bank grab just as they did in Cypress a few years back.

Is all this too hard to fathom? Is it one of those conspiracy theories? Not!

A Huffington Post article from 2012 follows; said this: Entitled; *"It Can Happen Here: The Confiscation Scheme Planned for US and UK Depositors". The article pointed out that "A joint paper by the U.S. Federal Deposit Insurance Corporation (FDIC) and the Bank of England (Rothschild's bank), dated Dec. 10, 2012 shows that these plans have been long in the making; that they originated in the G20 Financial Stability Board in Basil, Switzerland...and that the result will be to deliver clear title to the banks of depositor's funds."*

Hmm, did you know that your deposits are the property and assets of the bank? Too bad, but the newer laws written by the bankers have made that a fact too! Your deposits are only "loans" to the bank! In a financial crash, your deposits take second seat to all other claims, even risky derivatives. If you think the FDIC will save you, think again. You'll probably get about ten cents on the dollar according to experts. They just don't have enough money, and neither does the government at this juncture when the big collapse comes soon.

In October of 2013, the IMF published a major report offering strategies to help pay down the debts for countries deeply in debt (as nearly all countries on earth are). Their solution was a one-time tax on the wealthiest in order to help pay off the debt, but with a sinister twist. On page 40 of said report, it iterates "if it's done before avoidance, and there is a belief that it will never be repeated, it shouldn't distort behaviors. All they have to do is convince the IMF that such a bailout would be limited to a one-time incident, never to be repeated.

Not advertised is the fact that the US already has the IMF ready to replace the dollar with a global currency should the dollar collapse. Remember the Hegelian Dialectic? This will be just another incident where that strategy is used. "Create a problem, offer the solution, fix the problem." In fact, plans are to replace the dollar with a IMF issued global currency. In the Cyprus fallout, people with over 100,000 euros took a 40% haircut! Lesser amounts were confiscated at a lowered, graduated rate depending on the amount. I don't know about you, but to me, even 1% is a crime. Many politicians use the number $250,000 dollars to describe the point that you are considered wealthy.

To put all this in perspective, consider how tempting this looks to our broken U.S. government. Our total immediate debt is "officially" about $20 trillion dollars. Trump or whoever is in the White House knows that in 2014 there was approximately $24 trillion dollars in private retirement accounts alone, and has been growing, according to Vera Gibbons, Fox contributor, 12/20/15. That doesn't count many other types of accounts. If they took half of retirement accounts, (12 trillion dollars), retirees would in all likelihood still have roughly the other half of their savings still intact plus all non retirement accounts would still be available. This is just a guesstimate to help make the point I have to make. However, they might divvy up the takings, you get the idea. There's enough money, but American and world's economies would likely fail completely at such a juncture. The big bet that big brother will take is that any damage such a huge action might cause on the economy might quickly fade once the public is given enough governmental assurance and guarantees that the (stolen) funds would be guaranteed by who else but the Federal Government themselves. So the your money isn't lost, it is just "borrowed.". Perhaps that might work? Other variations of a cure are likely to be utilized, but you get the idea.

Many smart economists think the idea isn't so preposterous at all, and neither do I, even though I detest it. This is what happens when a country allows a non-federal reserve outfit (that is owned by big banking interests) to control the value of the dollar. They take away the gold standard, and over time all we have left is fiat paper money and debt!

## .24

# THE FINAL WAR ON BANKING

Did it ever come to mind that maybe, just maybe, nearly all the wars throughout history have been carried out primarily for four things? Yes, banking, resources, drugs, and of course power! So when it comes to warring or nearly anything else, it can be traced to that old saying; *"money is at the root of all evil"*. Yet money is not all there is. Wars are <u>not</u>, as Ex- President Bush said, for "spreading democracy" or other such conjured up globalist lies. Here is something so profound that not even the mainstreet news sources or any other news out there is going to tell you, the general public. As a matter of fact, few in the highest positions even know of this story.

This is a blockbuster snippet of facts that might convince you once and for all that the Rothschilds, sometimes referred to as the owners of the world's central banking cartel, Aka (the Bank of International Settlements) has been creating wars for themselves, their banking partners, corporate thieves and the elites for over 200 years! This is not conspiracy mumbo-jumbo! The facts speak for themselves when any serious historian does his proper amount of diligence when uncovering the Rothshchilds and all the others mentioned. Are we to think that the following facts are just coincidence? This is something you just can't make up.

In 1990 there were just eleven countries that still had their own independent <u>non-</u>Rothschild banking systems. In other words, they were <u>operating outside</u> of the world's central banking system. All but nine had been convinced to play ball with the world banking system by that time. The same system that is controlled behind the scenes by the Rothschild's banking cartel. Yes, those whom invented and financed the Bank of International Settlements! Most people have no clue who that is. Otherwise known as the B.I.S. <u>This mother of all banks controls ALL central banks of the world.</u> It has been called the "central banker to ALL the central banks! Remember, Rothschild invention just before WWII. They created this mega power powerhouse and they built it in 1933 in Basil Switzerland, ostensibly to help launder dirty money and control ALL central banking. We do know that the B.I.S. laundered billions of dollars of stolen artwork, bonds, cash, loan payments, equipment, and you name it during WWII for Hitler in order that he could operate the war and do trade without the world watching. Remember, he was not allowed to legally trade with allied countries during WWII. This is all verified historically as accurate. Banking has always been the most lucrative scam ever devised!

In 2007, U.S. General Wesley Clark admitted in filmed interview with journalist Amy Goodman that in the year 2000 he had been told by the highest levels inside the Pentagon and State Department that the U.S. State Department had a plan to take out seven countries in the next five years. He didn't claim to know why there were seven or even why they were targeted. He did state who the seven countries targeted were though! Due to his high position, we can surmise he DID in fact know why but could not divulge more than he did. Nothing this big would be held from a top general that would be involved in its very applications.

Listed below are those countries. The general publically, openly spilled the beans during the filming of an interview that you can still find on YouTube. Democracynow.com/3/2/2007 /Interview with Amy Goodman and Gen. Wesley Clark.

We must remember that the entire lynchpin for a one world currency has always been the acknowledgement that the world must have a real, actual WORLD BANK that would be the end-all monopoly banking system of all time. They are so very close.

The plan has been successful to date, carried out by the U.S. State Department, U.S. Military, C.I.A. and the Pentagon. The centralized cooperation and planning of the C.F.R, Trilateral's, United Nations and other such non-governmental one world organizations would, and do, supplement as they can in the planning and the success of the operations.


These are the 7 countries that in the year 2000, General Wesley Clark prophesized to be taken out in that next 5 years.

Afghanistan

Iraq

Sudan

Libya

Cuba

North Korea

Iran


As of 2011, the only countries left without a Rothschild Central Banking system, Aka a private central bank! These are:

Cuba, North Korea, Iran

Let's see, does it now make sense that out of these three last countries, two are the primary enemies of America at this time, while Cuba will be the last to go without a fight? Once North Korea and Iran are crushed or negotiated with (in the best of world's), Cuba becomes just a military or signing ceremonial exercise, annexing that country to America or the new world order! All these countries taken out so far have been replaced with new leaders who are obedient to America's owners, the new world order primarily controlled by the Rothschild banking cabal! See, without a central banking system running the entire new world's movements of money, a new world order becomes incomplete.

Surprisingly, Russian banking is under the ownership of the Rothschilds in some sense and this is why Russia is not a part of the seven above. Surprisingly, under the Russian Constitution, the CBR belongs to a foreign state – the City of London, owned by the Queen and banking of the Rothschilds! Although Putin's banking system is quasi nationalistic, it is largely controlled behind the scenes by the City of London.. If Russia were ever to be 100% free of any ties with the Crown, this would have to be dealt with, for the fuzziness created by this semi-secret arrangement makes it next to impossible for Russia to be truly free of the one world banking system.

So, here is the crux of this conundrum. The City of London is a separate entity from the British Government much like Washington D.C. is also. (yes, I said that.) On a map you will see "City of London" as a extremely small area within the London that most of us are aware of. This is separate. Incredulously, and little known is that this lesser known City of London is owned by the Queen and the Rothschilds apart and separate from the U.K. government in order to conduct its often clandestine and oft incredulously secret dealings by the Queen and the Rothschilds dealings that go far, far back in time. I find this phenomenon quite interesting to say the least and purposely never discussed. This arrangement is bigger than another book perhaps!

Back to the CBR, this bank can only print money corresponding to its cash in foreign currency, which is not sufficient for Putin's purposes. The CBR even has to buy fiat US bonds for the dollars it receives for Russian oil. And in 1995 under Putin's directions, the CBR stopped financing shortfalls in the Federal Budget! This told the Central Banking cartel and the BIS that he was dead serious about staying clear of massive debts which could conceivable make Russia pawns to those scoundrels! Since 2008 when Russia and its ruble collapsed, Putin has blamed the Rothschild bankers for. The purposeful and largely artificial manipulation downwards upon the Ruble, banks, real estate and far more caused the collapse. It made Western banks and bond dealers filthy rich! Putin and many other claim with good proofings that it was all an attempt to overthrow Russia and depose Putin. And it nearly did. The plan included foremost to rid Putin and take Russia into the arms of the one world agenda including Rothschild nationalist banks aka the Bank of International Settlements. That would have put Russia right in place to join in with the one world order platform, leaving only Iraq and North Korea. That claim has much validity if one wishes to study it.  So, when and how will these last two countries, both posed as enemies of the United , and independently separate in their banking business models,  be able to remain independent of the private bankers the Rothschilds?

Putin is between a rock and a hard spot.  He must somehow manage to nationalize his banks without triggering war brought on by the West.  Yet, he at times seems intent on nationalizing the Rothschild controlled Central Bank of Russia (CBR) in an effort to stabilize the declining Ruble.  Brave Vladimir Putin has banned Jacob Rothschild and his New World Order banking cartel family from entering Russian territory "under any circumstances."  Putin played the New World Order game long enough to climb up to the position of President.  Now he has abruptly turned his back on them, prompting Jacob Rothschild to accuse him of being a traitor to the New World Order!

Without bank nationalization he may not be able to afford the military he will need to defend against the bankers cabal and the U.S.  He knows he must build up an unrivaled military before he can pull this one off.  If not, he takes a big chance of becoming number four on the chopping block, sandwiched somewhere between Iran and North Korea.

During the 2016 St. Petersburg Economic Forum, Russian President Putin proclaimed to the worlds press agencies the following shocker statement.  If we listen closely, we know what Putin has been trying to say:

*"We know year by year what's going to happen, and they know that we know. It's only you that they tell tall tales to, and you buy it and spread it to the citizens of your countries. You people in turn do not feel a sense of the impending danger – this is what worries me. **How do you not understand that the world is being pulled in an irreversible direction? While they pretend that nothing is going on. I don't know how to get through to you anymore.**"*
*President Putin*

Call me crazy, but isn't he saying that so much of what goes on is all by inside of a truly "grand design" as I have iterated throughout this book?

# .25

# FEARING THE PATRIOT ACT AND FEMA

*"Those who give up essential liberty, to purchase a little temporary safety, deserve neither liberty nor safety"*

*Quote: Benjamin Franklin*

Arguably, the hastily passed Patriot Act(s) could be called two of the most dangerous pieces of legislation ever written and passed into law during America's entire history. In the aftermath of 9/11, the elites quickly and craftily moved to pass this legislation, some sniping that it was intended not so much to protect America from its true and real enemies but to intentionally inject numerous sections that would perhaps forever change our free country into one quite less so. Using an insane amount of nationalistic fire and fear propaganda as cover for the many unrequired erosions of civil liberties and economic devastation, congress (always looking at the next election), passed this overreaching legislation without hardly a thought, lest be labeled a traitor to America. Yes, even though hardly one signer actually had a chance to read it (or even offered it), it was passed under pretense of not being a patriot if one didn't pass it! Hitler said "the bigger the lie, the more believable it will be for the populace." This truism is what allowed our congress to pass it so easily without public scrutiny. I mean, it was called the "Patriot Act" for God's sake! Yes, Hitler would have been so proud on the day this legislation passed as law, for he gained much of his unstoppable power using his Enabling Act, a similar power grab.

Yet here we are today with a groundbreaking document that, even with its revisions, has already taken away some of our liberties such as being afforded the right to an attorney and the guarantee to be judged by a jury of your peers, for such is not the case in some cases wherein a person is simply thought to be an enemy of the United States, even a terrorist, perhaps by guilt of association. These are sometimes just thrown away into one of the many secret prisons across America and never seen again, sometimes for reasons we will never know. Our clandestine CIA amongst other near invisible defense agencies take care of this kind of dirty work. Why haven't you heard of these individuals? Because dead or lost men don't talk. Hitler had his SS for this kind of work. The truth is that the precious American liberties and freedoms contained within our own Constitution of the United States is year by year losing its steel armor shield against the abuse of its citizens. Chip by chip, it is being weakened.

As ridiculous as that may sound to many, remember that we have already given our presidential occupier the powers to abuse his office to a horrific point due in large part to our naïve responses to the 9/11 event, gladly giving up many extremely valuable freedoms in exchange for what is called "security." History repeats often, for instance we must remember that historic event when Hitler purposely ordered the burning down of the Weimar parliament building (similar to our White House) aka the Reichstag fire. It was a false flag event, likely by using an out of work anarchist to set the fire. It was used to secure the means for Hitler to obtain power to change and subvert Weimar laws and take control of Weimar legally under the immense powers given to him by ailing President Von Hindenburg and his eventual vote of victory at becoming Feurer.

As you will see, we have handed over enormous powers, and many of our rights, liberties and freedoms within what is many far reaching laws that perhaps started out with good intentions. But, the passage of the Patriot Acts I and revisions in the second version II, the Military Commissions Act and FEMA in particular have allowed many additionally worrisome, immense powers added to the arsenal of bad actors. Should a president wish to use one or more of them in nefarious ways to achieve a political or ideological agenda upon America then God help! How long can we just hope that no president will one day hold up his red pen and yell out "CODE RED?" All of us should worry that this never happens for the wrong reason. We should ask for an expert non-partisan blue ribbon commission, harnessed with the necessary specialized knowledge required, to review the holes in some of these areas and make sure that the most pressing dangers get addressed immediately before it it too late!

In case of such a claimed "emergency", the government has these and other actions including wide ranging, possibly dangerous executive orders in place. There are many known and unknown lethal forces, deep states actors and agencies in places of ultimate power such as these mentioned. Many inside government intelligencia worry about the outcomes to witness when the eventuality one or more official declaration(s) of emergency within or upon America, whether a real deal, a staged event, or government induced. Now that the public at large realizes full well that there is a significant percentage of bad wishers for the America we love, often within inside positions of the highest ranks of power, (think CIA, FBI, State Department, MCA, et.al., we know there is no guarantee that bad actors won't use cyber-warfare to foul up or sabotage well intended emergency operations for instance.

Literally thousands of people, representing a wide range of high government intelligencia have been warning that our government has been gearing up for large scale mass civil disorders for several years now. Do they know something we don't? I do hope it is all just for the sake of being prepared, and not a sign of their worries or worse yet their purposeful plans.

In a time of crisis (natural or conceived), once a green light is given via Presidential Code Red Alert, FEMA automatically kicks into high gear, taking top controls over all movement within the U.S. Once this occurs, FEMA will be handed over absolute control of all modes of transportation, highways, seaports, airports, aircrafts, the national media, all electrical power, petroleum, fuels and minerals, as well as all food sources and farms. In an emergency, there are at least fifteen executive orders that outline the powers of FEMA should the President set them in motion after a disaster or attack. Some are nebulous enough to encompass the decision to cancel a national election! With these two agencies and the immense powers written within them when put together, it gives the President and FEMA the powers to basically change us from a free nation into an authoritarian police state at the stroke of a pen, with no obligation to answer to Congress for 60 days as written into the law!

Hitler wrote in his (largely banned, yet truthfully telling) socialist playbook Mein Kampf the following quote:

*"In the size of the lie there is always contained a certain factor of credibility since the great masses of the people...will more easily fall victim to a great lie than to a small one."*

The Patriot Acts I & II and the Freedom Act is very similar to Hitler's "Enabling Act of 1933, but contains even more far reaching, newer and more potent powers.

When the 342 page monumentally important Patriot Act was hurriedly sent for signing to the Congress, it hadn't even reached the hands of many of our representatives to read until minutes before the actual vote on the rushed bill. Some claim to have never received it. Even the ACLU was upset at the rush! So in actuality, nearly none of our representatives actually read it before the vote took place.

Rep. Ron Paul was one whom didn't sign it for this very reason, saying *"It's my understanding the bill was not available to members before the vote, at least I couldn't get it."* A lot of games were played, like keeping the House in session all night trying to hurriedly piece together this very complicated bill in order to have it ready fot vote by the following morning. The delay was planned perfectly in order to allow quick, unnoticed unconstitutional passages at the last minute and leaving no time read it or debate it.

With the name Patriot Act, undue pressure was placed upon all representatives to quickly sign it when it was brought to the floor, or be labeled anti-American by the dumbed down public! Rep. Paul was justly upset that anyone would call him unpatriotic, of course. No details, no debate, nada, due to an artificial deadline on a piece of paper. This is just another one of those Washington tricks of the trade tactics to stall the reading of a controversial or wrongly named bill until or after vote time. And for the neo Deep State collectives, the tactic works darn well. For such a piece as this, it was priceless to the neo, most of whom seem to love anything that hands them more and more power from citizens simply by calling the need for more "security" and "defense". The parts of the bill that are most concerting to real patriots follow:

A. The Federal Government may monitor religious and political institutions without suspecting criminal activity to assist terrorism investigations (a violation of the First Amendments right of association).

B. The government may search and seize individual and business papers and effects without probable cause to assist an antiterrorism (a violation of the Fourth Amendment right against unreasonable searches and seizures).

C. The government can close public attendance immigration hearings and secretly detain hundreds of people without charge while encouraging bureaucrats to resist Freedom of Information requests, (a violation of the 5th and 6th Amendments guaranteeing due process, speedy trials and freedom of information.)

D. The government may prosecute librarians and other record keepers if they tell anyone that a government subpoenaed information related to a terrorism investigation (a violation of the First Amendment right to speech).

E. The government may now monitor conversations between federal prisoners and their attorneys and may deny access lawyers to Americans accused of crimes (a violation of the Sixth Amend to have legal representation. F. The government may now jail Americans indefinitely without a trial or charges (a violation of the Sixth Amendment right to a speedy trial and the individual right to be informed of the charges against them.

A portion of the Patriot Act, Section 201 called the "Authority for Delaying Notice of the Execution of a Warrant" is commonly called the "sneak and peek" provision. It allows for authorities to search personal property without warning, even jailing without reading out your Miranda rights or due process (like Hitler and all dictators also have done). Many of these differing acts and laws actually overlap their powers as you will notice.

The Military Commissions Act (MCA), was passed on September 2006, which created a new legal reality that could herald the end of America if used in the wrong hands. The freedoms we take for granted could be snatched overnight if our President decides rightly or purposely wrongly that we are in an "emergency". That one word is very, very loosely defined within the MCA Act and the Patriot Acts as well, offer foggy and in descript wording that does not necessarily fit into the category of an "emergency" by most of us. The law gives any President the authority to establish a separate justice system for trying alien "unlawful enemy combatants". Furthermore, the actual verbiage allows the arrest of anyone, even under dreamt up charges. Even American citizens as well. Even if you have never committed a crime of any kind, "enemy combatant is a "status offense". Meaning that if the President or his cabinet says you are one, then you are assumed to be one!

The President and his lawyers now have the authority to designate any American citizen to be an "enemy combatant"; and to define both "torture" and "material support" broadly. Anyone within the executive branch can knock on your door, seize you on the street, or grab you as you change planes: take you to a secret cell in a navy prison or elsewhere, keeping you in complete isolation for months or years, delay your trial again and again and make it hard for you to see or communicate with your lawyer. Obviously, this act could be used as a possible infringement upon innocent foreign detainees. Most people have no idea of the passage of this act and even less know what is contained in it, sadly. This sad fact is repeated again and again with most all of the laws under the guise of fighting terrorism. Again, these types of new laws are exactly what regimes such as Hitler legally, but nefariously used onto his unsuspecting citizenry when the time was right. These dictators "used the law to subvert the law". Since 9/11/2001 American's are experiencing a government that has the legal right to squash nearly anything resembling Americana!

With the Military Commissions Act that was passed by Congress in 2006, the freedoms we take for granted were snatched away overnight if our President decides we are in an "emergency". That term can be used to describe an endless amount of situations that could be described as foggy, indescript and perhaps not falling into most minds as a "national emergency". These provisions in the Patriot Act as well as the Military Commissions Act, passed in 2006 plus several Executive Orders passed by Pres. Bush and Obama now give the President unlimited power to dictate nearly anything he wants, anytime, on anybody, in the name of " an enemy combatant" or similar terminology as he sees as acceptable. He or his henchmen attorneys can indefinitely jail anyone using this term. Your trial can be delayed and delayed, making it hard or impossible to communicate with a lawyer. Enemy combatant is now considered simply as a "status offense".

So if the President says you are one, then you are, period. No charges required, no attorney or court trials for an undisclosed period of time, etc. One could just get lost in one of our secret prison system facilities around the country. Yes, they exist, more than you'd feel comfortable with. These tactics are already widely used toward actual enemy combatants from the Middle East. Others just "disappear". With these extreme powers, you could feasibly be held to the same standard. We have many other such prisons that are designed for such uses, some secret, and may include any one of the dozens of the FEMA Camp Facilities that are throughout the United States (largely unused at this point in time). These facilities are largely older facilities on closed bases, but have been converted to hold undesirables during civil warring or any number of other situations i.e. any way the government deems necessary, as authorized by the Patriot Act or the President with the many other expanded uses of powers contained within the Patriot Act and other laws and Executive Orders like these I list. Can one imagine that scene? Many remember the U.S. encamping American Japanese during the duration of WWII. Imagine how much worse it could become if actual trouble comes about inside our borders. Many think rightfully that as the world and our own country become more dangerous for all the obvious reasons, the use of armed forces will very conceivably be used on our own citizens or groups who get targeted as protestors, rebel rousers, anti-government agitators as just a few examples. It's very conceivable that in the case of a gov't rebellion, civil war, a serious change of policies that threaten our freedoms, etc. that a Marshall Law situation could take place. At the point of Marshall Law, (total control of all movements brought about by the gov't) all bets are off. Again, these developments since 9/11 are all eerie signs of an impending takeover of civil rights, freedoms and more under the right circumstances. The exact type of civil war could come in one of several possible versions and not simply a black on white or vice-versa scenario. There are many huge frustrations across the whole spectrum of big issues facing Americans and all those special interest groups. Especially amongst those who don't care for the America that our Founding Fathers created! But something is surely coming down the pike!

Samplings of just Patriot Act laws already in place follow: Civilian Inmate Program-Army Regulation 210-35, HR 645 internment camps, HR 428, and HR 2479 indefinite sentencing NDAA. These are all reminiscent of Nazi Germany.

Again, these types of changes in law, including executive orders, are exactly what Hitler did legally and nefariously upon his own unsuspecting citizenry when the timing was right to abuse the same laws. Hitler famously "used the law to pervert the law" as I just exemplified, and just as we have all witnessed occurring on both sides of the political aisle . History is repeating itself.

A scary example of the mindset and possibilities that are talked of too often by our leaders was just how close Americas walk toward totalitarian rule is, consider this bill that was considered in 2010. The Constitution was aggravated with the near passage of a bill called the Belligerent Interrogation, Detention, and Prosecution Act of 2010, and was introduced March 4, 2010. Written by neo-cons Rep. John McCain and Rep. Lindsey Graham, it would have been the most extremist, tyrannical and dangerous bill to be passed perhaps ever in America.

Unbelievably, these are written by our representatives that the we the people put into Washington. The proposed legislation called to expand the Bush era term "enemy combatant" to "enemy belligerent", towards any individual, including American citizens, suspected of any affiliation with terrorism or supporting "hostilities against the United States or its coalition partners." Under these laws, anyone called a suspect must be turned over to military authorities and can be detained without charge, denied the Miranda warning of self-incrimination, any chance of legal representation and held for "the duration of the hostilities." So, anyone whom the administration or authorities don't like or want around, including dissidents or objectors, could be jailed indefinitely without representation or justice, until the end of the hostilities. In this never ending war on terrorism, you or I could be locked up for perhaps 20 or 30 years even though we are innocent! As scary as this sounds, perhaps it shouldn't. It is almost word for word what the Patriot calls out for except that the term "belligerent" is a more inclusive, wide open term. Who is to decide is qualifies as a belligerent? According to the rules as their written, virtually anyone can be if the President or his minions say so!

Most everyone appreciates the need to give our government added powers during an emergency even such as a terrorist attack. But this bill goes far, far beyond powers allowed within the Constitution of the United States. Going even farther, we can see just how easily all or parts of these allowances explained above could be abused by those in power!

Saving up on food, water and supplies is, as the Red Cross advises to all, obviously a good idea. And remember:

*"Government is not reason, it is not eloquence, it is force. Like fire, a troublesome servant and a fearful master. Never for a moment should it be left to irresponsible action".*     President George Washington.


## CAMP FEMA... HERE TO SAVE YOU?

There is an honest joke of sorts that circulates amongst serious prepper types. *"If the FEMA truck pulls up, DON'T GET ON!* While many think of FEMA as a benevolent government service that will come to your aid in case of a hurricane, flood or some other natural disaster such as they did in New Orleans and Hurricane Sandy, this Federal agency also has immense power bestowed on it, even the ability to run our entire government in a large enough "crisis". This agency has been a lifesaver for millions of people perhaps when tragedy strikes upon cities hit by hurricanes, flooding and such. But on the flipside, this agency has the power of God when called to do so in the case of a national emergency when directed to by executive decree. Obviously, many patriotic and freedom loving Americans are rightly concerned that one day all this power could feasibly be wrongly and terribly used in a horrific way upon average citizens by a Hitleresque President or Vice President should an assassination be in the cards. The Patriot Act is written in such a way that it leaves the door open to any one of a hundred different scenarios being used to abuse it.

If a Presidential declaration of "Code Red" alert is ever issued by a U.S. President, (which indicates a "severe risk of imminent terrorist/homeland or civil attacks") even elections could be suspended indefinitely. The Posse Comitatus Act could be suspended or nullified as spelled out within the Patriot Act, and would allow the military to engage in aggressive domestic law enforcement (danger!). In case of a ISIS attack, such an "outside enemy" could very easily trigger a Code Red Alert and trigger Marshall Law. If such an incident was facilitated by any twisted person or group such action would not seem out of reason for naïve citizen's to accept under such false pretenses. You say it couldn't happen? Well, it's been done plenty of times throughout history in order to enact a police state or some gigantic change of government. The Reichstag fire in Germany was a staged event by Hitler. It was the firestorm (literally) event that propelled Hitler forward, making it possible for him to assume the power to cause the removal of most of those within the dominant political party. Any such event seem doubtful, yet should we ignore the Constitution and take the chance?

FEMA would get the first phone call from the President if a Code Red is declared and would be empowered with immense duties and responsibilities. FEMA is tasked with numerous duties including the *Continuity of Government (COG)* in the event of a crisis and would spark off a "neutralization" of key leaders and/or institutions. It also maintains contact between dozens of secret governmental command centers. In a declared emergency event(s), of any form, anywhere on the earth, FEMA's authority would divide up the nation into ten regions under FEMA control and would work autonomously with the military. A map of the 10 regions is available for anyone to see on the internet or by simply going into the FEMA website.

The agency was created through Executive Order by President Nixon's administration and has been the product of over 40 years of various legislations, executive orders and Presidential Decision Directives, and was originally created as a result of the cold war and the threat of a nuclear strike. In 2004 Professor Michel Chossudovsky of the University of Ottawa, editor of Globalresearch.com was asked to provide a report to the White House, Homeland Security and the Department of Justice, specifically to provide the authorities what is needed to cancel elections, place the country under Marshall Law and suspend the Constitution. He disclosed that all these authorities were already in place within FEMA powers extending over to all modes of transportation including cars, trucks, vehicles of any kind, total control of highways, seaports, airports, aircraft, trains, subways, national media, all electrical power, gas, petroleum, fuels and minerals, along with all food resources and farms, the ability to round up forced civilian labor on government projects, seizures of personal property including food & waters and the appropriation of food and water supplies.

The president can declare a national emergency, evoke Executive Order 11490 and take over the country without deferring to Congress or the Constitution. Bingo! New World Order in a couple of days! How many people have any idea of these many laws and executive orders in place and on standby mode?

FEMA would also have absolute power over all health, education and welfare functions and can develop plans to control all the mechanisms of production and distribution, wages, salaries, credit and flow of moneys in US financial institutions in any defined emergency. There are over fifteen executive order giving total authority to the president or FEMA. Just a few of the most powerful, far reaching Executive Orders are numbers 11051, 11320, 11921 and many more.

President Obama enacted E.O. 13606 (executive order) which could easily change America into a dictatorial country extremely easily, without the need to even call out a Code Red alert for it is stand alone! This order seems to double up on the above E.O.'s and takes complete control over all civil transportation, all water from all sources, "all commodities and products that are capable of being ingested by either human beings or animals". "Health resources, including all drugs, biological products, medical devices, materials, facilities, health supplies, services at the Presidents choosing." Section 601 states calls for a civilian security force with forced inscription if deemed necessary with no compensation. Any needed factories are for the taking over by government. This reflects Pres. Obama's 2008 campaign pledge to put in place a "National Civilian Security force just as strong, powerful, just as well funded, as the military". This scenario would be Nazi Germany and Stalinist Russia all over again. What could be just a strong as the U.S. military for God's sake? Now perhaps we know.

Enacting any or all of these E.O.s would basically deny all citizens the rights provided in the Constitution and the Bill of Rights. And what really constitutes an "emergency"? It is described fairly vaguely and non-descript in the Patriot Act, so even a threat of an attack could be construed as one. Much like in Hitler's Germany, all the powers are at the president's fingertips to engage in pretty much any act he wishes to carry out upon an unsuspecting public in order to gain, or even change, the government or its power structures.

The rushed-through Patriot Act left no time for the signers of the act to even read it. Again, this is purposefully done in order to pass what never could be passed if our representatives had the time to scrutinize its language. Such disregards for the Constitutional for political expediency and secret agendas is every bit as important as the economic inequalities that the same system creates. In January 2016 Pres. Obama had talked of permitting himself to unilaterally invade foreign countries with American troops even without Congressional approval! He certainly had the power to do so!

I sincerely hope that at this turning point in Americas history we don't see an assassination of a president or a presidential candidate, a Supreme Court judge, or any number of other last ditch efforts by the globalist elites to hold onto their political party and its platform, the good old boy system, or the globalist agenda. The global elites (the owners of most of the D.C. political class) already see that their new world order plans are becoming more visible. So America is at a turning point. What comes after will not be pleasant I assure all. Remember what the financial man behind the globalist one world government had to say about their end game…


*"The supranational sovereignty of an intellectual elite and world bankers is surely preferable to the national auto-determination practiced in past centuries."* David Rockefeller, Memoirs. WOW!


With so much history behind the globalists plans of a one world government, it definitely seems that time is not on our side at this point. American and worldwide bankruptcy unto the International bankers/Rothschild/Royal Family cabal clearly looks more and more eminent! The pain and losses resulting from this fall could be tenfold the 2008 crash! Will they get the immense powers they want? In the aftermath of this coming colossal depression, will much of the world be forced to become virtual slaves to the International globalists as they make claim to own everything including our own sweat labor? Will this be the "New World Order" so talked of? We know that this same leach's upon societies, the big bankers, the predatory elites, have for 100 years already profited in the hundreds of trillions of dollars and brought America and the world unto their financial knees due to their paper printing Ponzi scheme while indebting the peoples into hundreds of trillion of dollars of debt that they have thrown onto society! We know they have greatly profited from the engineered mass stealing's every single American's wages or income via their insanely usurious un-Federal Reserve System.

Why does it seem that hardly a young soul today has read this history noticed that history repeats itself over and over again? And why hasn't there been a citizen revolt by now? I believe that upon the next crash, one that will assuredly be larger than the Great Depression, we will finally see huge screams of change! Americans are great and patient people, but once they've had enough, look out! Hopefully, whatever comes at America, it won't be too large for the good American citizens to overcome for they are the fiercest fighters if need be. In upcoming elections, help kick out both the socialist one world leaning Rino's and Democrats in Washington and local politics. We need new blood that isn't tainted with money, illusions of a global utopia, and corrupted habits. This is the only surefire and effective way to move ahead should the masses have the chance.


*"Dissent is the highest form of patriotism"* - Thomas Jefferson

## .26

# THE FIGHT TO REGAIN OUR COUNTRY

**"The greatest danger to American freedom is a government that ignores the Constitution."**

**Thomas Jefferson**

Our Founding Fathers warned us of the dangers and risks down the line in the new country they founded. Many times in fact. The fact that we have strayed so very, very far away from the principles of the U.S. Constitution and Bill of Rights is testament to their warnings and to the upside down world we live in today. They wrote the most intelligent political document ever written, full of painstakingly arrived at principles for the new nation to abide by. They warned incessantly that the Republic would not stand if we strayed away from the principles within that very Constitution. This was an experiment of offering freedoms the world had never known.

America is representative republican form of democracy, a different animal than just pure democracy, not to be confused with what many have called "mobocracy." Again, this was an experiment! This was radical because it requires citizen's involvement, even revolt if needed in order to keep the representatives from destroying it. They knew that pure democracy was seriously flawed. It was H.L.Mencken who said: *"Democracy is a pathetic belief in the collective wisdom of individual ignorance."* Without an empowered citizenry and a set of just principles to abide by, politicians could cow tow to political expediencies and vote buying's.

And, there was absolutely no guarantee that the Founding Fathers would get back to Britain if this new government failed to materialize. Furthermore, if we had lost the revolutionary war they would've been hung as traitors of the British Monarchy. These were Radicals with a big R! They were Radicals for liberty, freedom, limited government by the people, democracy, backed up by a Constitutional republic. These great men were from all walks of life, mostly very well educated, extremely well read on the government histories of the world. Armed with historic knowledge and experience, it seems that these were ordered for the job. The founders had a profound awareness and disdain for big centralized, all powerful government and felt inspired to protect the newly found nation against tyranny, loss of liberty and free will. They took every precaution they could muster in the drawing up and approving's within the founding documents. If one reads about the negotiations during the assemblage of our Constitution, you will find that it was very contentious, filled with arguments and disagreements. Some founders leaned too far one way or the other as to the government's new role in the life of its citizens. Some longed for a little of the old British parliamentary traditions to be inserted into the new Constitution and eventually the Bill of Rights. Luckily, the latter group didn't get much traction and we became a nation with newly found liberty, basic rights and all the other freedoms granted.

Our job is to go all back to their great visions and the Constitution that had served us so well until the last 100 years or so. To look at their writings and backgrounds, one could very well make the statement that these men possessed a very special set of knowledges due to their own experiences with the corrupt, all powerful and abusive British government they had endured.

*"No one pretends that democracy is so perfect or all wise. Indeed, it has been said that democracy is the worst form of government except those other forms that have been tried from time to time" by Winston* Churchill

We should be so lucky in today's White House to find even one politician alive who could display the statesmanship, honesty and wise judgement that most of these icons possessed. Today politicians are short sighted, continually in campaign mode, watching which way the wind blows, bought off and indebted to their financial sponsors in campaigns of deception and partners in fraudulent corporate profits and patsies for the globalists. Reelection is the name of the game. It seems so miraculous that these particular men got together, each having his own special part to play at this special time. It seems that God divinely chose this particularly suited and select group from Britain into the positions they were employed with. Their wisdoms achieved a most unique form of new government based on God given freedoms and liberties, both of which were employed

My heartfelt desire is to help wake up people out of their slumber and complacency enough to understand the urgent nature of our countries huge and imminent dangers and challenges, including the 100-year-old plans of the New World Order agenda that is nearly completed, ready to be foisted upon us all. Today, losing our freedoms is just one big "emergency" or several concurrent "emergencies" away.

My hope is also that you and your families can begin to prepare in whatever ways are relevant to your life. And knowing what the challenges are, I hope this book helps you understand the enemy's game plans, take notes and notice when they are being played on you. Hopefully you have learned a lot about the real world around you that the globalists have engineered, how you are being played, and how to fight it, push it back by getting even a little bit more involved even at a local level. Are you prepared? Do you now have awareness of the new world plan so you can be ahead of the crowd in recognizing it and dealing with it? Might you be one to take up the fight to save our nation at whatever level you can? It really doesn't take very long in your community or at higher levels by letting them hear your voices! Are you ready to tell your children as they become young adults why and where America went wrong? And if things haven't change yet for the better, why must they now suffer?

Much of what I write on is focused on driving home the fact that our world is very uncertain today, that individuals are responsible to take a bit more time at trying to make a difference. They need to make time to be more involved, become more educated voters, do some adequate research, really look hard at the issues come election time. Unless you are a communist or die in the wool socialist, see if the candidates or issues to be voted upon hold true to the U.S. Constitution. Checking their voting records is now as easy as 1-2-3. It is after all the very document that made America great. Don't just be another wasted, ignorant vote, let it be known at the voting booth. Be aware of groups whom claim to represent fair sounding change, yet vote opposite when they cast their votes for their district or country.

A groundbreaking debate on the unfairness of the delegate voting system is ready to explode. The public is ever more aware how the elites are able to manipulate elections polls and results, buy delegates votes and much more. A cry for a simple majority vote is being screamed about. Nevertheless, we must vote or else we have nobody to blame but ourselves. Become proficient at reading and understanding the U.S Constitution and the Bill of Rights. Be sure your representatives are voting according to the wise founder's doctrines, or else reject them and try to kick out. Those with the time and vigor (you know who you are), should get involved "hands on" at whatever levels you are comfortable with. An important part is joining in on blogs, on Facebook sites, joining into political focus groups or other types of political activist groups who share your idea of what America should look like. Join groups that align with your political beliefs, try to get involved in local government groups. Write and call your Congress people. Just do what you can! Even far, far back it was known how crooked politicians can be.

It was H.L. Mencken who said of elections… "American elections are an advanced auction of stolen goods."

This is where America has gone wrong. Today, most voters don't know or don't care about the Constitution after being inundated for many years by leftist schools of thought all around them. They buy into any old politician who makes music to their ears! Depending on the area they reside, they can be made to feel foolish for being conservative. These often only take notice of who offers the most goodies without regard of anything else. The globalists, the elites, the leaders in Washington are counting on you continuing to be ignorant and trusting of them in order for them to continue the con game called corporate fascism that has now gone bankrupt. Go beyond the establishments biased misinformation machine. Do some reading. Read their votes.

The news manipulators have their own self-interests at heart. If you want yours, you need to go find it yourself and not believe their propaganda. Expand your limits and think with your head. Read, read and read more. These aren't your allies, you're not part of their elite club, and you're never going to be invited to the party! Only then can we citizens take our nation back.

Remember, when you hear someone calling a Constitutional zealot as an extremist, remember that the Founding Fathers were called extremists when they proposed our style of government. And for those of you who likes socialism or communism, please go to where it already exists for goodness sakes and don't try to change the freedoms that America stands for!

If our Founding Fathers were here today, they would assuredly call the people running Washington D.C. today as "traitors" of the worst type!

*"He who in given cases consents to obey his fellows with servility, and who submits his will, and even his thoughts, t0 their control, how can he pretend he wishes to be free?"*

— Alexis de Tocqueville, Democracy in America


Here is my own, personal list of top priority actions that I feel need to be tackled very soon by our leaders in order to save America from the one world agenda. There are many ways to help effectuate change, so ask yourself if you can do even a very small part on your own.

1. Lobbyist reforms must be installed that severely limit the influence of money. Personal caterings, free trips, free loans, free jet flights, lying in front of Congress must be strictly enforced using a policy of no tolerance, irregardless of how high a position a government employee holds. Fair jail or prison time must quickly be applied to those found ignoring such rules of conduct! Hillary Clinton is a prime example. America's representatives must finally realize that their job requires utmost honesty and the real concerns of the American people again, or they will pay a steep price!

2. Limit Congress people and representatives to two terms. Supreme Court Justices twelve years only.

3. The Patriot Act should be thrown away and rewritten after laborious debates. It was purposely passed without enough time for the hugely important document to be read and contains dozens of examples that are Constitutionally forbid! It sets a unprecedented threat upon every citizens rights and liberties if we should have another "emergency" which is loosely defined. The entire 9/11 event has more holes than Swiss cheese. The many losses of constitutionally guaranteed rights and liberties contained within the Patriot Act were politically impossible, that is, unless there was a good reason. The 9/11 event provided that event. The truths are finally coming out. Example: According to Former New Jersey attorney general John Farmer in his 2009 *book The Ground Truth: The Story Behind America's Defense on 9/11* wrote that by 2010 even top officials of the 9/11 commission, including commission co-chairman Lee Hamilton and Farmer himself, had publicly questioned the conclusions of the commission. Briefly, he explained that in the course of the investigation into the national response to the attacks, the 9/11 Commission staff discovered that the official version of what had occurred that fateful morning was almost entirely, inexplicably untrue. Further iterating that "at some level of the government, there was an agreement not to tell the truth about what had happened." The 9/11 event and the follow up response of creating a freedom robbing so-called Patriot Act seems to assuredly to have been part of a planned event by elites including

Pres. George W. Bush, for reasons of which we will never know the whole story. This is standard procedure in order to hide pertinent facts. We now know at least that the whole 9/11 event(s) and responses were likely part of the same tactic nearly always connected with any firestorm event. Yes, the Hegelian Dialectic, the tactic of "create a problem, offer a solution, fix the problem." The Patriot Act(s) should be thrown away and replaced with a new document that has been argued at length in Congress. Of note; The Patriot Act was apparently written in large part before the 9/11 tragedy!

4. All regional and global trade agreements, pacts, and treaties such as NAFTA, CAFTA, NAU and the TPP should be redrafted by a blue ribbon committee of perhaps 100 different experts with extensive business experience and wide knowledge on free markets. And all anti-Constitutional provisions should be rejected. President Trump seems to have begun the process. We must be assured that any trade agreement ensures FREE trade, in contrast to "managed trade" run by, and for, the sole benefit of the globalist corporates as I expounded upon it in previous chapters.

   This will bring jobs back to America in droves. America CAN compete if they don't have to compete with the ten cent per hour slave labor that the globalists expect. Independent trade experts, patriots, Constitutional scholars and an array of non-corporate, non-political advisors should have the final word on all trade deals. Of course, a transparent endeavor such as this is unlikely to occur without voter revolts. This is what Trump is up against!

5. Rid the nation of the un-federal reserve. Get back to the Constitution and return that job back to the government! We could stop paying interest on phony fiat money that the Rothschild's and the International banking cabals have cleverly foisted upon America for the last 100+ years, and of which is now driving America past the point of simple bankruptcy. This would be such a huge win for America. Far bigger than most can imagine.

6. Rid Obamacare and replace it with a private healthcare system that works and creates free choices through real competition amongst insurance providers, guaranteed placement and no allowance for cancellation or unreasonable premium hikes. Medical savings accounts need to be encouraged as well. No system will be perfect, but Obamacare has proven to be unfixable and unaffordable. So much so that President Obama had to illegally raid the profits of Fannie May and Freddie Mac to keep the plan from sinking! The cost of medical care has gone up over 300 percent since the year 2008. It is a failed idea that was always intended to become a single payer plan foisted upon us all by the left. Obamacare has driven up costs for paperwork, allowed medical providers, drug providers and health insurance companies to charge nearly whatever they want. Drug companies should be forced charge Americans the same rate as they do Canada (nearly half)!

7. Medicare must be forced to use their immense buying power to negotiate far better drug prices. Drug price gouging on particular drugs must be regulated. Example: The 62 yr. old drug Daraprin price was raise from $3.50 to $750.00 in one day after being bought out by a hedge fund company. Another: Cycloserine, previously priced at $50.00 for a bottle of 30 pills. An investment company bought its manufacturer and raised the price to $750.00. Doxycycline, an antibiotic went from $20.00 a bottle made by Mylan in 2013 to $1,849.99 by 2016! The list goes on. Investors are raking in obscene profits at the cost of taxpayers, the dying and sick. This is probably an extreme example but the new

cancer drug, Campath, which sells for $600 to $700 in Canada. Its U.S. price is $2,400. (Excerpt from Why are pharmaceuticals cheaper in Canada?)

Another example is the drugs needed for Parkinson's disease Mirapex, for Parkinson's disease: $157 in Canada vs. $263 in the USA, Celexa for depression: $149 in Canada vs. $253 in the USA. Diovan for high blood pressure: $149 in Canada vs. $253 in the USA. Oxazepam for insomnia: $13 in Canada vs. $70 in the USA. Seroquel, for insomnia: $33 in Canada vs. $124 in the USA. Critical Condition: Cheaper in Canada https://www.wsj.com/articles/why-the-u-s-pays-more-than-other... The price Medicare pays for these drugs must at least be competitive to other nations whom pay far less for the same exact drug, as well as limit usurious charges. Same goes for other obscene charges within the system. When will the dumbed down and politically unread American public wake up and demand all this? Oh, do you think that the existing system which simply passes the costs (no matter how insanely expensive), is designed to make it extremely easy for the average taxpayers to just shrug the costs off using ill-logic i.e "the government pays for it?" Using the one-eye-closed and crony endorsed payment system presently raping us all off is not a good alternative to be peddled onto hard working Americans! Stand up people.

8. Asset Forfeiture laws should be overhauled even further. Currently suspects are assumed guilty before being tried, often losing everything. Originally designed towards drug dealers, there are today more than 200 federal forfeiture laws applied to non-drug related crimes. (Inside IRS and Seizure Abuses)

9. Major campaign reforms, ending Super-Pac's such as Citizens United with its false cliché title. Limit all campaigns unto a reasonable, set dollar limit in order to encourage more competition from other smart contestants whom have good ideas to debate. Allow free airtime for more contestants whom are running for the public office. The public does in fact own the airwaves after all.

10. End the Common Core Educational Program and return education to the states. Basics should be prioritized, English should be the official language, students should be encouraged to think critically instead of just regurgitating names and dates that are irrelevant to life. Questioning authority should be encouraged rather than following an official state pushed and politically correct one world socialistic inspired agenda. Instead of pushing students hard to prepare every child for college, schools should offer vocational schooling during high school and into college. Enact more common-sense changes that are aimed at actually preparing young people for real life, and stop the politically correct agenda.

11. Outright ban G.M.O.s and potentially dangerous vaccines by following the lead of most of developed countries around the world. rest of the world. Stop the use of all vaccines and vaccine cocktails invented and marketed for the last 20 years that are suspected of being dangerous to our health. Only resume the production of those vaccines once they have gone through rigorous, long term testing's carried out by multiple, independent, non-drug industry affiliated test labs in order to truthfully see their long term effects.

12. Stop unconstitutional importations of illegals. Join Pres. Trump in his plans to build more and bigger walls, provide better monitoring abilities, untie border agents hands.

Help President Trump to overturn all the various bad border policies that have allowed hundreds of thousands of criminal aliens to sneak into our country and creating havoc. Support him as well in stopping unvetted refugees from war torn countries from entering the U.S. as I covered in the book. President Trump has made the border issue a major part of his referendum voiced by Americans and we must help him fight the opposition on both sides of the isle.

13. Reform the jail and judicial system completely. Reverse the current course of using these two agencies to serve as profit generating centers for cash strapped local governments. A serious assessment should be made towards reducing the fines and jail terms for first time minor drug charges. We must take a look at who really belongs in jail, and who doesn't.

14. Restore the Glass-Steagall Act and rewrite the Net Capital Rule to restore sanity within lending, Wall Street and the banking industries with the aim of reducing the common practices of huge risk takings on the backs of citizen's savings and retirement accounts, such as we saw in 2008. The situation today is far more perilous. Finally, find more ways to stop the elites practice of "All risks to the taxpayers, all profits to the bankers" with as little negative effect on the real economy as possible.

15. Last but not least, citizens should force our politicians to abide by the 10th Amendment which reads: *"The powers not delegated to the United States by the Constitution, nor prohibited by it to the States, are reserved to the States respectively, or to the people.".* The **10th Amendment** was designed to keep the federal government from interfering with states' rights as defined. This oh so important document was ratified on December 15, 1791. It expresses the principle of federalism and states' rights, which strictly supports the entire plan of the original Constitution for the United States of America, stating that the federal government possesses only those powers delegated to it by the United States Constitution. All remaining powers are reserved for the states or the people. This is a warning that this principle has been trampled on around Washington, too often sending America into the arms of the globalists! The Tenth Amendment Movement group is great place to get involved in this fight.

These are my top fifteen but not all, not by a longshot. Can you name more? I am sure you can, and I urge you to get involved with whatever inspires you when it comes to fixing America!

It is my earnest desire that people wake up to the blatant attempts by the power structures and the globalists to change America into something much different. Take heed of the chaos and civil unrest soon to come. Remember, the crisis precedes the calm. I have hope that once all this dust settles, there will be a new awakening of brotherhood, connectedness, compassion and a greater purpose than what the godless corrupted leaders of this world have tried to push upon us all.

And remember that old adage... *"Those who fail to prepare are planning to fail."* As Americans became more awake during the run up to the Trump election, so must they take that extra 20 minutes a day to try and stay up with the accurate news. Write a congressman or call him once in awhile! It doesn't take a retired person to do this. Retired people have much more time to save their grandkids future! What good is a stash of money in a trust for the children if their freedoms and the value of their money is swept under the carpet upon the next big fall?

The power elites see their powers being threatened like never before. Yet people are waking up to the long running frauds these have engineered for so long. Their public admissions of their plans in fact reveal that they are feeling emboldened at this time in history. Time is close and they know it. As already mentioned, President Trump will need to pull off a miracle if he can slow down the speeding freight train of globalism! We will all have to wait and see. And when someone says, *"Do believe all that stuff in that book?"*, kindly remember the following saying:

**"First they ignore you. Then they laugh at you. Then they fight you. Then you win", Mohanda Gandhi.**

### FINAL WORDS

Be concerned, involved and amply prepared to deal with the upcoming once-in-a lifetime changes coming at you from all angles. There is a quickening today that futurists predicted many years back. Changes and challenges such as America has never seen or heard of are directly ahead. History does repeat, albeit will be on a larger scale than we could have imagined perhaps. What is to come, and in what form, is largely predictable unless great resistance is exercised against the one world forces. Keep up the fight good friend!

*Please be kind enough to write a positive review of this book on Amazon if you enjoyed the information presented in this book! And watch for a follow up book soon to come at Amazon.com!

## REMEMBER: ETERNAL VIGILANCE!

# ADDITIONAL SOURCES, BOOKS, ARTICLES

## INTRODUCTION

Tumped Up, How Criminalization of Political Differences Endangers Democracy Alan Dershowitz ISBN 9781974617890

## SWAN SONG OF GLOBALISM-

The Fall of the American Empire... And What We Can do About ...

www.globalresearch.ca/the-fall-of-the-american-empire-and...it/5385506

Why the Globalists Selected Obama to be President - DaGlobalization -The Economic Collapse theeconomiccollapseblog.com/archives/tag/globalization

GlobalizationTheEconomicCollapsetheeconomiccollapseblog.com/archives/tag/globalizati

## WORLD MONEY-

Paul Craig Roberts, *"The Money Changers Serenade: A New Plot Hatches,* "Infowars.com December 1, 2013.

Sweden leads the race to become cashless society ...www.theguardian.com › Business › Banking

UN backs new global currency reserve currency. The Financial Times: March 23, 2009

www.cnbc.com/2013/12/12/cashless-society-a-huge-threat-to-our.
www.thenewamerican.com/...pushing-cashless-society-to-control-humanity

A New Digital Cash System Was Just Unveiled at A Secret Meeting for Bankers In New York, article by Michael Snyder/Theeconomiscollapse.com May 02/2016

## CONSPIRACY? -

Mike Adams on normalcy bias: http://www.naturalnews.com

Dave Hodges on common foe is the elite: http://www.thecommonsenseshow.com 2014/04/26/will-humanity-survive-the=depopulation-agenda-of-the-elite/

Jim Marrs- The Trillion Dollar Conspiracy- How The New World Order, Man Made Diseases, and Zombie Banks Are Destroying America, HarperCollins Publishers ASIN: B003P2VYJG

## THE SYSTEM IS THE PROBLEM

The Corporation Named America/The Royals and Vatican Connection: Quotations and writings from numerous sources such as Jordon Maxwell, David Icke, World Book Encyclopedia, Encyclopedia Britannica, The Atlantean Conspiracy

DEMOCRACY INCORPORATED: MANAGED DEMOCRACY AND THE SPECTER OF INVERTED TOTALITARIANISM SHELDON WOLIN (AUTHOR) **ISBN:** 0691178488

CLASS DIVISIONS, POVERTY AND COLLAPSE-

INSPIRATIONS FROM CHRIS HEDGES BOOK *THE DEATH OF THE MIDDLE CLASS* CHAPTER 1 ENTITLED RESISTANCE.

*"The Obama Stimulus Impact? Zero."* John F. Cogan and John B. Taylor, *Wall Street Journal* 12/9/10

Taylor, Kristinn, "Black Labor Force Participation Rate Under Obama Hits Rock Bottom-Lowest Ever Recorded," *Gateway Pundit*, January 13, 2014.

Jim Marrs- The Trillion Dollar Conspiracy- How The New World Order, Man Made Diseases, and Zombie Banks Are Destroying America, HarperCollins Publishers ASIN: B003P2VYJG

Taylor, John B. *Getting Off Track: How Government Actions and Interventions Caused, Prolonged, and Worsened the Financial Crisis,* Stanford, Calif.: Hoover Institution Press, 2009

Reinhart, Carmen M., and Kenneth S. Rogoff. *This time is Different: Eight Centuries of Financial Folly.* Princeton, N.J.: Princeton University Press, 2009

FEDERAL RESERVE-

Record profits for Fed: http://finance.yahoo.com/news/Fed-posts-record-profit/bernie-sanders 791091.html

Fed Monetizing U.S. debt: http://seekingalpha.com/article/158330-how-the-federal-reserve-us-monetizing -debt

Converting debt into money: G. Edward Griffin, *The Creature from Jekyll Island* (Westlake Village CA.: American Media, 1994) pg,207

*Congress outflanked and outfoxed*: Griffin. p.469

Tower of Basel: *The Shadowy History of the Secret Bank That Runs the World.* New York: Public Affairs, 2013 Lebor, Adam

*Paper Promises: Debt, Money and the New World Order.* New York: Public Affairs, 2012 Coggens, Phillip

*The House of Morgan: An American Banking Dynasty and the Rise of Modern Finance.* New York: Simon & Schuster, 1999. Chernow, Ron.

Congress outflanked and outfoxed: Griffin. Rep. Ron Paul introduces audit the Fed bill: http/www.house.house-gove/list/speech/tx14__paul/AdittheFedBill.shtml

Bernanke not knowing where the money went: http. //prisonplanet

Web of Debt: The Shocking Truth About Our Money System and How We Can Break Free. *Her websites are webofdebt.com and ellenbrown.com.*


AGE OF DISINFORMATION, MEDIAS, GOVERNMENTAL


## CONTROLLING THE OPPOSITION

"NSA Spying Did Not Result in a Single Foiled Terrorist Plot," *Washington's Blog*, Oct 15, 2013

Chris Hedges on surveillance state:http:truthdig.com/report/item/what_obama_really-meant-was-20140110

WilliamBinney:http://www.theguardian.com/comments          free/2014/jul/11/the-ultimate-goal-is-total-population-control

Anthony Gucciardi on kicking out mainstream media: http://www.storyleak.com/gallup-poll-virtually-no-one-trusts-the -media

Michael Crichton on junk media: http://www.slate.com/articles/new-and-politics-press-bpx 2008/05

Manufacturing Consent, book by Noam Chomsky, Edward S. Herman Isbn.0-375-71449-9


THE FIGHT TO REGAIN OUR COUNTRY- Intelligent insights from Chris Hedges book "The Death of the Liberal Class", chapter 11 entitled "Rebellion."


## THE FRANKFURT SCHOOL/CULTURAL MARXISM-

Marx, Karl. *Selected Writings*. Edited by David McLellan. Oxford: Oxford University Press, 1977

How the Frankfurt School Changed American Culture, Garret-Galland Investments, article, 8/12/16 by David Galland

The Devils Pleasure Palace, Michael Walsh. The cult of critical theory and the subversion of the West. ISBN 978-1-59403-769-6

Tavistock Institute: Social Engineering the Masses, Daniel Estulin ISBN:63424043X


## CORPORATE FASCISM TAKEOVER-

Truthdig article "The revenge of the Lower Classes and the Rise of American Fascism" by Chris Hedges March 2, 2016

The Truth About the Robber Barons, Mises Institute

Mises.org/library/search.asp?+robber+barons

The Rise Of The Fourth Reich, Jim Marrs 2008 ISBN: 0061245593 ASIN:B0018QUCWQ

## UNEMPLOYMENT

*More job seekers than jobs*: http//www.whotv.com/business ct-biz-1208-gail-unemployment-20101208.0.2069895.column

Unemployment figure second highest since WWI: http://finance.yahoo.com/new/what recovery-unemployment-apf-5632122944.html?x=0

## BANKS / BAILOUTS / BIS / FEDERAL RESERVE

Hank Paulson on safe banking system: http://cbs5/national/henry.paulson.economy.2.776329.html

BIS report on unstable system: http//www.telegraph.co. ul/finance/newsbysector/banksand finance/6184496/Derivatives_still_pose_huge_risk_says_BIS.html

*BIS is a Nazi bank*: Jim Marrs, *The Rise of the Fourth Reich, 00.24-28*

*The Death of Money*. The Coming Collapse of the International Monetary System. James B. Rickards ISBM1591846706

Marilyn Barnewall on central bankers http:newswithviews.com/Barewall.marilyn103.htm

Jim Marrs- The Trillion Dollar Conspiracy- How The New World Order, Man Made Diseases, and Zombie Banks Are Destroying America, HarperCollins Publishers ASIN: B003P2VYJG

The New Financial Deal: Understanding the Dodd-Frank Act and Its (Unintended) Consequences, David Skeel Wiley; 1st edition (December 7, 2010) **ISBN:** 0691178488

Whithouse, Michael (May 1989). *"Paul Warburg's Crusade to Establish a Central Bank in the United States"*. Minnesota Federal Reserve.

## NEEDIEST SUFFER THE MOST

Wiley; 1st edition (December 7, 2010)Adults and children on food stamps: http://www.nytimes.com /2009/11/29/us/29foodstamps.html

Snyder, Michael, "The More Illegal Immigrants That Go on Food Stamps, the More Money JP Morgan Makes," Theeconomiccollapse.com article 4/28/13

"Blame Rich, Overeducated Elites as Our Society Frays," Bloomberg *View, 11/20,13*

*More Americans Receive benefits than they pay in taxes*: http:taxfoundation.org/article/accounting-what-families-pay-taxes-and-what-they-receive-government-spending-0

Dorothy Stoneman on ending poverty: http: ..www.huffingtonpost.com/Dorothy-stoneman/poverty-gun-violence_3528888.html

Death of The Middle Class, Chris Hedges **Page Numbers Source ISBN:** 1568586442 Nation Books (October 19, 2010)

Americans on food stamps and unemployment: http://www.statisticbrain.com/welfare- statistics/

*82nd Annual Report, 1995,* Board of Governors of the Federal Reserve System, U.S. Government Printing Office.

Galbraith, John K. (1990), *A Short History of Financial Euphoria.* New York: Whittle Direct Books.

Kah, Gary (1991), *En Route to Global Occupation.* Lafayette, La.: Huntington House.

Mullins, Eustace (1983), *Secrets of the Federal Reserve.* Staunton, Va.: Bankers Research Institute.

Schauf, Thomas (1992), *The Federal Reserve*, Streamwood, IL: FED-UP, Inc.

Woodward, G. Thomas (1996), "Money and the Federal Reserve System: Myth and Reality." Congressional Research Service.

United States Code Annotated, 1994. U.S. Government Printing Office.

Economic Collapse in Argentina- http://.telegraph.co.uk/finance/comment/6146873/Adam-Smith-would -not-be-optomistic-in-todays-economic-world.html

Web of Debt: The Shocking Truth About Our Money System and How We Can Break Free. *Her websites are webofdebt.com and ellenbrown.com.*

CORPORATISM/FASCISM-

How the World Really Works: Noam Chomski

Lenin on subservience to the State: http://www.fff.org/freedom/0198d.asp; http;//www.time.com/time/magazine/article
*Neo-Colonialism, the Last Stage of Imperialism*, Kwame Nkrumah.


Catherine Austin Fitts on global financial coup d'e`tat:http;//solari.com

Larry Flynt on government by corporations: http://huffingtonpost.com/larry-flynt/common-sense-2009_b_264706.html

Fascism VS. Capitalism: Lew Rockwell Jr.

Jim Marrs- The Trillion Dollar Conspiracy- How The New World Order, Man Made Diseases, and Zombie Banks Are Destroying America, HarperCollins Publishers ASIN: B003P2VYJG

Corporate Fascism Takeover Truthdig article "The revenge of the Lower Classes and the Rise of American Fascism" by Chris Hedges March 2, 2016

The End Of America, Naomi Wolf, 2007 ISBN 978-1-933392-79-0

UNITED NATIONS/CFR/TRILATERALS/BILDERBERGS

U.S. Bilderberg attendees Violating Federal Law, Activists Say. Article by Alex Newman/The New American.com June 02,2012

Walter Cronkite on America's ruling class: http://www.newswatc.org/

CFR explains the president's agenda for Paulson: http:www.cfr.org.publication/11165/what_the_boss_wants_from_hank_paulson.html

Adolph Hitler on New World Order: http://hitlersDiariesPhilosophy2.html

Joan Veon and the transfer of America's sovereignty:

http//www.newswithviews.comVeon/joan156.htm

Woodrow Wilson on committee of men like J.P. Morgan: http: http: ..www.latimes.com/latimes/Global_Economy/JA30Dj02.html

Carrol Quigley, *Tragedy and Hope: A History of the World in our Time (New York: MacMillan, 1966)*

Alex Jones on "scientific dictatorship" https://www.youtube.com/watch?=vxqODoYUDGk

*Neo-Colonialism, the Last Stage of Imperialism*, Kwame Nkrumah. ISBN-13: 978-0717801404

New World Order Agenda: Obama's Reckless Roadmap to World ...The New Agenda: Agenda 21 and the U.N. One World www.renewamerica.com/columns/cobb/130219

*Neo-Colonialism, the Last Stage of Imperialism*, Kwame Nkrumah.

Obama's Unconstitutional Agenda: Plan for A New World ...

www.infowars.com/obamas-unconstitutional-agenda-plan-for-a-new

Rule By Secrecy: The Hidden History that Connects the Trilateral Commission, The Freemasons & The Great Pyramids by Jim Marrs **ASIN: B00X7YN69I**


POPULATION CONTROL/AGENDA 21-

G. Griffin on Holden's plans for population reduction:  http:www.heart.org/choice4health.htm

Bill Gates Foundation Announces Population Control ...

www.riseearth.com › conspiracy

Catherine Austin-Fitts on population control means: http://www.scoop.co.nzstories/HL0907/S00250.htm thetruthwins.com/archives/category/eugenics

Population Control/How corporate owners are killing us / Jim Marrs ISBN 978-9-06-235989-6

William Binney: http://www.theguardian.com/comments free/2014/jul/11/the-ultimate-goal-is-total-population-control

The Man-Made Origin of Aids: Are Human and Viral Experiments Responsible For Unleashing The HIV Holocaust? Alan Cantwell, Jr. MD/www.Rense.com

Jim Marrs- The Trillion Dollar Conspiracy- How The New World Order, Man Made Diseases, and Zombie Banks Are Destroying America, HarperCollins Publishers ASIN: B003P2VYJG

DERIVATIVES-

Ambrose Evans-Prichard, Derivatives still pose huge risk, says BIS. The Telegraph: Sept. 13, 2009

Hearing before the Joint Economic Committee, "Financial Regulatory Reform: Protecting Taxpayers and the Economy," Nov 19, 2009

Stiglitz, Joseph, "Capitalist Fools," *Vanity Fair,* January 2009

Blinder, Alan, "It's Broke, Let's Fix It: Rethinking Financial Regulation," Prepared for the Federal

Reserve Bank of Boston, Oct. 23, 2009

Sens. Warren, McCain, Cantwell and King, "We Need to Rein In 'Too Big To Fail' Banks," U.S. Senate documents, July 17, 2014

Phone interview with Karen Shaw Petrou, Federal Financial Analytics

Kuttner, Robert (October 2, 2007), *"The Alarming Parallels Between 1929 and 2007"*, The *American Prospect*: 2, *retrieved February 20, 2012.*

Stiglitz, Joseph E. (January 2009), *"Capitalist Fools"* (PDF), *Vanity Fair*: 2, *retrieved February 20, 2012.*

Stiglitz, Joseph E. (2010), Freefall: America, Free Markets, And The Sinking Of The World Economy, New York: W.W. Norton & Co., pp. 15 and 82–83, *ISBN 0-393-07596-6.*

The New Financial Deal: Understanding the Dodd-Frank Act and Its (Unintended) Consequences, David Skeel

WALL STREETS VAMPIRE SQUID-Matt Taibbi's "Vampire Squid" Takedown Of Goldman Sachs …

www.businessinsider.com/matt-taibbis-vampire-squid...goldman-sachs..The Great Vampire Squid Keeps On Sucking - Forbes

www.forbes.com/.../2013/08/08/the-great-vampire-squid-keeps-on-sucking

DOJ Will Not Prosecute Goldman Sachs in Financial Crisis …

abcnews.go.com/blogs/.../08/doj-will-not-prosecute-goldman-sachs-in...


ELITES ENGINEERED VIRUSES/VACCINES-

Catherine Austin- Fitts on pandemics as depopulation method: http:..www.scoop.co.nz/stories/HL0907/S00250.htm

Katie Keranen on events caused by injection: http:..www.motherjones.com environment 03/13

CDC patent on Ebola virus: http//wwwgoogle.com/patents/CA2741523A1?cl+en

The Ebola Conspiracy Theories - The New York Times www.nytimes.com/.../sunday-review/the-ebola-conspiracy-theories.html

The Man-Made Origin of Aids: Are Human and Viral Experiments Responsible For Unleashing The HIV Holocaust? Alan Cantwell, Jr. MD/www.Rense.com

Jim Marrs- The Trillion Dollar Conspiracy- How The New World Order, Man Made Diseases, and Zombie Banks Are Destroying America, HarperCollins Publishers ASIN: B003P2VYJG

GLASS STEAGALL ACT-

Weissman, Robert (November 12, 2009), *Reflections on Glass–Steagall and Maniacal Deregulation*, CommonDreams.org, *retrieved February 26, 2012.*

Kuttner, Robert (October 2, 2007), *"The Alarming Parallels Between 1929 and 2007"*, The *American Prospect*: 2, *retrieved February 20, 2012.*

Stiglitz, Joseph E. (2010), Freefall: America, Free Markets, And The Sinking Of The World Economy, New York: W.W. Norton & Co., pp. 15 and 82–83, *ISBN 0-393-07596-6.*

Hearing before the Joint Economic Committee, "Financial Regulatory Reform: Protecting Taxpayers and the Economy," Nov 19, 2009

Blinder, Alan, "It's Broke, Let's Fix It: Rethinking Financial Regulation," Prepared for the Federal Reserve Bank of Boston, Oct. 23, 2009

Sens. Warren, McCain, Cantwell and King, "We Need to Rein In 'Too Big To Fail' Banks," U.S. Senate documents, July 17, 2014

Phone interview with Karen Shaw Petrou, Federal Financial Analytics Fact Check: Did Glass-Steagall Cause The 2008 Financial Crisis? Oct. 14, Jim Zarroli NPR

## GUNS / MILITARIZED STREETS-

John W. Whitehead on arms and ammunition for federal agencies:http://w.lewrockwell.com/2014/06/john-w-whitehead-/you-trust-the-government/

Mass Shootings every sixty-four days since 2011: Http/www.huffington-post.com/2014/10/15

David Price and American Anthropological Association concerns: http://wwwrawstory.com/rs/2014/o6/12/defense-dept-studying-protestors-to-prepare-for -mass-civil-breakdown/

ACLU study on over aggressive domestic policing: https://www.aclu.org/criminal-law-reform-/war-comes-home-excessive-militarization-american-police-report

How the Order Creates War and Revolution, June 19, 1984, by Antony C. Sutton (Author) ISBN-10: 0914981021 ISBN-13: 978-0914981022

Syrian rebels linked to al-Qaeda: http:..www.washingtonexaminer.com/Obama-waives-ban-on-arming-terrorists-to-allow-aid-to-syrian-opposition/article/2535885

White House: http://wwwwnd.com/2015/01genrals-conclude-Obama-backed-al-qaida

How the Order Creates War and Revolution, June 19, 1984, by Antony C. Sutton (Author) ISBN-10: 0914981021 ISBN-13: 978-0914981022

## ON GOLD-

Greenspan on gold: http:..www.restore_government_accountability.com/greenspan-on-gold.html

Any financial instrument subject to seizure: http://www.gata.org/node/5606

The Federal Reserve Conspiracy- Antony C. Sutton

William Still, *"The Money Masters: How International Bankers Gained Control of America"*, Still Productions, 1996.

Minework's Media Group Inc for The History Channel, *"Decoding the Past: The Templar Code, the crusade for secrecy"*, A & E Television Networks, 2005.


ON COLLEGE-

Highest paid college professors: CNN Money U.S. The Future of America? -

More Than Half of All U.S. Young Now Reject Capitalism, economiccollapse.com/ Michael Snyder, April 27th, 2016


GMO'S, POPULATION CONTROL, VACCINES-

How Corporate Owners are Killing Us: Jim Marrs, ISDN; 9780062359896

Katie Kernen on events caused by injection: http://www.motherjones.com 2013/03

Dr. Helen Wallace on government-GMO collusions:

http://www.dailymail.co.uk/news/article-2621058


GLOBAL WARMING / CLIMATE CHANGE

Sun Scientists debate Whether Solar Lull Could Trigger Another "Little Ice Age", Huffington Post, January 24, 2014 by Macrina Cooper-White

Michael Bastach, *"Global Warming? Satellite Data Shows Arctic Sea Ice Coverage Up 50 percent!*

Steven Goddard, *"2013 Will Finish One of the Ten Coldest Years in US History, with the Largest Drop in Temperature,"* Real Science, Dec. 20,2013.

Joel B. Pollack, *"2014 is Global Warmings Worst Year Ever."*

*Steve Watson article: "Professor Calls for Climate Change 'Deniers' to be imprisoned.* Infowars.com

Cracking Big Green: To Save The Earth From The Save-The-Earth Money Machine Ron Arnold and Paul Dreissen (authors)

*Dark Winter*, author John L. Casey, a former White House national space policy advisor, NASA headquarters consultant, and space shuttle engineer tells the truth about ominous changes taking place in the climate and the Sun. Humanix Books (August 19, 2014)

This Changes Everything: Climate Vs. The Climate: Naomi Klien 9/16/2014 **ASIN: BOOJHIDON6**

The Deniers: The World Renowned Scientists Who Stood Up Against Global Warming Hysteria, Political Persecution, and Fraud**And those who are too fearful to do so 1st.

"IPPC Official: 'Climate Policy Is Redistributing the World's Wealth," 11/19,2010 *US Message Board*

Greenpeace Co-Founder: No Scientific Evidence Humans Are Dominant Cause of Warming Climate," Fox News/science/2014/02/26

Watson, Steve, "Professor Calls for Climate Change 'Deniers' to Be Imprisoned,"*Infowars.com* March 17, 2014

Pollak, Joel "2014 Is Global Warming's Worst Year Ever*," Brietbart*, February 19,2014 (http://nypost/2013/12/04americas-greenest-energy-source/).

Fumento, Michael, "Global-Warming 'Proof' Is Evaporating," *New York Post*, 12/5/13

American Boomer author, Charles C. Reich, entitled 'The Greening of America'.

The Deniers: The World Renowned Scientists Who Stood Up Against Global Warming Hysteria, Political Persecution, and Fraud**And those who are too fearful to do so 1st. Lawrence Solomon (Author) ISBN-13: 978-0980076318

ISBN-10: 0980076

Climate Change: A Failed Attempt To Establish "Scientific Dictatorship" Infowars

Global Political Awakening Mark Daniels, August 31, 2010 **ASIN:** B00X7YN69I

Lawrence Soloman (author), ISBN-13: 978-0980076318 Richard Vigilante Books; 1 edition (April 1, 2008)

"Regional climate impacts of a possible future grand solar minimum", Sara Ineson et al, *Nature Communications*, 23 June 2015.                    "Predicted slowdown in the rate of Atlantic sea ice loss", Yaeger et al, GRL, 28 December 2

THE COMING CIVIL WAR

ISBN-10: 098007631 Simon Schama, The world teeters on the brink of a new age of rage, The Financial Times, May 22

On The Precipice Of Widespread Civil Unrest, economiccollapse.com Michael Snyder, January 29th, 2017

Why The Banking Elite Want Riots in America. February 11, 2013 Civil War 2: The economic imperative for mass social unrest Paul Joseph Watson & Alex Jones, Infowars.com

Edmund Conway, Moody's warns of 'social unrest' as sovereign debt spirals.  The Financial Times, December 15, 2009

Charles C.W. Cooke on police gearing up for invasion:

http://www.nationalreview.com/article/381445/barney-fife-meets-delta-force-charls-c-w-cooke

William Norman Grigg on state-licensed aggression: http://.lewrockwell.com

Stop The Coming Civil War, Michael Savage ISBN 978-1-4555-8243-3

JAMES TRAFICANT/1933 Bankruptcy of The United States

1.        Van Susteren, Greta (2009-09-10). *"Exclusive: Traficant – 'I Was a Target. ... I Must Have Been Doing Something Right'".* Fox News. *Retrieved 2009-11-13. Buy American: The Untold Story of Economic Nationalism – Dana Frank – Google Books.* Books.google.ca. *Retrieved 2013-03-27.*Jump up ^ Milan Simonich, Pittsburgh Post-Gazette, Rep. James Traficant: 'He's perceived ... to have almost magical powers', April 12, 2002

## OBUMMERCARE & V.A. CRIMES

John Dickerson on growing VA scandal: http;//www.slate.com/articles/news_and-politics-politics/2014/05/veterans_affairs_scandal_why_the_treatment_of_
pir_veterans_is_a_genuine.html

Michelle Malkin, "How America Treats Illegal Aliens vs. Veterans," Creators.com, May 23, 2014(http://Michelle-malkin/how-america-treats-illegal-aliens-vs-veterans.html

## PATRIOT ACT & FEMA

The End of America- Naomi Wolf ISBN 10-1033392797

The Patriot Act-Key Controversies NPR, article by Larry Edelson/Maria Godoy2/4/06

## RIGGED INEQUALITIES AGAINST THE 90%

*Noah*, Timothy. The *Great Divergence, America's Growing Inequality Crisis and What We Can Do About It.* New York: Bloomsbury, 2011

## ON WARRINGS

Chris Hedges, book "Death of the Middle Class". **ISBN:** 1568586442 October 19.2010, Nation Books, Hachette Book Group /General takes on chapter 2 entitled ".Permanent War"

The EMP Threat: Sending America Back to The 1800s | Zero Hedge

www.zerohedge.com/news/2015-04-07/emp-threat-sending-america-back...

Neoliberalism and the Globalization of War. America's ...

https://southfront.org/neoliberalism-and-the-globalization-of-war

Chuck Baldwin on perpetual war:http://chuckbaldwin

winlivecom/Articles/tabid/109/ID/1203/Globalist-Pounce-On-Rand-Paul.aspz

## HEGELIANISM/ORDER OUT OF CHAOS

The Hegelian Dialectic https://www.fhu.com/hegelian.html

"Crisis is an Opportunity": Engineering a Global Depression to Create a Global Government by Globalresearch.com article- October 26, 2010

## CIVIL WARRING-

# Planned Collapse of Americanism

[Type here]

Stop the coming Civil War, book by Michael Savage ISBN 978-1-4555-8241-

How the Order Creates War and Revolution, June 19, 1984, by Antony C. Sutton (Author) ISBN-10: 0914981021 ISBN-13: 978-0914981022

PATRIOT ACT/FEMA

Stop the coming Civil War, book by Michael Savage ISBN 978-1-4555-8241-

FABIANISM

The Crimes of the Fabian Socialist NWO 6/24/09 Centurean2

'Welcome to 1984'. Article / Truthdig, Chris Hedges May 14, 2016

Barack Obama, Fabian Socialist-Forbes article 11/03/01 by Jerry Bowyer, Contributor

The Webb's, Fabianism and Feminism Peter Bielharz, Chris Nyland ISB: 9781840143072

Made in the USA
San Bernardino, CA
28 September 2018